Young Adulthood Across Digital Platforms

Young Adulthood Across Digital Platforms: Digitally Constructing Gender and Sexualities

EDITED BY

INÊS AMARAL
University of Coimbra, Portugal

RITA BASÍLIO DE SIMÕES
University of Coimbra, Portugal

AND

ANA MARTA M. FLORES
University of Coimbra, Portugal

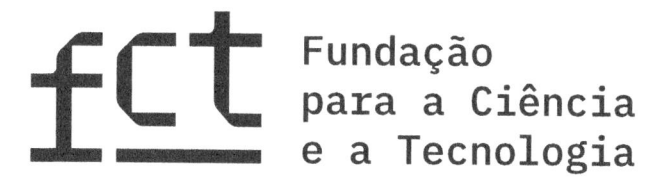

fct Fundação para a Ciência e a Tecnologia

emerald PUBLISHING

United Kingdom – North America – Japan – India – Malaysia – China

Emerald Publishing Limited
Emerald Publishing, Floor 5, Northspring, 21-23 Wellington Street, Leeds LS1 4DL

First edition 2025

Editorial matter and selection © 2025 Inês Amaral, Rita Basílio de Simões and Ana Marta M. Flores.
Individual chapters © 2025 The authors.
Published under exclusive licence by Emerald Publishing Limited.

Reprints and permissions service
Contact: www.copyright.com

No part of this book may be reproduced, stored in a retrieval system, transmitted in any form or by any means electronic, mechanical, photocopying, recording or otherwise without either the prior written permission of the publisher or a licence permitting restricted copying issued in the UK by The Copyright Licensing Agency and in the USA by The Copyright Clearance Center. Any opinions expressed in the chapters are those of the authors. Whilst Emerald makes every effort to ensure the quality and accuracy of its content, Emerald makes no representation implied or otherwise, as to the chapters' suitability and application and disclaims any warranties, express or implied, to their use.

British Library Cataloguing in Publication Data
A catalogue record for this book is available from the British Library

ISBN: 978-1-83753-525-5 (Print)
ISBN: 978-1-83753-524-8 (Online)
ISBN: 978-1-83753-526-2 (Epub)

Printed and bound by CPI Group (UK) Ltd, Croydon, CR0 4YY

INVESTOR IN PEOPLE

Contents

List of Figures and Tables   *vii*

About the Editors   *ix*

About the Contributors   *xi*

Acknowledgement   *xv*

Chapter 1   Reimagining Identity in Mobile Apps: The Intersection of Gender and Sexuality Among Young Adults   *1*
Ana Marta M. Flores, Inês Amaral and Rita Basílio de Simões

Chapter 2   Young Adulthood Digital Cultures and Practices: An Overview   *19*
Eduardo Antunes and Frederico Fonseca

Chapter 3   Gender Across Digital Platforms   *35*
Inês Amaral, Ana Marta M. Flores and Eduardo Antunes

Chapter 4   The Storefront of Gender in the Portuguese Google PlayStore   *57*
Ana Marta M. Flores, Sofia P. Caldeira and Elena Pilipets

Chapter 5   Young Adults' (Re)Negotiation of Gender and Sexual Identities Across Mobile Apps in Portugal   *75*
Rita Alcaire, Sofia José Santos and Filipa Subtil

Chapter 6   Fostering Intimacy in a Digital Environment: Couples, Mobile Apps and Romantic Relationships   *93*
Rita Sepúlveda

Chapter 7 Monitoring Bodies and Selves: Unveiling Menstrual
Tracking Apps Under Foucault's Concepts   111
Juliana Alcantara

Chapter 8 Doing Gender in WhatsApp Homosocial Groups   127
Cosimo Marco Scarcelli

Chapter 9 Community Engagement With Health Messages on
Reproductive Health in an Age of Misinformation and Political
Polarisation: A Case Study of the US NGO Open Arms in Florida   145
Carolina Matos

Chapter 10 Views From Inside: Young Adults' Practices of
Self-Governance on App-Based Platforms   165
Rita Basílio de Simões, Inês Amaral and Ana Marta M. Flores

Index   179

List of Figures and Tables

Figures

Fig. 4.1.	Visual Research Design.	60
Fig. 4.2.	Visualisation of Combined App's Icons by Hue and Most Frequent Terms in Their Descriptions.	63
Fig. 4.3.	Unique and Shared App Recommendations Network for the Five Gender Queries.	68
Fig. 6.1.	Available Apps Found Using the Term 'Couple', Presented According to Year of Release and Category.	98

Tables

Table 3.1.	Sample Distribution.	40
Table 3.2.	Mean Levels of Agreement on Several Burden Experiences of Hate, Harassment and Bullying.	42
Table 3.3.	Mean Levels of Agreement on Content Creation and Sharing Patterns.	44
Table 3.4.	Mean Levels of Agreement Regarding Digital Interaction and Socialisation Experiences.	45
Table 3.5.	Mean Levels of Agreement on Intimate and Sexual Digital Lives.	47
Table 4.1.	Gender Bias in Google PlayStore App Recommendations.	70
Table 10.1.	Summary of Participant Profiles.	170

About the Editors

Inês Amaral is an Associate Professor at the Faculty of Arts and Humanities of the University of Coimbra. Inês holds a PhD in Communication Sciences from the University of Minho and is a Researcher at the Centre for Social Studies. She has developed research on sociability in digital social networks, participation and social media, gender and media, feminist media studies, masculinities, media and digital literacy, technologies and active ageing, audiences and disinformation. She is the PI of the project MyGender and a member of the Masculinities Observatory and Cyberjournalism Observatory teams. Among her latest publications are articles published in journals such as *Social Media + Society*, *Social Sciences*, *El Professional de la Información*, *International Journal of Communication* and *European Journal of Women's Studies*.

Rita Basílio de Simões holds a PhD in Communication Sciences and is an Assistant Professor at the Faculty of Arts and Humanities of the University of Coimbra (FLUC) in the Department of Philosophy, Communication and Information. She is a Researcher at the Centre for Social Studies (CES) and collaborates with CEIS20, also from the University of Coimbra, and ICNOVA, from the Nova University of Lisbon. She is the National Coordinator of the 'Global Media Monitoring Project – Who Makes the News?' She leads the Working Group on Gender and Sexualities of the Portuguese Association of Communication Sciences (SOPCOM).

Ana Marta M. Flores holds a PhD in Journalism and is a Researcher at ICNOVA/iNOVA Media Lab, affiliated with NOVA University Lisbon. She is also a Research Collaborator at the Trends and Culture Management Lab, part of the University of Lisbon's CEAUL. Currently, Ana Marta is a Postdoctoral Researcher in the MyGender project at the University of Coimbra while also assuming the role of Communication Officer for the Digital Culture and Communication section of the European Communication Research and Education Association (ECREA).

About the Contributors

Rita Alcaire is a Postdoctoral Researcher at the Centre for Social Studies (CES) and a Collaborator Researcher at the Centre for Interdisciplinary Studies (CEIS20), University of Coimbra (Portugal). Her research interests lie in the study of gender and sexualities, mental health and pop culture, using media as a privileged way to engage with them. She is a Researcher in the *UnCover – Sexual violence in Portuguese media landscapes* (2023–2026) project. She participated in national (Ouvir Vozes, MyGender, Equal.STEAM) and European (ReMO, CILIA LGBTQI+ and KINDER) projects as a Researcher and a Consultant. She is a Guest Lecturer on MA and PhD programmes in (mental) health, media and communication and contemporary studies. She holds a PhD in Human Rights in Contemporary Societies (CES/III, 2019) and a Master in Cultural Psychiatry (FMUC, 2011). She is developing a postdoctoral project entitled *ENGAGE – Promoting gender equality and social justice through transmedia storytelling and social science communication* (2022–2025) that aims to propose changes in how research and scholarship in gender studies are co-produced and co-performed in and beyond academia.

Juliana Alcantara holds a PhD in Communication Sciences at the Faculty of Arts and Humanities of the University of Coimbra (FLUC, Portugal). She holds a Master's degree in Journalism and Communication at the same institution, where she received the Top 3% of Students Award. She has a postgraduate degree in Business Communication and Higher Education Teaching. She also has more than 10 years of professional experience as a Public Relations Officer and a Journalist in the Brazilian media. She is part of the Interuniversity Network for Journalist Studies (RIEJ) in Portugal. Her academic interests have been directed to communication sciences, gender, health and democracy issues. Among her latest publications are articles published in *Journalism, Journalism Practice* and *International Journal of Communication*.

Eduardo Antunes is a Research Fellow and a doctoral student in Communication Sciences at the University of Coimbra, where he completed his Master's degree in Journalism and Communication. Additionally, he is a Radio Broadcaster and an author at RUC, where he previously served as the Programme Coordinator. He seeks to develop studies on the dynamics of orientalism and gender in the media, with a particular focus on examining identity construction processes, having published works in journals like *Social Sciences, Social Media + Society, Lecture Notes in Computer Science, Media & Jornalismo* and *Comunicação e Sociedade*.

Sofia P. Caldeira is a Marie Skłodowska-Curie Postdoctoral Fellow at CICANT, Lusófona University [g.a. 101,059,460]. She holds a Communication Sciences PhD from Ghent University, Belgium (2020). Her research focuses primarily on feminist media studies, social media practices and politics of gender representation. She currently serves as the Chair of ECREA's Digital Culture and Communication section.

Frederico Fonseca is a doctoral student in Communication Sciences at the Faculty of Letters of the University of Coimbra and has a degree in Multimedia. He is a Professor in public and private higher education and a Researcher in Communication Sciences and Information and Communication Technologies. He has recently been part of the research team for three funded projects, two national and one international (ERASMUS+). He is interested in topics related to algorithmic governance, datafication, m-apps, (in)fertility, serious games and active ageing.

Carolina Matos is a Senior Lecturer in Media and Sociology at the Department of Media, Culture and the Creative Industries (MCCI) at the School of Communication and Creativity at City, University of London, and also a former Visiting Associate Professor in Global Communications at the School of Communication, University of Miami, US. Matos' research is in the area of gender, media and development and international communications. She investigates the role of communications for social change in processes of development, paying particular attention to structural inequalities of gender, race and class. A previous Journalist, Matos is the author of four books, various chapters and articles, including the book *Gender, Health Communications and Reproductive Health in International Development* (McGill Queen's University Press, 2023).

Elena Pilipets is a Postdoctoral Researcher in Digital Media and Methods at the Department of Media Studies, University of Siegen (PhD in Media Studies, University of Klagenfurt). Her work focuses on the processes of social media circulation, with particular attention to the study of platforms through combinations of visual and digital methods. This includes online-grounded empirical investigations of internet memes, platform subcultures and social bots, the latter being studied in a working group funded by the Centre of Advanced Internet Studies (CAIS) in Bochum.

Sofia José Santos is an Assistant Professor of International Relations at the Faculty of Economics of the University of Coimbra and a Researcher at the Centre for Social Studies. Sofia studies the politics of media representations and media production from a critical and feminist perspective, focusing on international relations; peace, violence and security studies; masculinities; and technopolitics. Within CES, she is currently the PI of the project 'UNCOVER: Sexual Violence in Portuguese Mediascape' and a co-editor of *Alice News*. She has a PhD in International Relations from the Faculty of Economics of the University of Coimbra and a diploma in Advanced Studies in Communication Sciences from ISCTE-IUL. She was a Visiting Scholar at the Flemish Peace Institute, Belgium, and a Marie Curie Fellow in the Anthropology department at Universiteit Utrecht, the Netherlands. Her research has been published in academic journals such as *Media and Communication*, *European Journal of Women's Studies* and *Contexto Internacional*.

Cosimo Marco Scarcelli, PhD, is an Associate Professor at the Department of Philosophy, Sociology, Education and Applied Psychology of the University of Padua (Italy). He teaches Media, Gender and Sexuality (BD in Communication) and Digital Culture, Gender and Society (MD in Strategies of Communication) and is a member of the board of PhD Programme in Social Sciences. His research deals with sexuality, gender and digital culture, intimacies, pornography, masculinities, love and emotions and young people. He is particularly interested in qualitative and participatory research. He is an Editor of *Journal of Gender Studies*. From 2016 to 2021, he served as the Vice-Chair and then the Chair for ECREA's Gender, Sexuality and Communication section.

Rita Sepúlveda is a Postdoctoral Researcher at ICNOVA, Instituto de Comunicação da Nova, Nova University of Lisbon (Ref: ICNOVA/PÓSDOC/2022). She holds a Communication Sciences PhD from ISCTE-Iul, Portugal (2021). Her research focuses on collective and dynamic expressions in digital environments regarding the transformation of intimacy in the context of digital platforms appropriation. She is an Associate Researcher at Cies (ISCTE-Iul) and coordinator of the MetDigi project (Cies-Iscte). Since 2019, she's been lecturing in postgraduate degrees on communication, social media, and methodologies subjects.

Filipa Subtil is a Coordinator Professor at Escola Superior de Comunicação Social, Instituto Politécnico de Lisboa, and a Researcher at LIACOM and ICNOVA. She holds a PhD in Social Sciences from the Universidade de Lisboa. Her research interests include the sociology of communication, social theory of communication in the United States and Canada, and media frameworks on gender issues. Her work has been published in academic journals such as *Journalism Practice*, *Journalism Studies*, *History of Media Studies*, *Media e Jornalismo*, *Revista Famecos* and *Revista Brasileira de Ciências da Comunicação*. She is also co-editor and author of *Os três D's dos media: desigualdade, desprofissionalização e desinformação* (2021) and *Media and Portuguese Empire (2017)*, among others.

Acknowledgement

Portuguese national funds through FCT (Fundação para a Ciência e a Tecnologia) provided financial support in the framework of the project 'Mediated young adults' practices: advancing gender justice in and across mobile apps' (PTDC/COM-CSS/5947/2020). https://doi.org/10.54499/PTDC/COM-CSS/5947/2020

Chapter 1

Reimagining Identity in Mobile Apps: The Intersection of Gender and Sexuality Among Young Adults

Ana Marta M. Flores, Inês Amaral and Rita Basílio de Simões

University of Coimbra, Portugal

Abstract

The influence of digital media and mobile technologies on the interpersonal dynamics of young individuals across various aspects of their daily lives underscores the significant role of digital media in shaping their experiences. Research exploring how individuals engage with mobile applications (m-apps) has revealed the constraining effects of platform norms and politics on users' expressive identities. This chapter examines the evolving landscape of media consumption, engagement and civic participation amidst the proliferation of new media modalities, focussing on m-apps. The authors highlight the pervasive adoption of mobile apps across diverse categories and the escalating temporal investment individuals allocate to these platforms for fostering interpersonal connections. Drawing from a feminist and intersectional perspective, the authors explore how young adults navigate the technicity and imaginaries of m-apps, incorporating them into their daily routines and (re)negotiating their gender and sexual identities. Through the MyGender project, the authors investigate the relationship between m-apps and power dynamics, examining the construction and reconstruction of gender and sexuality across platforms. The findings underscore the need for critical engagement with digital technologies as sociocultural products actively reshaping gender relations and sexual practices. The text ends with an overview of the book, briefly presenting the remaining nine chapters.

Keywords: Gender; MyGender project; society; mobile apps; self-expression; social media

Introduction

The transformative impact of digital media and mobile-based technologies on the interpersonal dynamics of young individuals within various spheres of their daily existence underscores the pivotal role of digital media in shaping their lived experiences. Research into the nuanced ways individuals engage with the technical intricacies and conceptual frameworks embedded within m-apps, seamlessly integrating them into their quotidian routines, has enlightened the constraining effects of platform grammars and politics on users' expressive identities as digital technologies exert regulatory control over the interpretations and appropriations afforded by these platforms. The evolving landscape of media consumption, engagement and civic and political participation has remained a persistent concern amidst the proliferation of new media modalities.

The widespread adoption of m-apps across diverse categories, spanning social networking, dating, gaming, health, fitness and self-tracking domains, underscores the escalating temporal investment individuals allocate to these platforms for fostering interpersonal connections. These mobile-centric technologies have transcended the realm of mere tools to become indispensable extensions of individuals' selfhood, intricately interwoven into the fabric of their daily existence. Consequently, unravelling the multifaceted layers of individuals' utilisation and diverse appropriations of m-apps is paramount in elucidating how these technologies either challenge or circumscribe their personal narratives.

Interactions within the realm of mobile application platforms (m-apps) intricately interlace with collective narrative processes, exerting a reinforcing influence on prevailing power dynamics and perpetuating hegemonic ideals of masculinity and femininity deeply entrenched in heteronormativity (Amaral et al., 2021). These constructions of masculinities and femininities represent culturally constructed norms, semiotically and discursively transmitted ideals dictating how individuals should embody and enact gender roles as either masculine or feminine entities (Amaral et al., 2019). Given the socially constructed nature of gender (Butler, 1990), it is imperative to acknowledge that these notions of masculinity and femininity are not innate, fixed or immutable; instead, they undergo continual evolution through dynamic social and cultural processes, susceptible to contestation, reconstruction and transformation (Boni, 2002).

Consequently, the integration of technical features and visual representations within m-apps into individuals' daily routines incites a reassessment of their sexual and gender identities. How individuals engage with the technological functionalities and visual elements of m-apps, alongside their interactions with fellow users, has garnered considerable attention amidst the emergence of novel forms of social interaction (Ohme, 2020). The pervasive adoption of m-apps across diverse categories, ranging from social media platforms and dating applications to gaming apps, health and fitness tools and self-tracking applications, underscores the escalating temporal investment individuals dedicate to these platforms for interpersonal connectivity and multimedia engagement. Consequently, these mobile technologies have evolved into indispensable extensions of individuals' identities, seamlessly woven into the fabric of their daily lives (Zhang et al., 2018). Within this framework, it becomes imperative to probe how individuals' utilisation of and varied appropriations of m-apps play a pivotal role in elucidating how these technologies either challenge or constrain their personal experiences, particularly concerning renegotiating their sexual and gender identities. By being rooted in a new materialist feminist perspective and from a feminist and intersectional perspective, this book explores how young adults engage with the technicity and imaginaries of m-apps, incorporating them into their daily lives, embodying them in their everyday practices and (re)negotiating from it their gender and sexual identities.

Exploring young adults' interactions with m-apps within the uses and gratifications theory framework or the risks and advantages paradigm has constituted a focal point of scholarly inquiry. However, this book adopts a critical lens towards contemporary digital media, rooted in an understanding of technology as a potent generator of meaning, subjectivity and agency intricately intertwined with power dynamics.

Young Adulthood Across Digital Platforms: Digitally Constructing Gender and Sexualities is framed within the project 'MyGender – Mediated Young Adults' Practices: Advancing Gender Justice in and across Mobile Apps', which aimed to understand the relevance of m-apps in the lives of Portuguese young adults and how their use dialogs with their contexts and experiences. Across 10 chapters, the book embarks on a feminist and intersectional exploration of how individuals navigate digital technologies and m-apps' technicity and conceptual underpinnings, seamlessly integrating them into their daily routines and utilising them as conduits for the (re)negotiation of their gender, sexual identities and intimacy, as well as to create engagement between communities that promote health and deconstruct myths of disinformation disorder.

Mediated Interfaces and the Extension of the Self

Technological uses are intricately interwoven with specific cultural and ideological contexts, engendering diverse social structures and hierarchies (Simões & Amaral, 2022). M-apps often prompt users to interpret their data through normative constructs of masculinity and femininity, fostering behaviours entrenched in conventional gender norms and power dynamics, thereby delineating gendered social spaces.

Research delving into how individuals engage with the technical intricacies and visual elements of m-apps, integrating them into their daily lives, has unveiled that the grammatical structures and platform regulations inherent in these apps can constrict users' expressions of identity, as digital technologies govern and oversee their utilisation (Correa et al., 2010). Consequently, a comprehensive analysis of the impacts of these applications necessitates a dual perspective: one that acknowledges the symbolic nature of m-apps as digital communication environments and another that delves into their experiential dimension as technological tools. Drawing from a new feminist materialist standpoint (Lupton, 2019), individuals' interactions with people and objects are viewed as profoundly generative (Bennett, 2010). When individuals engage with digital technologies, they adopt prevailing modes of thought and experience and internalise affective amalgamations of material, ideas and language (Lupton, 2019), thereby cultivating capacities for agency and reasoning to navigate the notions of masculinity and femininity.

As technology assumes roles in shaping meaning, subjectivity and agency, digital practices are intricately intertwined with the technical aspects and imaginaries of the social milieus in which they operate, influencing personal decision-making in individuals' everyday lives (boyd, 2015). The intricate interplay between technological tools and their utilisation and appropriation necessitates a deeper understanding of digital practices as sociocultural artefacts shaped by power dynamics (Lupton, 2019). Within this context, feminist media studies challenge the naturalised status of gender disparities, recognising that all significant social attributes are actively constructed and not inherently biological, socially ingrained or structurally predetermined (Silveirinha et al., 2020).

Digital technologies present new avenues for engagement in gender politics, fostering more emancipatory social contexts, behaviours and relationships (Simões & Amaral, 2022). Moreover, digital environments offer novel avenues for identity expression and subjectivity. Given that the Internet serves as both a producer and reproducer of social roles, practices, identities and forms of oppression, digital feminist research provides a unique lens for dissecting the intricate ramifications and mechanisms of the digital environment. M-apps must be recognised as mediated interfaces for gender identity performances, yet studies on their usage, appropriation and impacts remain varied and often lack a gender-focused perspective.

A substantial body of research on m-apps has predominantly focused on utilising social networks and visual representations (Berry, 2017). Drawing from the uses and gratifications theory, numerous studies have explored the appropriation of specific platforms by young adults, encompassing social networks (Khadir et al., 2021), social media (Ash et al., 2020; Moreno & Whitehill, 2016; Song et al., 2021), news media applications (Antunovic et al., 2018) and home banking (Prom Tep et al., 2020).

Scientific inquiry into integrating m-apps into the daily lives of young adults is entwined with the usage of information and communication technologies and social media. However, m-apps encompass a broader spectrum and permeate various facets of young adults' lives. From gaming to shopping, dating to health and nutrition, and fitness to self-monitoring, many m-apps are used daily by young adults. danah boyd (2015) asserts that mobile communication is restructuring socio-technical practices, leading to the construction and reconstruction of sociability cultures (Amaral, 2012, 2016), social structures and hierarchies, thereby embedding technology in different realms of daily life (Simões & Amaral, 2022).

Given the hybrid nature of the new media ecosystem, scholarly literature has examined how young individuals utilise digital technologies, interact with others, incorporate digital devices into their daily routines, alter their perspectives and behaviours based on networked practices, participate in civic and political movements (Ohme, 2020), consume news, follow trends and influencers, form friendships and engage in digital intimacy within a multiplatform paradigm that fosters active experiences (Gerlich et al., 2015).

Considering the central role of digital platforms in young people's lives (Jenkins et al., 2016) and their extension as embodiments of the self (Zhang et al., 2018), risks and opportunities have emerged as prominent research areas. Risks often feature prominently in discussions surrounding youth technology usage. Concerns regarding addiction, cyberbullying, hate speech, online sexual exploitation, sedentary lifestyles, depression and suicide are frequently cited in research on youth and technology (Amaral & Simões, 2021; Sinkkonen et al., 2014; Thulin & Vilhelmson, 2019; Twenge, 2017). Conversely, another line of study emphasises the positive aspects of digital media usage, highlighting digital activism, public and civic engagement, and social and political participation (Bouliane & Theocharis, 2020; Ekström et al., 2014; Lee et al., 2013).

Given the diverse patterns of media consumption fostered by the digital ecosystem (Gurevitch et al., 2009) and its constant evolution (Thulin & Vilhelmson, 2019), various theories on social media effects (Bouliane, 2015) posit their potential impact on civic and political engagement (Bouliane & Theocharis, 2020), the creation of new engagement repertoires (Cammaerts et al., 2014), incidental news exposure (Boczkowski et al., 2018; Gil de Zúñiga et al., 2017) and the strengthening of social bonds (Amaral, 2016). It should also be noted that other research strands explore the immersion of young individuals in digital media within their daily lives, acknowledging that while technologies promote social interaction, they may also foster isolation and loneliness (Thulin & Vilhelmson, 2019). Additionally, research on youth also delves into networked sexual identities and the Internet as a realm of digital intimacy (De Ridder & Van Bauwel, 2015).

Regarding young adults, a substantial research domain has focused on examining the use and appropriation of m-apps by men who have sex with other men (Blackwell et al., 2015), often explored through studies on health and risks associated with sexual behaviours, frequently framed as pathologies. However, these inquiries have expanded to encompass questions centred on digital sexual cultures from a 'data culture' perspective (Albury et al., 2017). This viewpoint pertains to the digital mediation of intimacy and the manner in which algorithms capture user data, monitoring habits and routines to 'suggest' other users and activities (Albury et al., 2017; Light, 2014). Thus, the negotiations and renegotiations of gender and sexual identities that young adults undergo on mobile apps directly intersect with their cultures of intimacy and sexuality through pronounced technological intrusions into their daily lives (Gillespie, 2014; Mollen & Dhaenens, 2018).

Gender and Sexuality Across Mediated Mobile Interfaces

The dizzying evolution of technology and the proliferation of mobile communication have profoundly altered the landscape of human interaction, ushering in new paradigms of usage, practices and consumption behaviours. The ubiquitous presence of smartphones and tablets has engendered a thriving market for competitive m-apps, spanning various categories whose functionalities, structures, policies and content pose challenges to users and their utilisation of these applications. Moreover, m-apps, characterised by their user-friendly interfaces and mobility, have emerged as a prevailing trend, owing primarily to their versatile features surpassing conventional devices (Gerlich et al., 2015).

Furthermore, mobile-based technologies facilitate the convergence of media content, functionalities and features from disparate platforms onto a singular device, fostering seamless integration of diverse digital experiences (Deng et al., 2019). Indeed, smartphones and other mobile devices excel in multitasking capabilities, enabling users to concurrently engage in multiple activities, thereby optimising time utilisation and consolidating tasks previously performed using separate devices.

The evolution of media consumption, engagement and civic and political participation has become a perennial concern amidst the proliferation of new media modalities (Ohme, 2020). These mobile-based technologies have transcended mere utility to become indispensable facets of individuals' lives, serving as extensions of their identities and augmenting their digital self-expression and interaction capabilities.

The use of technology is intricately entangled within specific cultural and ideological contexts, which actively (re)generate diverse social frameworks and hierarchies (Simões & Amaral, 2022). Numerous m-apps prompt users to interpret information through the lens of conventional conceptions of masculinity and femininity, resulting in behaviours rooted in established gender norms and power dynamics that sculpt gender-specific social environments.

Research delving into how individuals integrate the technical features and visual aspects of m-apps into their daily routines has unveiled how the structures and guidelines inherent to these apps can constrict users' expressions of identity as digital technologies oversee and regulate their utilisation (Correa et al., 2010). Consequently, it becomes imperative to evaluate the impact of these applications from a dual perspective: one acknowledging the symbolic role of m-apps as digital communication environments and another recognising their experiential dimension as technological tools.

Drawing upon the perspective of new feminist materialism (Lupton, 2019), individuals' interactions with other people and objects are perceived as profoundly generative (Bennett, 2010). When individuals engage with digital technologies, they are not merely adopting prevailing modes of thinking; they are also experiencing and internalising affective amalgamations of material, ideas and language (Lupton, 2019), thereby cultivating capacities and reasoning to grasp the concept of being and behaving as a man or a woman. In this framework, gender is constructed as a construct intricately interwoven with specific social elements and the power dynamics they instantiate.

As technology evolves into a source of meaning, subjectivity and agency, digital behaviours become intimately intertwined with the technical elements and the constructs of the social contexts in which they are employed, subsequently influencing individual decisions in people's daily lives (boyd, 2015). The intricate interplay between technological instruments and their usage and adaptation necessitates a deeper understanding of digital behaviours as sociocultural artefacts shaped by power dynamics (Lupton, 2019). Within this milieu, feminist media studies challenge the taken-for-granted nature of gender disparities, acknowledging that all significant social attributes are actively constructed and are neither biologically inherent, permanently socialised nor structurally predetermined (Silveirinha et al., 2020).

Digital technologies present new avenues for active participation in gender-related issues, fostering more emancipatory social environments, behaviours and relationships (Simões & Amaral, 2022). Furthermore, digital realms offer novel pathways for expressing identity and subjectivity. Acknowledging that the Internet produces and reproduces social roles, practices, identities and forms of oppression, digital feminist research provides a unique perspective for scrutinising the intricate ramifications and mechanisms of the digital environment. It is essential to recognise m-apps as mediated interfaces for performing gender identities. However, research on their utilisation, adaptations and consequences remains diverse and often lacks a gender-oriented perspective.

Research concerning m-apps has primarily focused on the uses of social networks and visual representations (Berry, 2017). Leveraging the uses and gratifications theory, numerous studies have explored how young adults appropriate specific platforms, including social networks (Khadir et al., 2021), social media (Ash et al., 2020; Moreno & Whitehill, 2016; Song et al., 2021), news media applications (Antunovic et al., 2018) and home banking (Prom Tep et al., 2020).

Within feminist media studies, surveillance technologies have consistently functioned as tools of discipline. Consequently, investigations into inequalities, power dynamics and commodification have revolved around how digital technology fosters particular practices and conceptions of identity and subjectivity. This perspective posits that digital technologies are (re)shaped within social contexts defined by gender expectations and norms governing individuals' engagement (Simões & Amaral, 2022).

Sexual identity and sexual orientation play pivotal roles in shaping young adults' interactions with m-apps, particularly evident in dating platforms and social media. Research by Chester et al. (2016) suggests that sexual identity, including LGBTQ+ identities, influences app usage preferences and online profile presentation strategies. Furthermore, studies such as Light (2014) shed light on how geolocation technologies embedded in dating apps impact digital intimacy experiences, providing unique opportunities for interactions based on physical proximity and shared interests.

Digital intimacy, as an emerging interdisciplinary field, explores how digital technologies reshape and redefine forms of intimacy and interpersonal connection. Research from Mollen and Dhaenens (2018) investigates how instant messaging apps and social networks facilitate the expression of affection and emotional support in online relationships, challenging traditional notions of physical closeness. Additionally, Albury et al. (2017) research examines how recommendation algorithms in dating apps shape online interactions, influencing matchmaking dynamics and virtual intimacy experiences.

However, it is imperative to acknowledge that digital intimacy may pose challenges and risks, especially concerning online privacy and security. Scholars such as De Ridder and Van Bauwel (2015) delve into the complexities of sexual and gender identities in digital spaces, highlighting how social norms and gender expectations manifest and are contested in online interactions. Moreover, works like those of Blackwell et al. (2015) investigate the experiences of men who have sex with men on dating apps, examining issues related to sexual health and informed consent in digital contexts.

MyGender project aimed to explore how these apps relate to power relations, examine the construction and reconstruction of gender and sexuality across these platforms and scrutinise their enactment and reenactment within the realms of app imaginaries and utilisation. Additionally, the project considered how these processes manifest in data monitoring and mining, ultimately forming distinct sociability and intimacy domains.

While existing critical research on digital surveillance technologies has primarily focused on the broader sociocultural impact of m-apps, shedding light on their potential to either combat or reinforce social inequalities (boyd, 2015; Correa et al., 2010; Wajcman, 2007; Whiting & Williams, 2013), we argue that, without diminishing the value of these studies, there is a pressing need for a critical examination of digital technology tools as sociocultural products actively reshaping gender relations and sexual practices. The results of this project show that personal technological agency in people's everyday practices (boyd, 2015) is influenced in different ways by sociodemographic factors such as gender, sexual orientation and living with parents.

Through mixed methods and within a multidimensional and holistic approach, MyGender has examined mobile app affordances, grammars, platform politics and content and their uses, appropriations and embodiment. The overall research design combined qualitative and quantitative data collection methods, analysis and inference within different phases and axes of the research process. The research design encompasses an analysis of m-apps to examine the technicity of a sample of apps through the interfaces and five fieldwork studies implemented to investigate how young adults engage with technicity and imaginaries of mobile apps: a survey to a representative sample of Portuguese young adults between 18 and 30 years, six focus groups, a tracking survey and two ethnographic studies – one centred on semi-structured interviews to investigate the issues in-depth and the other centred on diary records to address emotional and interpersonal.

In the survey, we found that m-apps directly interfere with the gender identities and sexual practices of young adults, depending on the affordances of the platforms, which substantially shape, condition and constrain how these identities are (re) negotiated and imagined in mediated experiences, in perceptions of others and their self-representations. We also identify digital dependency and anxiety when separated from their mobile phones, highlighting the role of technology in shaping emotional well-being. The several studies demonstrated that m-apps have a direct impact on the sexual and gender identities of young Portuguese adults. The affordances and grammars of these platforms play a pivotal role in shaping how individuals negotiate and imagine their identities in digital spaces. Likewise, sociodemographic factors, such as gender, sexual orientation and living situations, influence the use and agency of m-apps. This research contributes to a better understanding of how technology and digital environments intersect with personal identities, relationships and societal norms.

In the 25 semi-structured interviews developed, our primary objective was to elucidate the underlying power dynamics inherent in digital practices, revealing a predominant adherence to gender-conforming behaviours among participants despite sporadic instances of countering hegemonic gender scripts, often due to a lack of recognition of the power dynamics influencing their actions. While the affordances of digital platforms did not singularly determine behaviour, they did foster compliance with prevailing gender norms, as evidenced by participants' narratives, which frequently overlooked the multifaceted realities of young adults' lives and the diversity of their identities. Consequently, by inadvertently perpetuating normative gender scripts instead of capitalising on opportunities for reshaping identity performances, participants unintentionally reinforced culturally ingrained patterns of relational behaviour, highlighting the intricate interplay between social context and digital technology.

The data from the diary records ($N = 16$) revealed a pervasive presence of mobile apps in daily activities, communication patterns and self-expression. It was also found that private corporations' commodification of user data has led to asymmetrical power dynamics. Despite concerns about privacy infringement, there is a prevailing acceptance of corporate surveillance practices, highlighting the normalisation of data commodification. Participants demonstrated varying levels of engagement, with some providing rich and detailed entries while others exhibited sporadic involvement. Despite challenges in ensuring consistency and depth of engagement, the method enabled real-time documentation of experiences, offering researchers dynamic and evolving datasets. The participatory nature of the diary method facilitated a deeper understanding of participants' contexts and provided researchers with nuanced insights into their lived experiences. The method proved effective in capturing participants' reflections on mental health and wellbeing, showcasing their ability to engage in therapeutic self-expression within the constraints of digital platforms.

Data from tracking the mobile application usage of 342 young adults in Portugal highlights the dominance of social media platforms. Specifically, six apps garnered over 100 users throughout the tracking period: YouTube, Facebook, WhatsApp, Instagram, Messenger and TikTok. Despite YouTube being the most utilised app in the sample, the findings indicate that it is accessed less frequently daily than Facebook. While gender differences in app usage are relatively minor based on descriptive statistics, some notable variations exist. For instance, on average, women spend over double the amount of time per day on YouTube compared to men. This dominance of social media indicates a prevalence of daily usage among approximately one-third of the sample population. While other app categories showed more uniform usage patterns, such as self-tracking apps being among the least used, variations based on sociodemographic factors were slight but discernible. Notably, the absence of individuals from lower socioeconomic classes using self-tracking apps suggests a correlation between app usage and socioeconomic status, consistent with previous research. Regarding the exploration of traditional gender roles through self-tracking app usage, the study identifies a gendered trend in the utilisation of fertility and menstrual cycle-tracking apps, predominantly by women. These results align with societal expectations of women's responsibility for reproductive health and self-care, as reflected in the focus on female bodies and fertility-related functionalities within self-tracking apps.

The analysis of the top six most utilised apps among Portuguese young adults reveals notable insights. These apps offer varying degrees of flexibility regarding gender identification during registration: some provide complete freedom to input gender, while others lack the option altogether. However, users have endless opportunities to shape their gender representation within these digital spaces, notably through content creation and interaction.

The focus group discussions ($N = 31$) with young Portuguese adults highlight divergent attitudes towards gender inclusivity within these platforms. While some advocate for an open and inclusive approach, others adhere to binary gender norms, reflecting broader digital gender scripts. Despite differing viewpoints, participants are willing to engage in dialogue and learn about gender diversity. However, the absence of gender identification fields in certain apps, such as TikTok and WhatsApp, raises questions about the alignment of these platforms with evolving notions of gender identity.

The studies carried out by the MyGender project show that mobile app usage has social and political implications (Alcaire et al., 2024; Amaral et al., 2023, 2024; Antunes et al., 2022; Simões et al., 2023).

Book Overview

Eduardo Antunes and Frederico Fonseca argue, in *Chapter 2*, that the pervasive integration of mobile devices and digital platforms into everyday life underscores the non-neutral political power embedded within technology, shaping societal processes and individual agency. The authors state that the concept of deep mediatisation underscores how digital media technologies, particularly social media platforms, play a pivotal role in shaping interactions, beliefs and values among young adults, termed 'digital natives'. From fostering digital cultures to catalysing civic activism, these platforms are presented as profoundly impacting identity construction and socialisation patterns. Despite concerns about data-hoarding business models, the inextricable link between young adults and the digital landscape lays the groundwork for understanding the intricate interplay between technology, culture and identity in the digital age.

In *Chapter 3* 'Gender Across Digital Platforms', the authors contend that the process of socialisation, vital for integrating individuals into society, is increasingly mediated by digital media technologies, perpetuating social norms and expectations. The concept of digital cultures encompasses the diverse ways in which digital media influences societal norms and values, continuously evolving in response to technological advancements and changing social dynamics. From fostering digital citizenship among young adults to shaping collective identities through online communities and subcultures, digital platforms play a central role in identity expression and socialisation practices. Despite filter bubbles and data hoarding concerns, these platforms serve as crucial loci for digital socialisation, reflecting broader cultural shifts and societal transformations.

Chapter 4, 'The Storefront of Gender in the Portuguese Google PlayStore', by Ana Marta M. Flores, Sofia P. Caldeira and Elena Pilipets adopts a mixed approach that combines digital methods and qualitative analysis to identify app categories and their visual and textual expressions related to gender spectra and to determine which apps are common across genders. The empirical procedure comprised three stages: query design, data scraping and analysis, extracting 1,013 unique apps and their subsequent visual and textual analysis. Through a detailed analysis of app icon images and the frequently repeated terms in their descriptions, the study revealed complex patterns in the curation of apps concerning gender identities, highlighting tensions between the flexibility and rigidity of gender representations in the digital storefront. The data analysis revealed how app recommendations in the Google Play Store reflect and reproduce established gender norms while offering potential spaces for resistance and subversion. For example, while apps targeted at 'woman' and 'man' identities tend to reinforce normative stereotypes of femininity and masculinity, respectively, apps aimed at 'queer' identities challenge these representations by addressing themes such as gender transitions and vocal modulation. However, the prevalence of dating and relationship apps within the 'queer' category suggests a limited and sexualised view of these identities, neglecting their diversity and complexity. The study highlights the intersection between technology, gender representations and individual resistance within the digital environment of the Google Play Store, emphasising the need for further research into how users navigate and negotiate these digitised spaces in their everyday lives.

Rita Alcaire, Sofia José Santos and Filipa Subtil are the authors of *Chapter 5*, which delves into integrating m-apps into the daily lives of young adults in Portugal, exploring their multifaceted roles in shaping identity, communication and social interactions. Through qualitative analysis of interviews and focus groups, the study uncovers how technology extends individuals' identities, facilitating connections and fostering authentic engagement. Despite the convenience and connectivity of apps, participants also navigate challenges such as maintaining privacy, managing gender and sexuality representations, and negotiating social expectations within digital spaces. The research underscores the nuanced ways in which technology both reflects and reinforces societal norms, particularly concerning gender and dating dynamics, while also providing opportunities for individuals to challenge and redefine these norms. The analysis highlights the complex interplay between technology, identity and societal norms, revealing the diverse strategies employed by young adults to navigate digital spaces. While apps offer avenues for self-expression and community building, they also present obstacles such as harassment and pressure to conform to conventional gender roles. Moreover, the study emphasises the gendered dynamics of online dating, with women prioritising safety and authenticity while men may pursue more casual encounters. The findings highlight the need for a nuanced understanding of technology's impact on identity formation and social interactions, emphasising the importance of balancing the benefits of connectivity with the challenges of managing online presence in today's digital landscape.

Chapter 6, 'Fostering intimacy in a digital environment: couples, mobile apps and romantic relationships', signed by Rita Sepúlveda focuses on apps available in the Apple App Store and collected data in April 2023 using a store scraper. First, a qualitative–quantitative exploratory analysis described the existing offer of apps for couples. Subsequently, a qualitative content analysis of app presentation was conducted, followed by an analysis of the top 10 apps in terms of rating to examine how they address gender, sexual orientation and relationship-type issues. The results revealed a diversity of apps predominantly offered by private companies, with a notable emphasis on heteronormative representations and a lack of inclusion of diverse gender identities.

The study found that while the supply of couple apps has grown over the years, many of them adhered to traditional gender and sexual orientation representations, thus excluding couples who do not fit into these norms. The analysis of app authorship highlighted the dominant presence of private companies, raising questions about the commercialisation of romantic relationships and user data collection. Despite offering a variety of features to promote communication and intimacy between couples, these apps often fail to be inclusive regarding diverse gender identities and sexual orientations. These findings point to the need for greater awareness of the importance of inclusion and diverse representation in apps aimed at romantic relationships and future research exploring these issues in different platforms and cultural contexts.

In *Chapter 7*, 'Monitoring bodies and selves: Unveiling menstrual tracking apps under Foucault's concepts', Juliana Alcantara delves into regulating women's bodies and minds through the everyday use of menstrual control applications. Building on the theoretical framework proposed by Michel Foucault, the examination explores the nuanced connection between women and their physical selves. Nevertheless, the scope of the study transcends beyond the physical body itself as it focuses on the formation of subjectivities. The research delves into various power dynamics, disciplinary and discursive practices, regimes of truth, biopower, biopolitics and governance. The study outlines the key tenets of Michel Foucault's examination of power and how these concepts intertwine with the tactics employed by menstrual tracking applications. It scrutinises how these applications influence the subjectivity of womanhood, moulding modes of cognition and behaviour. Furthermore, it explores the correlation between disciplinary techniques, knowledge-power dynamics and surveillance mechanisms concerning medicine, as elucidated by Foucault. The narrative underscores that the surveillance of data and corporate oversight facilitated by menstrual apps present unprecedented challenges to feminist advocacy. Consequently, the contention posited is that the technology underpinning menstrual tracking apps exerts a subtle and continuous influence in subduing female bodies and rendering them instrumental. To chart new avenues and remedies through a feminist and critical lens, the paper recommends further exploring the subject matter. It argues for a departure from liberal methodologies that rely solely on media literacy, instead advocating for a comprehensive understanding of technology and women's rights.

'Doing gender in WhatsApp homosocial groups' is *Chapter 8* of the book, signed by Cosimo Marco Scarcelli. This chapter explores the dynamics of gender management and expression within private WhatsApp groups, focussing on young adults' experiences and perceptions. Employing a qualitative approach, the study delves into the intricate interplay between gender identity and social media, unravelling adolescents' values, practices and cognitive dispositions. The research, part of a larger project involving 46 Italian residents aged 20–24, examines the nuances of gendered interactions within these digital spaces. Through semi-structured interviews conducted between March and September 2021, participants shared insights into their group dynamics and behaviours, shedding light on how WhatsApp groups serve as arenas for negotiating gender boundaries and reinforcing homosocial bonds. The findings reveal distinct patterns in how men and women engage with these platforms. Male-only groups often centre around humour and objectification of women, perpetuating hegemonic masculinity through practices like digital girl-watching. In contrast, female-only groups offer emotional support and mutual assistance, creating spaces for camaraderie and solidarity. These gendered practices within WhatsApp groups reflect broader societal norms and serve as sites for the continuous negotiation and performance of gender identities. Furthermore, they illustrate the interconnectedness of local group dynamics with larger cultural discourses surrounding masculinity and femininity, highlighting the complex interplay between global influences and localised practices.

Chapter 9, by Carolina Matos, shows that the Western world has witnessed a persistent escalation of social and economic disparities in recent decades, accompanied by a concerning regression in the advancements made in women's rights and reproductive health. Despite transitioning from a discourse centred on 'population control' to one rooted in human rights frameworks, this ideological shift has not fully materialised in practical implementation. Structural gender inequalities endure, underscoring the ongoing relevance of feminist critiques that challenge the predominance of empiricism in research. The imperative to engage with marginalised communities from their unique perspectives remains paramount, particularly within a landscape where societal inequalities persist and research in the social sciences disproportionately benefits privileged segments of society. Embracing a feminist epistemological standpoint advocating for 'situated knowledges', this study endeavours to elucidate how women in local communities interpret health communication messages on sexual and reproductive health and rights (SRHR), underscoring the enduring significance of feminist inquiries within the realm of social sciences.

The study, conducted through two focus groups with participants from disadvantaged communities in Miami, Florida, delves into the multifaceted dynamics shaping individuals' comprehension and engagement with SRHR-related information, particularly within the context of pervasive political polarisation and the proliferation of misinformation. Through a thematic analysis of the data, it becomes evident that participants possess a nuanced understanding of SRHR issues and are adept at discerning misinformation online and offline. Echoing findings from a parallel study in Campinas, São Paulo, participants highlight the deleterious impact of political populism on the public discourse surrounding SRHR, exacerbating media polarisation and hindering the advancement of women's rights. Importantly, participants underscored the need for concerted efforts to improve mainstream media coverage, enhance health literacy skills, and foster inclusive, participatory mechanisms in the construction of health communication messages, emphasising the pivotal role of feminist researchers in navigating these complex terrains and advocating for substantive social change.

Chapter 10, 'Views from inside: Young adults' practices of self-governance on app-based platforms', by Rita Basílio de Simões, Inês Amaral and Ana Marta Flores, lies on the interpretations that young adults attributed to their behaviours on mobile app-based platforms, using diary records as a recurring method of documentation. The chapter delves into the multifaceted dimensions of self-governance in digital contexts, aiming to uncover the underlying motivations and implications shaping contemporary subjectivity. Through qualitative methods, the authors offer an in-depth exploration of participants' discourses and behaviours, employing digital diary records as a means to capture immediate responses and minimise memory bias. The participant cohort, predominantly educated, urban, cisgender and white, offers rich insights into how app-based platforms intersect with everyday life in Portugal, encompassing diverse forms of self-expression, productivity and relationship management. The analysis reveals a pervasive emphasis on productivity as a cornerstone of contemporary digital practices, wherein participants navigate pressures to present curated images of efficiency and success online. This ethos aligns with neoliberal ideologies, where individuals are encouraged to optimise their economic value through entrepreneurial self-governance. Concurrently, the construction of online identities emerges as a strategic endeavour, reflecting calculated efforts to manage one's symbolic value in the labour market. Participants deploy various strategies, such as pseudonyms and persona curation, to navigate the intricacies of online self-presentation, often prioritising professionalism and networking. Moreover, the management of e-relationships underscores the blurring boundaries between work and leisure as digital technologies reshape social connections and communication patterns. Despite growing concerns about privacy infringement and data exploitation, participants exhibit a prevailing acceptance of corporate surveillance practices, indicative of the normalisation of data commodification within contemporary society.

References

Albury, K., Burgess, J., Light, B., Race, K., & Wilken, R. (2017). Data cultures of mobile dating and hook-up apps: Emerging issues for critical social science research. *Big Data & Society*, *4*(2). https://doi.org/10.1177/2053951717720950

Alcaire, R., Flores, A. M. M., & Antunes, E. (2024). Beyond words: Tapping the potential of digital diaries while exploring young adults' experiences on apps. *Societies, 14*(3), 40.

Amaral, I. (2012). Participação em rede: do utilizador ao "consumidor 2.0" e ao "prosumer" [Network participation: From user to "consumer 2.0" and "prosumer"]. *Comunicação e Sociedade, 22*, 131–147.

Amaral, I. (2016). *Redes sociais na internet: sociabilidades emergentes* [Social networks on the internet: Emerging sociabilities]. Editora LabCom.

Amaral, I., Antunes, E., & Flores, A. M. M. (2023). How do Portuguese young adults engage and use m-apps in daily life? An online questionnaire survey. *Observatorio (OBS*), 17*(2).

AmaralI., Flores, A. M., & Antunes, E. (Eds.). (2024). *Apps e Jovens Adultos: Contributos para um Mapeamento de Práticas Mediadas*. UMinho Editora.

Amaral, I., Santos, S. J., Daniel, F., & Filipe, F. (2019). (In)visibilities of men and aging in the media: Discourses from Germany and Portugal. *Lecture Notes in Computer Science, 11593*, 20–32.

Amaral, I., Santos, S. J., Simões, R. B., & Brites, M. J. (2021). Digital aging: Reinforcing normative masculinities on Instagram. *Lecture Notes in Computer Science, 12786*, 335–348.

Amaral, I., & Simões, R. B. (2021). Violence, misogyny, and racism: Young adults' perceptions of online hate speech. In J. S. Sánchez & A. Barrientos (Coord.), *Cosmovisión de la comunicación en redes sociales en la era postdigital* (pp. 869–881). McGraw-Hill.

Antunes, E., Alcaire, R., & Amaral, I. (2022). Wellbeing and (mental) health: A quantitative exploration of Portuguese young adults' uses of M-Apps from a gender perspective. *Social Sciences, 12*(1), 3.

Antunovic, D., Parsons, P., & Cooke, T. R. (2018). 'Checking' and googling: Stages of news consumption among young adults. *Journalism, 19*(5), 632–648.

Ash, G. I., Robledo, D. S., Ishii, M., Pittman, B., DeMartini, K. S., O'Malley, S. S., Redeker, N. S., & Fucito, L. M. (2020). Using web-based social media to recruit heavy-drinking young adults for sleep intervention: Prospective observational study. *Journal of Medical Internet Research, 22*(8), e17449. https://doi.org/10.2196/17449

Bennett, J. (2010). *Vibrant matter: A political ecology of things*. Duke University Press.

Berry, M. (2017). *Creating with mobile media*. Palgrave Macmillan.

Blackwell, C., Birnholtz, J., & Abbott, C. (2015). Seeing and being seen: Co-situation and impression formation using Grindr, a location-aware gay dating app. *New Media & Society, 17*(7), 1117–1136.

Boczkowski, P. J., Mitchelstein, E., & Matassi, M. (2018). "News comes across when I'm in a moment of leisure": Understanding the practices of incidental news consumption on social media. *New Media & Society, 20*(10), 3523–3539.

Boni, F. (2002). Framing media masculinities: Men's lifestyle magazines and the biopolitics of the male body. *European Journal of Communication, 17*(4), 465–478.

Boulianne, S. (2015). Social media use and participation: A meta-analysis of current research. *Information, Communication & Society, 18*(5), 524–538.

Boulianne, S., & Theocharis, Y. (2020). Young people, digital media, and engagement: A meta-analysis of research. *Social Science Computer Review, 38*(2), 111–127.

boyd, d. (2015). Social media: A phenomenon to be analyzed. *Social Media+ Society*, *1*(1). https://doi.org/10.1177/2056305115580148

Butler, J. (1990). Gender trouble, feminist theory, and psychoanalytic discourse. *Feminism/postmodernism*, *327*, 324–340.

Cammaerts, B., Bruter, M., Banaji, S., Harrison, S., & Anstead, N. (2014). The myth of youth apathy: Young Europeans' critical attitudes toward democratic life. *American Behavioral Scientist*, *58*(5), 645–664.

Chester, M. R., Sinnard, M. T., Rochlen, A. B., Nadeau, M. M., Balsan, M. J., & Provence, M. M. (2016). Gay men's experiences coming out online: A qualitative study. *Journal of Gay & Lesbian Social Services*, *28*(4), 317–335.

Correa, T., Hinsley, A. W., & De Zuniga, H. G. (2010). Who interacts on the Web?: The intersection of users' personality and social media use. *Computers in Human Behavior*, *26*(2), 247–253.

De Ridder, S., & Van Bauwel, S. (2015). Youth and intimate media cultures: Gender, sexuality, relationships, and desire as storytelling practices in social networking sites. *Communications*, *40*(3), 319–340.

Deng, T., Kanthawala, S., Meng, J., Peng, W., Kononova, A., Hao, Q., Zhang, Q., & David, P. (2019). Measuring smartphone usage and task switching with log tracking and self-reports. *Mobile Media & Communication*, *7*(1), 3–23.

Ekström, M., Olsson, T., & Shehata, A. (2014). Spaces for public orientation? Longitudinal effects of internet use in adolescence. *Information, Communication & Society*, *17*(2), 168–183.

Gerlich, R. N., Drumheller, K., Babb, J., & De'Armond, D. A. (2015). App consumption: An exploratory analysis of the uses & gratifications of mobile apps. *Academy of Marketing Studies Journal*, *19*(1), 69–79.

Gil de Zúñiga, H., Weeks, B., & Ardèvol-Abreu, A. (2017). Effects of the news-finds-me perception in communication: Social media use implications for news seeking and learning about politics. *Journal of Computer-Mediated Communication*, *22*(3), 105–123.

Gillespie, T. (2014). The relevance of algorithms. In T. Gillespie, P. J. Boczkowski, & K. A. Foot (Eds.), *Media technologies. Essays on communication, materiality, and society* (pp. 167–193). MIT Press.

Gurevitch, M., Coleman, S., & Blumler, J. G. (2009). Political communication – Old and new media relationships. *The Annals of the American Academy of Political and Social Science*, *625*(1), 164–181.

Jenkins, H., Ito, M., & boyd, d. (2016). *Participatory culture in a networked era*. Polity Press.

Khadir, F., Ravindranath, V., & Sen, R. (2021). Factors that influence users in selecting mobile apps – A study on Facebook and Facebook Lite. *Journal of Public Value and Administrative Insight*, *4*(1), 24–36.

Lee, N. J., Shah, D. V., & McLeod, J. M. (2013). Processes of political socialization: A communication mediation approach to youth civic engagement. *Communication Research*, *40*(5), 669–697.

Light, B. (2014). *Disconnecting with social networking sites*. Palgrave Macmillan.

Lupton, D. (2019). 'It's made me a lot more aware': A new materialist analysis of health self-tracking. *Media International Australia*, *171*(1), 66–79.

Mollen, A., & Dhaenens, F. (2018). Audiences' coping practices with intrusive interfaces: Researching audiences in algorithmic, datafied, platform societies. In R. Das & B. Ytre-Arne (Eds.), *The future of audiences: A foresight analysis of interfaces and engagement* (pp. 43–60). Palgrave Macmillan.

Moreno, M., & Whitehill, J. M. (2016). #Wasted: The intersection of substance use behaviors and social media in adolescents and young adults. *Current Opinion in Psychology*, *9*, 72–76.

Ohme, J. (2020). Mobile but not mobilized? Differential gains from mobile news consumption for citizens' political knowledge and campaign participation. *Digital Journalism*, *8*(1), 103–125.

Prom Tep, S., Arcand, M., & Diotte, S. K. (2020). The smartphone, not the tablet, now rules the mobile banking experience. *Journal of Digital Banking*, *5*(2), 155–162.

Silveirinha, M. J., Simões, R. B., & Santos, T. (2020). Him too? Cristiano Ronaldo and the news coverage of a rape case allegation. *Journalism Practice*, *14*(2), 208–224.

Simões, R. B., & Amaral, I. (2022). Sexuality and self-tracking apps. Reshaping gender relations and sexual and reproductive practices. In E. Rees (Ed.), *The Routledge companion to gender, sexuality, and culture* (pp. 413–423). Routledge.

Simões, R. B., Amaral, I., Flores, A. M. M., & Antunes, E. (2023). Scripted gender practices: Young adults' social media app uses in Portugal. *Social Media+ Society*, *9*(3). https://doi.org/10.1177/20563051231196561

Sinkkonen, H. M., Puhakka, H., & Meriläinen, M. (2014). Internet use and addiction among Finnish adolescents (15–19 years). *Journal of Adolescence*, *37*(2), 123–131.

Song, S., Zhao, Y. C., Yao, X., Ba, Z., & Zhu, Q. (2021). Short video apps as a health information source: An investigation of affordances, user experience and users' intention to continue the use of TikTok. *Internet Research*, *31*(6), 2120–2142.

Thulin, E., & Vilhelmson, B. (2019). More at home, more alone? Youth, digital media and the everyday use of time and space. *Geoforum*, *100*, 41–50.

Twenge, J. M. (2017). *iGen: Why today's super-connected kids are growing up less rebellious, more tolerant, less happy – And completely unprepared for adulthood*. Simon and Schuster.

Wajcman, J. (2007). From women and technology to gendered technoscience. *Information, Community and Society*, *10*(3), 287–298.

Whiting, A., & Williams, D. (2013). Why people use social media: A uses and gratifications approach. *Qualitative Market Research: An International Journal*, *16*(4), 362–369.

Zhang, J., Calabrese, C., Ding, J., Liu, M., & Zhang, B. (2018). Advantages and challenges in using mobile apps for field experiments: A systematic review and a case study. *Mobile Media & Communication*, *6*(2), 179–196.

Chapter 2

Young Adulthood Digital Cultures and Practices: An Overview

Eduardo Antunes and Frederico Fonseca

University of Coimbra, Portugal

Abstract

Digital technologies have impacted our culture by expanding into every interstice of everyday life. Mobile gadgets for communications, work and leisure, social media, apps and platforms – the diverse array of items that we usually refer to as digital media and that keep people permanently connected – are at the core of a wider change that goes beyond the use of technology. These technologies provide the material structure for the complex and constant fluxes of information that permeate people's lives, originating new dynamics that impact people's relations, beliefs, practices, representations and identities, bodies or creative and political expressions. Understanding technology as a producer of meanings, subjectivities and agency that are shaped by power relations is central to the MyGender project. Hence, technology is not seen as neutral but as a place of political power. This chapter places young adults at the centre of the changing environment as main cultural and media producers and traces their practices, discourses and representations. By integrating diverse theoretical and empirical contributions that focus on the most relevant aspects of this changing environment, analysing significances, practices and negotiations related to digital cultures and young adults, this chapter proposes a narrative critical literature review that aims to provide a solid framework for the remaining chapters, within the theoretical horizon of the MyGender project.

Keywords: Digital socialisation; digital cultures; young adults; subcultures; digital disconnection

Introduction

From mobile devices facilitating communication to the immersive realms of social media and other digital platforms have immersed themselves into the very fabric of everyday life. However, technology is not neutral; rather, it is imbued with political power, shaping meanings, subjectivities and agency within common societal processes. The omnipresence of digital media technologies – the idea of deep mediatisation (Hepp, 2019) – shapes how people interact and share individual practices, beliefs, values and, therefore, even socialisation patterns. This chapter begins with the contributions of media to socialisation. The focus is set on young adults, who may be called 'digital natives' (Smith et al., 2015), due to their digital abilities that are the foundation of their technological presence that involves forming and strengthening bonds not restricted to physical and geographical proximity. Social media platforms arise as one of the key places for young adults to gather with others in common, developing digital cultures (Bollmer, 2018) and even digital subcultures (Haenfler, 2014), both not static in time and place (Sadiku et al., 2017), likewise the concept of culture as stated by Hall (1997). This comprehensive review of the dynamic interplay between digital cultures and young adulthood even led to approaching extreme phenomena like digital civic activism (Hutchinson, 2021) but also digital disconnection as a possible strategy for young adults to opt out of that ever-increasing immersion in the digital realm (Bucher, 2020). Thus, this chapter discusses social media and other digital platforms' business models that rely on hoarding data. Nonetheless, there is an inescapable bond between the digital landscape and young adults. By situating their engagement within the broader context of digital culture, we lay the groundwork for deeper analyses and discussions. The authors intend to provide a robust foundation for understanding the intricate interplay between technology, culture and identity in the digital age.

Digital Socialisation

The technological and cultural artefacts and contexts play a part in the process of socialisation. Socialisation is the exercise through which people are taught to be proficient members of society (Ashley, 2022). This does not mean it is a necessarily conscious exercise, as it gathers both conscious and unconscious practices. It also does not mean that it has an endpoint. Socialisation has the starting and ending points as life itself, just as inheriting and disseminating customs, norms, ideologies and common thought processes is a lifelong journey.

Media, in general, comply with functions of social reproduction and integration of individuals, as do digital media technologies, particularly as media contributes to socialisation as an endless flow of messages about social norms and expectations (Ashley, 2022). Digital media technologies are part of that, as the Internet has increased the possibilities and desires of being everywhere and every time since the beginning of its widespread use. Even almost 20 years ago, studies were being published regarding the Internet and computer-based technologies' role in social interaction processes (e.g. Brignall & Van Valey, 2005; Lee & Conroy, 2005;

Thomson & Laing, 2003). In the case of Brignall and Van Valey's (2005) and Lee and Conroy's (2005) studies, the focus was precisely on the technology's impact on younger generations' socialisation patterns, thus establishing a connection with the work of this chapter.

Referring to socialisation implies considering that it always involves the connection between the individual and the group and between the citizen and society. Such connection implies social and individual (self) identity construction, both by opposition and by similarity with others (Giddens, 2008). The self has been described as saturated and dissolved in post-modern society (Gergen, 1991). Hall (2006) pointed out that the postmodern subject has no fixed or permanent identity. Digital media arose after postmodernism, a sociological and philosophical thought developed during the 1980s and 1990s (Mirchandani, 2005). The current context of deep mediatisation (Hepp, 2019) is one where social media platforms play a crucial role, including in identity construction and expression processes and overall socialisation practices (Amaral, 2016). Understanding identity as constructed requires promoting the individual as being through an infinite process of formation, in a mediatised environment and culture (Poster, 1995).

Convergence culture and participatory platforms support a socialisation-oriented model based on social software and user-created content (Amaral, 2016). Between the conceptualisations of 'prosumer' (Toffler, 1981), later reappropriated in the convergence culture context (Jenkins, 2006), or 'produse' (Bruns, 2009), the involvement of users as producers and as well consumers is the common denominator. The extent of technological involvement is such that critical concerns and visions are needed in the face of the intrusive nature of technology, which mediates virtually any aspect of life, transforming it into a technological artefact (Ytre-Arne & Das, 2018). Those artefacts can be seen as ways of quantifying the social world, thus transforming it into data that serves power asymmetric relations, therefore possibly gaining the connotation of 'bits of power' (Mansell, 2017). Social media platforms are an example of particular importance in this case, as they are based on the datafication of the social world (Mejias & Couldry, 2019) and are one of the primary loci of digital socialisation (Amaral, 2016), especially for young adults (Amaral et al., 2023; Antunes, Amaral, et al., 2023).

The variety of processes of digital sociability tends to be presented and analysed as a general unifying characteristic of young adults (Mestre-Bach et al., 2020). This trend is not necessarily new. Coyne et al. (2013) focused on media habits and made use of the conceptualisation of 'emerging adulthood', an alternative term to refer to young adults, which, according to Arnett (2014), is a period of development between the ages of 18 and 29. In this context, it was stated that young adults spend more time using the Internet, within the context of media use in general, mainly intending to satisfy certain needs, the most important of which are related to their autonomy, identity and intimacy (Coyne et al., 2013). For Smith et al. (2015), young adults' usage of Internet-based technologies is, in itself, the definition of digital socialisation. In their study, qualitative interviews were carried out to follow 20 young adults who had been initially recruited when they were teenagers. According to them, the young adults in question are socially engaged users, in a sense, 'digital natives', as a result of using technology in a more personal and intrinsically motivated way, revealing a greater openness to innovations in usage. Their findings demonstrate that young adults can be influential in shaping the norms and standards of online behaviour among their peers, with the most socially committed ones standing out and consequently gaining status among them (Smith et al., 2015).

There has been a growing body of work consistently focused on the relationship between young generations and their usage of social media platforms (Zhou et al., 2022) although spreading a variety of social consequences as civic (un)involvement (Amaral, 2023; Mustapha & Mustapha, 2017; Wray-Lake & Abrams, 2020) and digital literacy (Garcia & Mirra, 2021; Roberto et al., 2015). Such topics can be addressed while simultaneously approaching socialisation, which is the true focus of social media platforms. Indeed, social media platforms offer digital socialisation and interaction processes for users, while retaining data as their business model (Assensoh-Kodua, 2020), with that data hoarding model being termed by authors as 'Big Social Data' or 'Social Big Data' (Olshannikova et al., 2017).

Whilst discussing digital socialisation involves forming and strengthening bonds in more or less virtual relationships, it is also interesting to consider the idea that a relationship, just like but not limited to a romantic/love relationship, is perceived as stronger the greater the geographical proximity and consequent physical tangibility between it and the people involved (Kolozsvari, 2015). The conceptual idea of digital social media platforms relies on making available the possibility of contacting, meeting and developing a social bond with supposedly almost anyone. Nonetheless, although that possibility exists, people tend to connect with other people they find to be similar to them in a variety of matters. The notions of filter bubbles and echo chambers (Cinelli et al., 2021; Kahne et al., 2013) tend to emphasise the flow of information in digital spaces between groups of people with common interests, but they can also be relevant to understanding the idea that people end up interacting in digital spaces, above all, with those who are similar to themselves or, at least, with those who share similar views. Indeed, Chambers (2013) emphasised that despite the purpose of these platforms, people used these technologies above all to maintain or deepen existing pre-digital ties. The interest in the geographical community has resulted in the creation of online neighbourhood social networks (ONSNs) (or hyperlocal social networking platforms), which can be categorised as niche social media platforms, which cater to specific society niches, compared to mainstream social media platforms.

ONSNs allow interaction with neighbours in a geographically limited range, mostly for information sharing, with the biggest example being Nextdoor (Vogel et al., 2020). If Nextdoor is the most popular ONSN platform, other competitors arose, like Neighbors by Ring and Nebenan (Vogel et al., 2020, 2021). Although supposedly created to strengthen hyperlocal bonds, some of those examples of ONSN platforms are focused on local crime and public safety issues. Lillie and Achhammer (2023) argue that Nextdoor, despite being popular, fails with being able to get people together to tackle neighbourhood issues, which is the main idea of community networks, mainly due to the technical and social design of the app that left out an array of topics. The results of Ohmer et al.'s (2021) study revealed privacy and safety concerns of adolescents and young adults regarding Nextdoor. Research has shown that the younger generations, like young adults, may use social media platforms to help increase awareness of social issues, but they usually do it on a bigger scale than a neighbourhood and also through mainstream social media platforms which are better suited to that idea of large scale digital activism (Hutchinson, 2021; Xu & Saxton, 2019).

Digital Cultures

Both the shapes of virtual civic participation and the various patterns of digital socialisation can be inserted into a framework of culture whose precise definition is always difficult to pin down, as everything and nothing seems to fit into or be absent from the same concept. According to Hall (1997), culture, by itself, is multifaceted, reflecting different methods of coping with peculiar constellations of social and material life experiences, thus never being a homogeneous structure, at least in an industrial society.

Regarding the concept of 'digital culture', according to Bollmer (2018), it lies at the intersection of three main elements: (1) narratives about technologies; (2) material infrastructures that shape communication and (3) the physical capacities of bodies (human or otherwise), in their ability to move and perform specific acts. However, the concept of 'digital culture' arose in the 1990s and 2000s as one of the definitions indistinctly used to refer to the cultural impact of computational technologies (Bollmer, 2018), alongside terms like 'cyberculture' (Bell, 2001) and 'technoculture' (Penley & Ross, 1991) and even others that gained popularity more recently as 'internet culture' or 'information culture' (Sadiku et al., 2017). Bollmer (2018) alerts us to the greater theoretical clarity of the plural formulation 'digital cultures' instead of the singular. The reason is that there is not just one digital culture, since the plural idea of digital cultures addresses how digital media influence cultures, resulting in different ways in different and specific places and times. Sadiku et al. (2017) reinforce this idea suggesting that, therefore, digital cultures are drastically and permanently changing, not only because digital technologies are changing but also because social norms and values change. One possible example could be the use of digital platforms for performing, expressing, exposing and, consequently, socialising one's sexual and/or romantic identity and intimacy. The ideological matrices of the social norms in force allow readings on whether or not these practices fit into different cultural contexts (Antunes, 2023).

Theoretical discussions about digital cultures began with the growing trend towards the digitalisation of socialisation processes (Bollmer, 2018), which historically envisioned the disappearance of the physical and tangible imprint of bodies, replaced by digital avatars that virtually reflected the identity of people, in this case, turned into users (Stone, 1995; Turkle, 1995). Even though this idea of bodily/avatar replacement has not been fully achieved, digital socialisation has prevailed and currently prevails across generations. However, in the particular case of the younger generations, stronger links have been established between the role of the use of digital technologies in the general dynamics of young adults' lives. For example, younger generations are more able to overcome the idea of a fragile bond if it exists merely in the virtual realm (Hart, 2015).

As we discussed the conceptual notion of digital cultures, Wijaya (2023) focused on young citizens' perception of such a notion. Wijaya (2023) conceptualised young citizens as Indonesian university students, as young citizens and digital cultures compose digital citizenship. Accordingly, the idea of digital citizenship requires users to work with supposed shared values towards a globally networked and multicultural society across time and geographical boundaries (Wijaya, 2023). Mihailidis (2020) addresses the idea that younger generations now have more ways of participating in matters of digital citizenship precisely because of how rooted they are in digital cultures and their technological practices. Particularly, Mihailidis (2020) focuses on what he understands to be the civic potential of memes and hashtags, arguing that those technological vehicles may be rooted in overall literacy practices, thus connecting civic participation with digital participation. In regards to young adults, civic participation tends to assume a noteworthy political almost activist tone (Hutchinson, 2021) although other forms of digital and online civic activity exist (Kahne et al., 2013). For the study of Kahne et al. (2013), to analyse digital civic participation, it is important to consider the digital flow of information and news, which circulates differently according to each one's digital footprint, as the previously mentioned filter bubbles and echo chambers may accomplish a sense of belonging to a digital subculture, even if that subculture is just a space for ideological and even partisan intervention and participation (Sunstein, 2007). Although technological innovations tend to be seen as overall promising, especially regarding the array of possibilities given to its users, there is still, at least, a need for reflecting on the societal consequences of digital cultures becoming, more and more, almost the same as the broader meaning of cultures. For example, authors like Xiaojuan (2023) state the need to consider the possibility of the increasingly powerful digital technologies resulting in prosaic and dull cultural expressions.

Early 21st-century studies like the ones of Ito (2005) and Li-Vollmer (2002) addressed how commercial products and brands were able to generate (sub)cultures mostly in younger generations, stating as examples YuGiOh and Pokemon, precisely focussing on the idea of those products being able to generate consumer cultures. The consumer imprint of (digital) cultures is still prevalent, as the *locus* of socialisation is rooted in market dynamics. By applying qualitative-based interviews with 32 young adults aged between 20 and 25 years old, Gangneux (2018) stated that the digital socialisation practices of young adults are, at least partially, embedded in the predominant neoliberal cultural discourse that is focused on individual responsibility for digital actions and behaviours, that sometimes mimics a one-person corporate digital management. Entrepreneurship and self-responsibility are part of young adults' practical knowledge of navigating both the offline world and the digital world, especially on social media platforms (Gangneux, 2018). The role of social media platforms is almost inevitable in current life practices, especially in the lives of young adults, as those media devices serve as an extension of themselves (Zhang et al., 2018). Regarding young adults' digital social media patterns of usage, there is also an important aspect of identity expression involved, both because those digital spaces evolved to being able to immerse people in an interactive reality of life so interwoven that it influences how someone considers and sees themself, and also because the ever construction of self-identity depends on interaction, i.e. socialisation practices which are being channelled to sorts of social media platforms (Brekhus, 2020; Wandel & Beavers, 2010). Those digital socialisation practices may be twofold in their purpose, as young adults understand social media platforms as places for creating and developing both professional and personal interactions (Gangneux, 2018).

Understanding young adults' digital cultures participation also requires understanding some of the shared values between most of them. According to Katz et al. (2022), Gen Z (although the exact date varies from scholar to scholar, in this case, they considered born 1997 onwards) is a generation where acceptance and respect are key values, from gender to religious beliefs, as their idea of reinforcing diversity and freedom may be their 'most widely shared worldview' (Katz et al., 2022, p. 193). At the same time, one should not believe that every young adult shares those values, as social generations should not be considered universal (Vieira, 2018), although some aspects tend to be presented and even critically discussed as somewhat general unifying characteristics of generations like it is the popularity of digital sociability practices for young adults (Mestre-Bach et al., 2020).

When one addresses culture, the hegemonic processes must be taken into consideration, i.e. the Gramscian idea of cultural hegemony. Between those power dynamics, subcultures arise, and the study of those subcultures was always inserted in youth studies. Generally, subcultures 'can seem alternately strange and silly, mysterious and dangerous, or all of the above. They appear as bizarre little worlds with secret signs, idiosyncratic rituals, fantastical styles, and arcane social codes. Yet popular perceptions of sub-cultures are often incomplete, little more than caricatures based upon half-truths or hysteria' (Haenfler, 2014). Definitions of a subculture have varied in academia theoretical movements, with the post-subcultural movement even introducing other substitute or complementary concepts as 'neo-tribes' and 'scenes' (Haenfler, 2014). In that post-subcultural context, the very own idea of 'subculture' may lose some relevance as a theoretical framework to understand youth, precisely because of the interpretations of younger generations as being more fluid and dynamic, more permanently constructed (Robards & Bennett, 2011) and view social identity as dynamic, not something we permanently belong to. This reflects the trend of increasing diversity, as noted by Katz et al. (2022) in the newer generations of young adults. Robards and Bennett (2011) reinforced the idea that social media platforms allow behaviours associated with neo-tribes, as young adults use those technologies to gather with others – socialise – and share a sense of social and collective identity (Haenfler, 2014). Digitalisation processes allow younger generations to develop a common shared interest in something fundamental to the creation of a social group, whether it is defined as a 'subculture', 'neo-tribe' or even a 'scene'. That shared interest tends to be something that is not seen as the mainstream cultural norm but encompasses an array of topics, for example, from music genres

(Guerra, 2020) to graffiti practices (Baird, 2022), to skateboarding (Dupont, 2020) and even bodybuilding (Wellman, 2020). Robards and Bennett (2011) reinstate that such social and cultural identification occurs due to the individual-centred systems basis of any social media platforms, thus always requiring socialisation and identity (re)negotiation from young adults.

The Political Power of Technology

Particularly in the last decade, algorithms, applications and data have become commodities, with added commercial value, while being easily tradable, thus compelling us to question the role of the vertiginously evolving technological digital realm in today's society. The literature in the field of digital studies has sought to reflect on the transposition we are witnessing from the digital to the algorithmic (Noble, 2018), as in a (digital) society, economy, culture and politics are increasingly linked to deterministic and predictive data flows of 'lively data' (Lupton, 2016). Our daily lives are increasingly designed to delegate human agency to digital technologies themselves, turning us into mere agents who act as communication channels between devices, the global digital world and technological determinism (Kuntsman & Miyake, 2019).

We live in the digitalisation age of infrastructures, including goods and services, and immersive datafication (Bucher, 2020; Ghita & Thorén, 2021; Kuntsman & Miyake, 2019). Nonetheless, increasing digitalisation may be contested, particularly by generations that are more aware of the technological and digital realms, their affordances and implications, like young adults. Both mental health and well-being have been acknowledged as popular expressions, mainly in young adulthood, especially since the COVID-19 pandemic, and have even motivated a plethora of platforms aimed to help deal with such matters (Antunes, Alcaire, & Amaral, 2023). Therefore, a choice to step back from digital technologies and platforms can be a response to the overwhelming presence of technology in young adults' lives, perhaps considering the potential negative effects of increasing digitalisation mainly concerning their mental health and overall well-being. However, the motivations, practices and experiences of digital disconnection are never fully realised because disconnection is intentionally premeditated and controlled by devices and platforms but also because the data left 'behind' continues to be used by the media (Kuntsman & Miyake, 2019). As soon as someone is connected, the disconnection is never fully achieved, since the persistent nature of today's interconnected world is immersed in the broader notion of a surveillance culture, as worked by Lyon (2017), which surpasses the ideas of surveillance state and surveillance society.

We are facing a continuous practice of digital disconnection, or even the so-called 'digital detox' (Syvertsen, 2020), in which it is necessary to imagine disconnection as a continuous challenge to the one-dimensional understanding of the 'non-use' of the digital realm, while at the same time acknowledging the possibility of destruction and reconfiguration of technologies, due to digital usages and consequential digital collapses. The same extends to an example of a mere technological platform or even a form of digital sociability being challenged (Kuntsman & Miyake, 2019). Cai and McKenna (2023) conceptualise disconnection as a form of resistance, building from Foucault's analysis of power and resistance. In that case, the focus relies on the fact that even in people's everyday lives and holidays, that break-away moment from the routine is digitally and technologically mediated, thus suggesting the imagination of 'digital-free tourism'. The disconnection has the potential to be a powerful tool for political mobilisation and social transformation, when intended to deepen individuals' critical engagement with technology, thus creating for them a better capacity for more global critical reflections, which can even result in other practices such as activism, change and critique (Natale & Treré, 2020). A kind of collective political responsibility aimed at producing social and political change, opening up 'new ways of imagining relations between technologies and freedoms, engagement and digitality and sociality and refusal' (Kuntsman & Miyake, 2019, p. 2).

There is a need to address the current digital platforms' power, especially in data aggregation, as human resistance becomes limited, due to algorithms and data mining powerfully and persistently infringing on individual and collective freedoms (Karppi et al., 2021). Platforms and digital data themselves, as non-human actors, may become the ones that determine our (im)possibilities of 'escaping' the digital (Karppi et al., 2021). The logic of datafication and predictive analysis makes it difficult to resist and opt out of digital platforms and services (Bucher, 2020). Digital solutionism as a support for a better life, a digital life, has reinforced the subjective power of data production in this type of activity. These practices, set in a context of capitalist time management, seek to collect and process data and then 'forward' it to the user (Kennedy et al., 2015). In academia, several discussions have revolved around neoliberal responsibilisation concerning media use and non-use, critiquing its tendency to strip dis/connection of its political significance (Moe & Madsen, 2021; Syvertsen, 2020). Some scholars examined how disconnection can function as a form of resistance (Cai & McKenna, 2023; Kaun & Treré, 2020) to the point that even Hesselberth (2018) considered it a fundamental right. While delving into the realm of digital disconnection, others have explored the extent of digital datafication of social and societal structures (Karppi et al., 2021; Mejias, 2013). The entanglements between digital disconnection and its commodification are ambiguous and unclear (Karppi et al., 2021). There are significant ethical and privacy implications arising from the use of these applications and the data they produce.

In the digital age, the power of digital technology is presented in the form of selective algorithms, persuasive apps, personalised ads, fake news, and, in broader terms, narratives that present technology as the solution to all our problems, among many other means through which power is exercised – the 'soft power' (Nye, 1990). Digital technology is primarily based on the so-called data economy, where a large part of that data is individuals' personal (often intimate) data – the previously mentioned idea of 'Big Social Data' (Olshannikova et al., 2017). The data trade as a business model has expanded throughout society in recent decades, transforming 'citizens into users and data subjects', and threatening 'freedom, equality, democracy, autonomy, creativity and intimacy' (Véliz, 2020, p. 7). Some scholars have discussed the ethical implications of technological implantation in society, such as data privacy, security, addiction to technology, hate speech and disinformation, manipulation and political influence. By analysing the relationship between privacy and (technological) power, it is possible to better comprehend how institutions accumulate, exercise and transform power in the digital age, understanding the type of domination fuelled by privacy rights violations. Thus privacy gains popularity as the 'only way' to regain control, allowing people to keep certain intimate things private, such as thoughts, experiences, conversations or plans. People may feel empowered by privacy to the point of contesting governments and companies, contributing to a feeling of regained control of their own lives and their presence in societal structures, including socialisation and culture-belonging processes. Sometimes, privacy may be envisioned as key in encouraging people to create a more egalitarian, democratic and just world. For example, for LGBTQIA+ youth, privacy invasion is a considerable risk from digital technology usage, even though digital platforms can allow for an important identity self-exploration and cultural belonging (Selkie et al., 2020).

Technology and data economy influence people through coercive and persuasive power while being the vehicles to normalise specific ways of thinking. A large part of the power of technology lies in the narratives it constructs, and the stories it tells about the importance of technological progress. Technology wants people to think that the innovations it introduces into the market are inevitable (Zuboff, 2020). Most companies incorporate narratives stating the importance of treating personal data as commodities as a minor evil for a future with an even increased incorporation of digital technologies since they symbolise progress. That is the narrative of progressive and, most of all, inevitable technology.

Conclusion

In today's rapidly evolving digital landscape, young adults find themselves deeply rooted in digital technologies, shaping their socialisation processes (Ashley, 2022) and, as a consequence, their cultural practices (Bollmer, 2018). Academics' interest in this topic is not new, as even the cases of Brignall and Van Valey's (2005) and Lee and Conroy's (2005) analysed the impacts of technologies on younger generations' socialisation patterns. Nonetheless, today's world may even be characterised by the prevalence of social media platforms, which intensified digital integration (Amaral, 2016; Mejias & Couldry, 2019), with young adults being often labelled as 'digital natives' that navigate dynamic digital cultures that continuously evolve in response to technological advancements and changing societal norms (Mihailidis, 2020; Sadiku et al., 2017). Precisely due to the mutation of social norms and values through time and place, Bollmer (2018) suggested using 'digital cultures' in a plural form that symbolises how digital technologies result in a wide variety of cultures and movements and not in a uniform singular culture. Social media platforms may function as conduits for the gathering of subcultures, or other substitute or complementary concepts such as 'neo-tribes' and 'scenes' (Haenfler, 2014), by enabling digital gathering, socialisation and sharing of thoughts, values, opinions and identities. As young adults engage with digital technologies, they participate in matters of digital citizenship and civic engagement, influencing political discourse and activism (Hutchinson, 2021).

Precisely because young adults seem more aware of the dynamic nature of digital cultures, and alongside the opportunities for connection and expression, digital technologies raise concerns about privacy, data ownership and the commercialisation of personal information (Lupton, 2016). That data hoarding model can be termed 'Big Social Data' (Olshannikova et al., 2017), alongside the idea of the inescapability of a digital surveillance culture (Lyon, 2017). The peculiar case of the COVID-19 pandemic has further increased the debate regarding peoples' relationship with technology, namely young adults, by underscoring the importance of mental health and well-being in the digital age (Antunes, Alcaire, & Amaral, 2023). By opting for digital disconnection, young adults reclaim agency over their digital lives, prioritising well-being, authentic connections and offline experiences.

In essence, while young adults remain deeply intertwined with digital technologies, the phenomenon of digital disconnection underscores young adults' agency in navigating the digital landscape. Digital disconnection/opt-out may represent a conscious choice to balance the benefits of digital engagement with the need for offline experiences and well-being in an increasingly digitised society. Likewise, that critical stance may even result in other behaviours like digital activism (Kaun & Treré, 2020; Natale & Treré, 2020), thus practising their digital civic citizenship (Hutchinson, 2021; Kahne et al., 2013; Mustapha & Mustapha, 2017; Wray-Lake & Abrams, 2020). Recognising that (sub-)cultures increasingly happen through digital technologies, young adults may opt out of that mediated presence (Bucher, 2020), especially aware of the big social data that in fact does never allow for a complete and total disconnection of that digital realm. Nonetheless, the digital realm seems inevitable. Within this context, projects like MyGender aim to explore the intricate intersections of technology, culture and identity, shedding light on the complexities of young adults navigating the digital era. Through (digital) socialisation processes, young adults are mostly immersed in an array of digital cultures that mutate over time, as their feeling of cultural belonging is permanently constructed (Robards & Bennett, 2011); likewise, their social identity belonging is not static but rather diverse (Katz et al., 2022).

References

Amaral, I. (2016). *Redes Sociais na Internet: Sociabilidades Emergentes.* LABCOM.
Amaral, I. (2023). #17Feb and the so-called social media revolution: A decade over the Libya's uprising. *Estudos em Comunicação*, (36), 1–15.
Amaral, I., Antunes, E., & Flores, A. M. M. (2023). How do Portuguese young adults engage and use m-apps in daily life? An online questionnaire survey. *Observatorio (OBS*)*, *17*(2), 245–263. https://doi.org/10.15847/obsOBS17220232141
Antunes, E. (2023). Foucault, sexualidade e intimidade mediada pelo digital. *Estudos Em Comunicação*, *2*(37), 104–115. https://doi.org/10.25768/1646-4974n37v2a06

Antunes, E., Alcaire, R., & Amaral, I. (2023). Wellbeing and (mental) health: A quantitative exploration of Portuguese young adults' uses of M-Apps from a gender perspective. *Social Sciences*, *12*(3), 1–14. https://doi.org/10.3390/socsci12010003

Antunes, E., Amaral, I., Simões, R. B., & Flores, A. M. M. (2023). Who are the young adults in Portugal? Daily usage of social media and mobile phones, in a no-kids and no-independent housing context—Results from a representative online survey. *Youth*, *3*(4), 1101–1120. https://doi.org/10.3390/youth3040070

Arnett, J. J. (2014). *Emerging adulthood: The winding road from the late teens through the twenties* (2nd ed.). Oxford University Press.

Ashley, S. (2022). *Society: A global introduction* (2nd ed.). https://pressbooks.bccampus.ca/society2/

Assensoh-Kodua, A. (2020). This thing of social media! Going business or socialisation? Solving the great dilemma. *Foresight*, *22*(3), 331–350. https://doi.org/10.1108/FS-04-2019-0028

Baird, R. (2022). Youth and social media: The affordances and challenges of online graffiti practice. *Media, Culture & Society*, *44*(4), 764–784.

Bell, D. (2001). *An introduction to cybercultures*. Routledge.

Bollmer, G. (2018). *Theorizing digital cultures*. SAGE Publications Ltd. https://doi.org/10.4135/9781529714760

Brekhus, W. H. (2020). *The sociology of identity: Authenticity, multidimensionality, and mobility*. John Wiley & Sons.

Brignall, T. W., III., & Van Valey, T. (2005). The impact of internet communications on social interaction. *Sociological Spectrum*, *25*(3), 335–348.

Bruns, A. (2009). From prosumer to produser: Understanding user-led content creation. In *Transforming audiences 2009*. https://eprints.qut.edu.au/27370

Bucher, T. (2020). Nothing to disconnect from? Being singular plural in an age of machine learning. *Media, Culture & Society*, *42*(4), 610–617. https://doi.org/10.1177/0163443720914028

Cai, W., & McKenna, B. (2023). Power and resistance: Digital-free tourism in a connected world. *Journal of Travel Research*, *62*(2), 290–304.

Chambers, D. (2013). *Social media and personal relationships: Online intimacies and networked friendship*. Palgrave Macmillan. https://doi.org/10.1057/9781137314444

Cinelli, M., de Francisci Morales, G., Galeazzi, A., Quattrociocchi, W., & Starnini, M. (2021). The echo chamber effect on social media. In A. Underdal (Ed.), *Proceedings of the national academy of sciences of the United States of America* (Vol. 118, Issue 9, pp. 1–8). https://doi.org/10.1073/pnas.2023301118

Coyne, S. M., Padilla-Walker, L. M., & Howard, E. (2013). Emerging in a digital world: A decade review of media use, effects, and gratifications in emerging adulthood. *Emerging Adulthood*, *1*(2), 125–137. https://doi.org/10.1177/2167696813479782

Dupont, T. (2020). Authentic subcultural identities and social media: American skateboarders and Instagram. *Deviant Behavior*, *41*(5), 649–664.

Gangneux, J. (2018). *Mediated young adulthood: Social network sites in the neoliberal era*. University of Glasgow.

Garcia, A., & Mirra, N. (2021). Writing toward justice: Youth speculative civic literacies in online policy discourse. *Urban Education*, *56*(4), 640–669.

Gergen, K. J. (1991). *The saturated self: Dilemmas of identity in contemporary life*. Basic Books.

Ghita, C., & Thorén, C. (2021). Going cold Turkey! An autoethnographic exploration of digital disengagement. *Nordicom Review*, *42*(S4), 152–167. https://doi.org/10.2478/nor-2021-0047
Giddens, A. (2008). *Sociologia* (6th ed.). Fundação Calouste Gulbenkian.
Guerra, P. (2020). Under-connected: Youth subcultures, resistance and sociability in the Internet age. In *Hebdige and subculture in the twenty-first century: Through the subcultural lens* (pp. 207–230). Palgrave Macmillan.
Haenfler, R. (2014). *Subcultures: The basics*. Routledge. https://doi.org/10.4324/9781315888514
Hall, S. (1997). Introduction. In S. Hall (Ed.), *Representation: Cultural representations and signifying practices*. SAGE Publications Ltd.
Hall, S. (2006). *A Identidade Cultural na Pós-modernidade* (1st ed.). DP&A Editora.
Hart, M. (2015). Youth intimacy on Tumblr: A pilot study. *Young*, *23*(3), 193–208. https://doi.org/10.1177/1103308815577878
Hepp, A. (2019). *Deep mediatization*. Routledge.
Hesselberth, P. (2018). Discourses on disconnectivity and the right to disconnect. *New Media & Society*, *20*(5), 1994–2010.
Hutchinson, J. (2021). Micro-platformization for digital activism on social media. *Information, Communication & Society*, *24*(1), 35–51. https://doi.org/10.1080/1369118X.2019.1629612
Ito, M. (2005). Technologies of the childhood imagination: Yugioh, media mixes, and everyday cultural production. *Structures of Participation in Digital Culture*, 88–111.
Jenkins, H. (2006). *Convergence culture: Where old and new media collide*. New York University Press.
Kahne, J., Lee, N. J., & Feezell, J. T. (2013). The civic and political significance of online participatory cultures among youth transitioning to adulthood. *Journal of Information Technology & Politics*, *10*(1), 1–20.
Karppi, T., Chia, A., & Jorge, A. (2021). In the mood for disconnection. *Convergence*, *27*(6), 1599–1614. https://doi.org/10.1177/13548565211034621
Katz, R., Ogilvie, S., Shaw, J., & Woodhead, L. (2022). *Gen Z explained: The art of living in a digital age*. University of Chicago Press.
Kaun, A., & Treré, E. (2020). Repression, resistance and lifestyle: Charting (dis)connection and activism in times of accelerated capitalism. *Social Movement Studies*, *19*(5–6), 697–715.
Kennedy, H., Poell, T., & Van Dijck, J. (2015). Data and agency. *Big Data & Society*, *2*(2), 1–7. https://doi.org/10.1177/2053951715621569
Kolozsvari, O. (2015). "Physically we are apart, mentally we are not." Creating a shared space and a sense of belonging in long-distance relationships. *Qualitative Sociology Review*, *11*(4), 102–115. https://doi.org/10.18778/1733-8077.11.4.05
Kuntsman, A., & Miyake, E. (2019). The paradox and continuum of digital disengagement: Denaturalising digital sociality and technological connectivity. *Media, Culture & Society*, *41*(6), 901–913. https://doi.org/10.1177/0163443719853732
Lee, C. K., & Conroy, D. M. (2005). Socialisation through consumption: Teenagers and the internet. *Australasian Marketing Journal*, *13*(1), 8–19.
Li-Vollmer, M. (2002). *The Pokémon phenomenon: A case study of media influence and audience agency in children's consumer culture*. University of Washington.

Lillie, J., & Achhammer, M. (2023). Nextdoor v. the community network literature: Do Nextdoor's uses match the potential envisioned for ComNets. *Convergence*, *29*(4), 901–918. https://doi.org/10.1177/13548565231174595

Lupton, D. (2016). *The quantified self*. Polity Press.

Lyon, D. (2017). Surveillance culture: Engagement, exposure, and ethics in digital modernity. *International Journal of Communication*, *11*, 824–842.

Mansell, R. (2017). Bits of power: Struggling for control of information and communication networks. *The Political Economy of Communication*, *5*(1), 2–29. http://www.polecom.org

Mejias, U. A. (2013). *Off the network: Disrupting the digital world* (Vol. 41). University of Minnesota Press.

Mejias, U. A., & Couldry, N. (2019). Datafication. *Internet Policy Review*, *8*(4), 1–10. https://doi.org/10.14763/2019.4.1428

Mestre-Bach, G., Blycker, G. R., & Potenza, M. N. (2020). Pornography use in the setting of the COVID-19 pandemic. *Journal of Behavioral Addictions*, *9*(2), 181–183. https://doi.org/10.1556/2006.2020.00015

Mihailidis, P. (2020). The civic potential of memes and hashtags in the lives of young people. *Discourse: Studies in the Cultural Politics of Education*, *41*(5), 762–781. https://doi.org/10.1080/01596306.2020.1769938

Mirchandani, R. (2005). Postmodernism and sociology: From the epistemological to the empirical. *Sociological Theory*, *23*(1), 86–115.

Moe, H., & Madsen, O. J. (2021). Understanding digital disconnection beyond media studies. *Convergence*, *27*(6), 1584–1598.

Mustapha, L. K., & Mustapha, M. L. (2017). Media and youths' political engagement during the 2015 Nigerian general election. *Estudos em Comunicação*, *24*.

Natale, S., & Treré, E. (2020). Vinyl won't save us: Reframing disconnection as engagement. *Media, Culture & Society*, *42*(4), 626–633.

Noble, S. U. (2018). *Algorithms of oppression: How search engines reinforce racism*. New York University Press.

Nye, J. S. (1990). Soft power. *Foreign Policy*, *80*, 153–171. https://doi.org/10.2307/1148580

Ohmer, M., Booth, J., & Farzan, R. (2021). R U connected? Engaging youth in designing a mobile application for facilitating community organizing and engagement. *Journal of Community Practice*, *29*(3), 257–279. https://doi.org/10.1080/10705422.2021.1963383

Olshannikova, E., Olsson, T., Huhtamäki, J., & Kärkkäinen, H. (2017). Conceptualizing big social data. *Journal of Big Data*, *4*(1). https://doi.org/10.1186/s40537-017-0063-x

Penley, C., & Ross, A. (Eds.). (1991). *Technoculture*. University of Minnesota Press.

Poster, M. (1995). *The second media age*. Polity Press.

Robards, B., & Bennett, A. (2011). Mytribe: Post-subcultural manifestations of belonging on social network sites. *Sociology*, *45*(2), 303–317. https://doi.org/10.1177/0038038510394025

Roberto, M. S., Fidalgo, A., & Buckingham, D. (2015). De que falamos quando falamos de infoexclusão e literacia digital? Perspetivas dos nativos digitais. *Observatorio (OBS*)*, *9*(1). https://doi.org/10.15847/obsOBS912015819

Sadiku, M. N., Tembely, M., Musa, S. M., & Momoh, O. D. (2017). Digital culture. *International Journal of Advanced Research in Computer Science and Software Engineering*, 7(6), 33–34.

Selkie, E., Adkins, V., Masters, E., Bajpai, A., & Shumer, D. (2020). Transgender adolescents' uses of social media for social support. *Journal of Adolescent Health*, 66(3), 275–280. https://doi.org/10.1016/j.jadohealth.2019.08.011

Smith, J., Hewitt, B., & Skrbiš, Z. (2015). Digital socialization: Young people's changing value orientations towards internet use between adolescence and early adulthood. *Information, Communication & Society*, 18(9), 1022–1038. https://doi.org/10.1080/1369118X.2015.1007074

Stone, A. R. (1995). *The war of desire and technology at the close of the mechanical age*. MIT Press.

Sunstein, C. R. (2007). *Republic.com 2.0*. Princeton University Press.

Syvertsen, T. (2020). *Digital detox: The politics of disconnecting*. Emerald Publishing Limited.

Thomson, E. S., & Laing, A. W. (2003). "The net generation": Children and young people, the internet and online shopping. *Journal of Marketing Management*, 19(3–4), 491–512.

Toffler, A. (1981). *The third wave*. Bantam Books.

Turkle, S. (1995). *Life on the screen: Identity in the age of the internet*. Touchstone.

Véliz, C. (2020). *Privacy is power: Why and how you should take back control of your data*. Random House.

Vieira, J. (2018). Media and generations in Portugal. *Societies*, 8(61), 1–19. https://doi.org/10.3390/soc8030061

Vogel, P., Grotherr, C., Kurtz, C., & Böhmann, T. (2020). Conceptualizing design parameters of online neighborhood social networks. In *Proceedings of 15th International Conference on Wirtschaftsinformatik*. https://doi.org/10.30844/wi_2020_o5

Vogel, P., Kurtz, C., Grotherr, C., & Böhmann, T. (2021). Fostering social resilience via online neighborhood social networks during the COVID-19 pandemic and beyond: Status quo, design dilemmas and research opportunities. In *Proceedings of the Annual Hawaii International Conference on System Sciences*, 2020-January (pp. 3037–3046). https://doi.org/10.24251/hicss.2021.370

Wandel, T., & Beavers, A. (2010). Playing around with identity. *Facebook and Philosophy: What's on Your Mind*, 89–96.

Wellman, M. L. (2020). What it means to be a bodybuilder: Social media influencer labor and the construction of identity in the bodybuilding subculture. *The Communication Review*, 23(4), 273–289.

Wijaya, A. K. (2023). Digital culture: The conception of young citizens. *International Journal of Education and Humanities*, 3(1), 99–111. https://doi.org/10.58557/(ijeh).v3i1.142

Wray-Lake, L., & Abrams, L. S. (2020). Pathways to civic engagement among urban youth of color. *Monographs of the Society for Research in Child Development*, 85(2), 7–154.

Xiaojuan, J. (2023). Technology and culture in the digital era. *Social Sciences in China*, 44(1), 4–24. https://doi.org/10.1080/02529203.2023.2192080

Xu, W., & Saxton, G. D. (2019). Does stakeholder engagement pay off on social media? A social capital perspective. *Nonprofit and Voluntary Sector Quarterly*, 48(1), 28–49. https://doi.org/10.1177/0899764018791267

Ytre-Arne, B., & Das, R. (2018). In the interest of audiences: An agenda. In R. Das & B. Ytre-Arne (Eds.), *The future of audiences: A foresight analysis of interfaces and engagement* (pp. 275–292). Palgrave Macmillan. https://doi.org/10.1007/978-3-319-75638-7_14

Zhang, J., Calabrese, C., Ding, J., Liu, M., & Zhang, B. (2018). Advantages and challenges in using mobile apps for field experiments: A systematic review and a case study. *Mobile Media & Communication*, 6(2), 179–196. https://doi.org/10.1177/2050157917725550

Zhou, Y., He, T., & Lin, F. (2022). The digital divide is aging: An intergenerational investigation of social media engagement in China. *International Journal of Environmental Research and Public Health*, 19(19). https://doi.org/10.3390/ijerph191912965

Zuboff, S. (2020). *A Era do Capitalismo da Vigilância: A Disputa por Um Futuro Humano na Nova Fronteira do Poder* (L. F. Silva, & M. S. Pereira, Trans.). Relógio D' Água Editores.

Chapter 3

Gender Across Digital Platforms

Inês Amaral, Ana Marta M. Flores and Eduardo Antunes
University of Coimbra, Portugal

Abstract

As younger generations navigate a blended reality, their interaction with digital content and apps is marked by multitasking. Gender intersects with media and individual preferences, shaping how people navigate digital realms. This chapter investigates how young adults perceive personal digital experiences, analysing them based on various socio-demographic factors. Using a quantitative approach, a survey was conducted with 1,500 young adults in Portugal in October 2021. The sample was representative of the population distribution by sex, age and region. Statistical analysis revealed correlations between digital behaviours and socio-demographic factors such as gender, sexual orientation and parenthood status. Results indicated significant differences in agreement levels among different groups, highlighting areas such as online harassment, content creation, social interaction and digital intimacy. The findings challenge assumptions of homogeneity in generational technology usage and underscore the importance of considering diverse demographic perspectives in digital research. This chapter sheds light on the interplay between technology, identity and social connections, emphasising the relevance of gender in digital platform studies.

Keywords: Gender dynamics; online intimacy; digital platforms; social relationships; young adults; online survey

Introduction

Media convergence prompts the hybridisation of channels (Chadwick, 2017), underpinning the argument that audiences are inherently cross-media (Schrøder, 2011). Younger generations inhabit a predominantly hybrid reality where consumption has evolved into a collective process (Jenkins, 2006), technology manifests increasingly individualised and performative uses (Livingstone et al., 2005) and engagement with content and applications operates within a multitasking logic (Van Dijck, 2014). In this regard, mediated choices (Hepp, 2013) and the usage practices and appropriations of technology by younger generations differ from those of previous generations (Pacheco et al., 2017).

Moreover, within this landscape of media convergence and hybridity, gender dynamics play a crucial role in shaping online interactions and intimacy. Media channels and individual preferences intersect with gender identities, influencing how individuals navigate and negotiate digital spaces. Scholars have highlighted how gendered norms and expectations shape online behaviours, affecting everything from content consumed to how individuals present themselves online (boyd, 2014; Herring, 2003). For example, research suggests that women may encounter different experiences and challenges in online spaces compared to men, particularly about issues of privacy, harassment and self-representation (Duguay, 2017). Similarly, studies have explored how gender identities intersect with online dating practices, revealing complex dynamics of attraction, communication and power dynamics (Ellison et al., 2012).

Furthermore, the notion of intimacy in the digital age is intricately intertwined with questions of gender and identity. As individuals navigate digital platforms and engage in online interactions, they negotiate notions of intimacy in diverse ways, influenced by cultural norms, societal expectations and personal preferences (Baym, 2015). Gendered perceptions and experiences of intimacy shape the types of relationships individuals seek and maintain online and the level of trust and vulnerability they are willing to exhibit (Ranzini & Lutz, 2017). Consequently, the intersection of media convergence, gender dynamics and online intimacy presents a rich terrain for scholarly inquiry, offering insights into the complex interplay between technology, identity and social relationships in the digital age.

Mobile applications have emerged as multifaceted entities, serving as media texts and extensions of the digital self. Within the realm of contemporary technological culture, these apps play pivotal roles in diverse spheres, such as entertainment, social interaction and health promotion. Understanding the implications of mobile applications (m-apps) in activities ranging from gaming and dating to fostering improvements in health and fitness demands a nuanced and interconnected analytical approach. Scholars Fotopoulou and O'Riordan (2017) argue that such an approach must encompass two key dimensions: first, an examination of the symbolic nature of apps as digital communication environments, and second, an exploration of their experiential dimension as technological tools. This dual perspective sheds light on the intricate ways in which apps shape individual experiences and societal dynamics.

Furthermore, research strongly indicates that usage patterns and engagement with popular apps exhibit gender-specific tendencies (Zhang et al., 2018). This underscores the critical importance of considering gender dynamics in mobile technology adoption and usage studies. However, despite the growing significance of mobile apps in contemporary society, there remains a notable gap in research within the context of Portugal. The absence of solid empirical investigations on these topics highlights the urgent need for further scholarly inquiry.

To address this gap, recent studies have comprehensively explored the interactions of various demographic groups, particularly young people, with mobile technologies. For instance, Amaral et al. (2017) delve into the intricate ways young adults navigate digital practices and consumption habits, shedding light on engagement and usage patterns. Similarly, Silveira and Amaral (2018) contribute to the discourse by examining the concepts of media and digital literacy among young adults, elucidating the skills and competencies necessary for effective engagement with digital technologies. Research within the Portuguese context extends beyond mere usage patterns to encompass broader societal issues. Nevertheless, most studies focus on the uses of social media (Pinto et al., 2021) and, more recently, on health-related applications (Bento et al., 2018). Vieira and Sepúlveda (2017) explore the complexities of online sexual identities, offering insights into how digital platforms shape individual self-expression and identity formation.

Without questioning the importance of these studies, this chapter argues for a critical understanding of digital technology tools as sociocultural products that influence the digital behaviours of young adults and their personal digital experiences. Given the lack of in-depth research on the personal implications of m-apps use among young Portuguese adults, this chapter aims to contribute to understanding the role of popular mobile applications in everyday life and how they relate to the contexts and personal experiences of this specific population, namely their socio-demographic factors, taking into account uses and perceptions considering power relations, creation of specific territories of sociability and intimacy, and how gender and sexuality may influence digital behaviours. Based on an online questionnaire survey with semi-closed questions administered to a representative sample of young adults in Portugal ($N = 1,500$), in this chapter, we aim to investigate the digital behaviours of young adults by addressing the following research questions: (*RQ1*): What behaviours emerge when assessing the levels of agreement among young adults? (*RQ2*): To what degree does gender play a primary role in influencing these digital behaviours as a socio-demographic factor? (*RQ3*): What impact do other socio-demographic factors have on these behaviours, if any?

State of Art

The study of the importance of gender in people's lives undoubtedly contributes to an understanding of its socially constructed nature. When the word 'gender' is articulated, there is an implicit reference to a set of components such as gender identity, sexual orientation or gender roles, which intersect with issues of race, sex, class, ethnicity and religion of discursively constructed identities that legitimise themselves as a system of social relations of domination and subordination (Simões & Amaral, 2022). From this, it follows that gender identities can even be contradictory (Connell & Messerschmidt, 2005) and, therefore, marginalised masculinities and femininities can influence dominant forms through power relations (Santos et al., 2021).

Masculinities and femininities embody an idealised concept shaped by cultural perceptions and communication patterns (Simões & Silveirinha, 2019), which dictate behaviours and identities associated with the binary perception of being male or female (Amaral et al., 2019). Since gender is socially constructed (Butler, 2016), these ideals are not inherent or fixed but evolve through societal influences. Consequently, individuals can challenge, reconstruct and transform these gender norms through dynamic social and cultural processes (Boni, 2002). This fluidity extends to how people interact with m-apps, integrating them into their daily routines and potentially reshaping their sexual and gender identities. As m-apps and digital technologies become increasingly pervasive, questions arise about how individuals engage with these platforms and interact with others, highlighting ongoing debates about the nature of social interaction in the digital age.

Therefore, online platforms serve as arenas for gender performances and dynamics to be enacted and negotiated. The anonymity and accessibility afforded by digital spaces can amplify and disrupt traditional gender norms, creating opportunities for individuals to experiment with and challenge established gender roles (Döring & Mohseni, 2020). However, these spaces are also fraught with risks, including the perpetuation of cyberbullying and harassment, mainly targeting individuals who deviate from normative gender expectations (Wolak et al., 2007). Consequently, the intersection of gender identities and online participation necessitates critical examination, considering both the transformative potential and the risks inherent in digital interactions.

Moreover, the ways in which individuals navigate online platforms and engage with mobile applications are deeply intertwined with broader questions of intimacy and social participation. The affordances of digital technologies enable new forms of intimate communication and connection, transcending geographical boundaries and enabling individuals to forge relationships across diverse contexts (Baym, 2015). However, the proliferation of online interactions also raises concerns about privacy, consent and the commodification of personal data (boyd, 2014). Thus, as individuals navigate the complexities of online intimacy and participation, they must negotiate a delicate balance between the opportunities for connection and the challenges posed by digital vulnerabilities.

The complexities of gender, online intimacy, cyberbullying and participation intersect in the digital realm, shaping individuals' experiences and interactions. Understanding these dynamics requires a nuanced approach that acknowledges both the transformative potential and the risks inherent in digital spaces. The intertwining of technology with societal constructs of meaning and identity has profound implications for individual experiences and interactions in the digital realm. As highlighted by boyd (2015), digital practices are not isolated occurrences but rather embedded within the broader context of social imaginaries and technical infrastructure. For instance, research by Döring and Mohseni (2020) emphasises the role of online platforms in shaping sexual identity management strategies, illustrating how individuals negotiate and navigate their identities in digital spaces. Furthermore, the affordances of digital technologies facilitate new forms of online intimacy and social participation, with platforms like social media offering spaces for individuals to connect and express themselves (Baym, 2015).

However, these spaces are not immune to issues such as online harassment and hate speech, which often target marginalised groups based on factors such as gender, race and sexual orientation.

In addition to influencing individual experiences, digital technologies also reflect and perpetuate societal inequalities and power dynamics. Research by Tynes et al. (2008) highlights the prevalence of online racial discrimination, demonstrating how racism manifests in digital spaces through discriminatory language and behaviour. Similarly, studies on gender-based online harassment underscore how misogyny and sexism are perpetuated through digital platforms (Citron, 2014). This reflects broader societal issues of gender inequality and discrimination, which are mirrored and exacerbated in online environments.

Moreover, the intersectionality of identity markers further complicates the dynamics of online interactions. Scholars like Nakamura (2014) argue that online spaces can serve as sites of resistance and empowerment for marginalised groups, allowing for the subversion of dominant narratives and the amplification of diverse voices. However, the same digital platforms can also reinforce existing power structures, with marginalised communities facing disproportionate levels of online abuse and harassment (Daniels, 2019). Therefore, while digital technologies have the potential to challenge and disrupt traditional power dynamics, they also perpetuate inequalities and marginalisation, highlighting the complex interplay between technology, identity and social justice. This idea underscores the importance of examining digital behaviours through a socio-demographic lens, as this study aims to understand better how different identity markers intersect and shape individuals' experiences in digital spaces. Through a quantitative methodology, the research explores young adults' perceptions of personal digital experiences, considering various socio-demographic correlations such as gender, sexual orientation and parenthood status. By analysing these intersections, the study contributes to a deeper understanding of the complexities inherent in digital engagement within mobile apps and its implications for personal experiences.

Methodology

This study aims to explore the perceptions of young adults regarding a set of personal digital experiences, analysing them from the point of view of various possible socio-demographic correlations. Using a quantitative methodological strategy, an online questionnaire survey with semi-closed questions was administered to a representative sample of young adults in Portugal ($N = 1,500$) through an external organisation that conducted the survey in October 2021. The sample was chosen based on quotas of the population distribution of the generation by sex, age and Portuguese regions (including mainland Portugal and the Autonomous Regions). The sampling guarantees a margin of error of $\pm 2.53\%$ and a confidence level of 95%. The statistical analysis is descriptive and inferential (bivariate), highlighting correlations through z-tests ($z = 1.96$) and calculating p-values that support comparisons in which certain results are statistically significantly higher or lower for at least 95% confidence levels. We have used the IBM SPSS statistical analysis software and other digital programs for the statistical procedures.

The following research questions have emerged: (*RQ1*): What kind of behaviours emerge when observing young adults' levels of agreement? (*RQ2*): Is gender the main socio-demographic factor for those digital behaviours? (*RQ3*): What type of influence may produce the other socio-demographic factors?

Table 3.1 reveals our sample distribution, mainly regarding the socio-demographical factors which produced more statistically significant results, in terms of the used inferential (bivariate) statistical analysis procedures. Although the sample was based on official quotas of the young adult population distribution of the generation by sex, age and Portuguese regions, we have used the self-constructed notion of gender instead of sex. This explains why, according to the sample distribution of Table 3.1, our sample of 1,500 young adults had 796

Table 3.1. Sample Distribution.

	Count *N*	**Count** **%**
Age		
18–24	747	49.8%
25–30	753	50.2%
Gender Identity		
Man	696	46.4%
Woman	796	53.1%
Non-binary	14	0.9%
Rather not answer	1	0.1%
Sexual Orientation		
Heterosexual	1,253	83.5%
Lesbian/Gay	64	4.3%
Bisexual/Pansexual	155	10.3%
Queer	11	0.7%
Asexual	12	0.8%
Demisexual	4	0.3%
Graysexual	1	0.1%
Rather not answer	46	3.1%
Do You Have Kids?		
Yes	247	16.5%
No	1,253	83.5%
Total	*1,500*	*100.0%*

people self-identifying as women (53.1%) and 696 identifying as men (46.4%). Of the remaining 15 young adults, 14 identified as non-binary (0.9%) and 1 young adult (0.1%) preferred not to disclose their gender identity. Tables 3.2–3.5 address the mean level of agreement with a total of 60 sentences regarding their digital lives. Gender, sexual orientation and having kids or not were the main socio-demographic drivers of statistically significant different levels of agreement. Even between those three socio-demographic drivers, some of the possible answers seen in Table 3.1 are not present in Tables 3.2–3.5, mostly due to their statistical insignificance (mainly since those do not reach the threshold of 30 respondents for z-tests).

The 60 affirmations of Tables 3.2–3.5 were presented to the respondents on a Likert scale, transformed into a scale from 1 to 5, with the following correspondence: 1: 'Completely disagree'; 2: 'Disagree'; 3: 'Neither agree nor disagree'; 4: 'Agree'; 5: 'Completely agree'. Mean responses were calculated, indicating that a lower mean close to 1 and 2 implies average disagreement with the statement and, in turn, a higher mean close to 4 and 5 should be read as average agreement with the personal experience in question. (A) or any other letter used indicates a statistically significant difference compared to the mean of the variable corresponding to that letter. Those comparisons in Tables 3.2–3.5 were only applied between different answers of the same socio-demographic driver. Thus comparisons are between man and woman, between heterosexual, lesbian/gay and bisexual/pansexual and between having kids and not having kids. This rule utilises the following correspondence to those letters: (A): Man and (B): Woman; (C): Heterosexual, (D): Lesbian/Gay and (E) Bisexual/Pansexual; and (F) Having kids and (G) Not having kids.

Results and Discussion

Even in academia, there is a common assumption that generations are homogeneous in their technological usage. These results challenge the common perpetuation of generations which do not consider their multifaceted dynamics (Amaral et al., 2020; Antunes et al., 2023; Loos et al., 2012; Vieira, 2018). Tables 3.2–3.5 gather 60 affirmations regarding digital experiences. Respondents' mean levels of agreement were the key measure unit, revealing correlations between it and some socio-demographical factors.

Table 3.2 details the mean level of agreement with 17 experiences of diverse types of digital burdens, from hate to bullying. Regarding gender differences, the array of mean levels of agreement ranged from the highest 2.63 mean level of women agreeing with the sentence 'I've been approached by someone because of my gender' (in that case, with statistical significance over the men's mean agreement), and the lowest 1.59 mean level of women agreeing with two sentences in which their agreement is statistically significantly inferior to the mean level of agreement of men. Those two sentences were 'I suffer online attacks because of my ethnicity' and 'I have been subjected to racist attacks offline'.

Table 3.2. Mean Levels of Agreement on Several Burden Experiences of Hate, Harassment and Bullying.

Question	Gender Man (A)	Gender Woman (B)	Sexual Orientation Hetero (C)	Sexual Orientation Lesbian/Gay (D)	Sexual Orientation Bi/Pansexual (E)	Do You Have Kids? Yes (F)	Do You Have Kids? No (G)
I try to identify my sexual orientation in my profile on the mobile apps I use	2.55 B	2.30	2.37	2.93 C	2.70 C	2.68 G	2.36
I'm interested in trying to identify the sexual orientation on the profiles of people I follow/connect with online	2.51 B	2.17	2.24	3.26 CE	2.70 C	2.57 G	2.29
I've been approached by someone because of my gender	2.39	2.63 A	2.42	3.22 C	3.14 C	2.65	2.50
I've been approached online because of my sexual orientation	2.18	2.04	1.96	3.27 CE	2.73 C	2.22	2.09
I've approached people because of their gender	2.34 B	1.85	2.03	2.30	2.45 C	2.27 G	2.05
I've tried to interact with someone because of their sexual orientation	2.53 B	2.03	2.14	3.51 CE	2.74 C	2.54 G	2.23
I have been sexually harassed because of my gender	2.08	2.59 A	2.25	2.95 C	2.84 C	2.65 G	2.29
I have been bullied because of my gender	2.05 B	1.74	1.79	2.96 CE	2.14 C	2.12 G	1.85
I have been sexually harassed because of my sexual orientation	1.95	1.81	1.77	2.98 CE	2.22 C	2.08 G	1.84

I have been attacked online because of my sexual orientation	1.97 B	1.67	1.73	2.64 CE	2.11 C	2.10 G	1.78
I have been stalked offline because of my online participation	1.96 B	1.67	1.76	2.51 CE	1.80	2.10 G	1.76
I suffer online attacks because of my ethnicity	1.95 B	1.59	1.72	2.26 C	1.89	2.08 G	1.71
I am a victim of offline harassment because of my sexual orientation	1.96 B	1.61	1.71	2.39 CE	1.93 C	2.07 G	1.74
My race is used as a justification for being attacked online	2.00 B	1.64	1.78	2.32 CE	1.91	2.25 G	1.74
I was attacked offline because of my ethnicity	1.95 B	1.60	1.73	2.20 C	1.93	2.07 G	1.72
I have been subjected to racist attacks offline	1.96 B	1.59	1.73	2.24 CE	1.86	2.09 G	1.71
I suffer racial discrimination online	1.92 B	1.61	1.72	2.21 C	1.94 C	2.06 G	1.70

Table 3.3. Mean Levels of Agreement on Content Creation and Sharing Patterns.

Question	Gender Man (A)	Gender Woman (B)	Sexual Orientation Hetero (C)	Sexual Orientation Lesbian/Gay (D)	Sexual Orientation Bi/Pansexual (E)	Do You Have Kids? Yes (F)	Do You Have Kids? No (G)
I feel confident with what I post on social media	3.58	3.68	3.66	3.92 CE	3.51	3.71	3.62
I keep my profiles private	3.37	3.61 A	3.51	3.54	3.52	3.44	3.51
The person I am online doesn't match the real me	2.41 B	2.02	2.17	2.41	2.40 C	2.44 G	2.16
I get anxious when I don't have my mobile phone	2.73	2.98 A	2.82	3.24 C	3.20 C	3.15 G	2.81
It disturbs me to see what people write about me in the comments	2.51	2.36	2.41	2.76 C	2.51	2.68 G	2.38
I feel I can be myself on the mobile apps I choose to use	3.52	3.61	3.59	3.57	3.47	3.65	3.55
I use some platforms just to see what other people are posting	3.14	3.16	3.15	3.07	3.37 C	3.22	3.14
I feel pressured to have social media accounts	2.54	2.53	2.49	2.86 C	2.81 C	2.73 G	2.49
I'm sure that my followers enjoy my content	3.24	3.25	3.24	3.49 CE	3.23	3.33	3.23
I don't care what others think of my posts	3.58 B	3.35	3.49 E	3.70 E	3.22	3.70 G	3.41
I spend a lot of time producing content to share with my followers	2.44	2.31	2.35	2.70 CE	2.35	2.78 G	2.30
The content I publish/share is different from one platform to another because of who follows me	2.97	3.08	2.98	2.98	3.56 CD	3.08	3.03
In some apps, I feel like I can really be me	3.42	3.59 A	3.52	3.66	3.57	3.57	3.50
I like to share my life on the internet	2.53	2.54	2.53	3.03 CE	2.57	2.82 G	2.49
I post content privately to avoid my family seeing it	2.59 B	2.35	2.39	2.86 C	2.99 C	2.57	2.45

Table 3.4. Mean Levels of Agreement Regarding Digital Interaction and Socialisation Experiences.

Question	Gender Man (A)	Gender Woman (B)	Sexual Orientation Hetero (C)	Sexual Orientation Lesbian/Gay (D)	Sexual Orientation Bi/Pansexual (E)	Do You Have Kids? Yes (F)	Do You Have Kids? No (G)
I think it's ridiculous for people to publish photos of themselves on social media	2.31 B	1.83	2.04	2.25	1.97	2.34 G	2.00
I don't accept friend requests on social media from people I don't know	3.16	3.49 A	3.37	3.42	3.20	3.50 G	3.30
I follow a lot of people because I like what they share	3.55	3.99 A	3.78	3.74	3.97 C	3.86	3.77
I feel inspired when I scroll through some people's profiles	3.23	3.84 A	3.53	3.79	3.81 C	3.56	3.56
I seek inspiration from social media	3.20	3.84 A	3.53	3.77 C	3.65	3.63	3.53
People are all different according to gender, race, ethnicity and social class and that's not a problem for me	3.76	4.22 A	3.99	4.46 CE	4.16	3.89	4.03
I hate people who stir up controversy on social media	3.42	3.49	3.46	3.70	3.45	3.49	3.46
It annoys me to read what others post on social media	2.85	2.81	2.83	2.93	2.84	3.02 G	2.79
When I don't like what I read or see, I leave criticising comments	2.41 B	2.00	2.18	2.60 C	2.36	2.54 G	2.12
I've insulted people on social media	2.60 B	1.87	2.19	2.25	2.46 C	2.54 G	2.15

(Continued)

Table 3.4. (Continued)

Question	Gender Man (A)	Gender Woman (B)	Sexual Orientation Hetero (C)	Sexual Orientation Lesbian/Gay (D)	Sexual Orientation Bi/Pansexual (E)	Do You Have Kids? Yes (F)	Do You Have Kids? No (G)
I don't accept people of other races or ethnicities assuming online that they have my nationality	2.13 B	1.77	1.93	2.04	1.83	2.19 G	1.89
I spend many hours watching what others share about their lives	2.64	2.90 A	2.76	3.11 C	2.93	3.06 G	2.73
I use social media to find people in the same situation as me	2.86	2.79	2.74	3.15 C	3.35 C	3.01 G	2.79
I'm certain that the people I meet through social media are my friends	2.88 B	2.56	2.69	3.08 CE	2.71	2.88 G	2.68
I'm afraid of what people might think of me when I post or share something on social media	2.71	2.77	2.70	2.76	3.13 C	2.80	2.73
I argue online with people who don't follow the norms and customs of my culture because they have different religious beliefs	2.22 B	1.75	1.97	2.12	1.93	2.35 G	1.91
I don't like to see people of other races or ethnicities writing comments about my country	2.34 B	2.03	2.19	2.35	2.06	2.46 G	2.13
I don't see colours or races: all people are the same	4.01	4.31 A	4.19	4.36	4.17	4.06	4.19

Table 3.5. Mean Levels of Agreement on Intimate and Sexual Digital Lives.

Question	Gender Man (A)	Gender Woman (B)	Gender Hetero (C)	Sexual Orientation Lesbian/Gay (D)	Sexual Orientation Bi/Pansexual (E)	Do You Have Kids? Yes (F)	Do You Have Kids? No (G)
I've had relationships with people I've met online and I felt good about it	3.13 B	2.83	2.90	3.84 CE	3.48 C	2.99	2.98
I don't dare to use dating apps	2.75	3.12 A	2.97	2.62	2.87	3.13 G	2.89
I feel comfortable in sharing my intimate life on some apps	2.48 B	1.96	2.16	2.73 C	2.43 C	2.38 G	2.18
I follow people who share their intimate lives online	2.87 B	2.48	2.65	2.77	3.02 C	2.72	2.67
My partner likes to share our life online, I do not	2.54 B	2.10	2.33	2.25	2.36	2.57 G	2.26
People have shared intimate photos/videos of me and I felt really bad	2.29 B	1.98	2.12	2.21	2.37 C	2.42 G	2.08
I like it when people share intimate photos/videos of me as long as I authorise it	2.43 B	1.81	2.08	2.37	2.23	2.40 G	2.05
I unfriend people who publish intimate content	2.72	3.17 A	3.00 E	3.06	2.76	3.19 G	2.91
I block people who send me sexual messages	3.41	4.27 A	3.88	3.92	4.04	3.90	3.87
I send sexual messages to other people	2.48 B	1.95	2.17	2.59 C	2.46 C	2.31	2.19

The extent of the mean level of agreements was bigger regarding sexual orientation differences. The highest mean level of agreement was registered by lesbian/gay young adults who averagely agreed in 3.51 with the sentence 'I've tried to interact with someone because of their sexual orientation', with it being statistically significantly superior to the mean level of agreement of both heterosexual (2.14) and bisexual/pansexual respondents with that sentence (2.74, which was also statistically significantly superior to the mean level of concurrence of the heterosexual respondents). The case of the lowest mean level of agreement regarding sexual orientation consisted of the mean level of 1.71 heterosexuals agreeing with the sentence 'I am a victim of offline harassment because of my sexual orientation', which was statistically significantly inferior to the agreement of both bisexual/pansexuals (1.93) and lesbian/gays (2.39, which was also statistically significantly different from the mean level of bisexual/pansexual respondents).

The range of mean level of agreements between people who have kids and who do not have kids was not particularly big. The highest mean level of agreement was 2.68 among young adults who have kids, regarding the sentence 'I try to identify my sexual orientation in my profile on the mobile apps I use', which was statistically significantly superior to the mean level of agreement between the respondents who do not have kids (2.36). The lowest mean level of agreement was registered by young adults who do not have kids for the affirmation 'I suffer racial discrimination online' (1.70), which was statistically significantly inferior to the mean level of agreement of respondents with kids (2.06).

Still, in the case of Table 3.2, between gender, sexual orientation and having kids or not, there is a bundle of statistically significant differences. Men had statistically significantly superior mean levels of agreement than women in 13 of the 17 sentences. Those include sentences like 'I've approached people because of their gender' and 'I've tried to interact with someone because of their sexual orientation', which may suggest greater comfort in navigating the digital realm. At the same time, there were several sentences in which the mean level of agreement of men was statistically superior to women, possibly suggesting the idea that despite that comfort, men still feel attacked and harassed digitally. Those sentences include, but are not limited, to the following: 'I have been bullied because of my gender', 'I have been stalked offline because of my online participation', 'I am a victim of offline harassment because of my sexual orientation' or 'I have been subjected to racist attacks offline'. Nonetheless, and despite the statistically significant differences, most of those sentences generated mean levels of agreement under the medium value of 2.5 (due to it being a scale from 1 to 5), which indicated low levels of mean agreement regarding respondents' gender.

There are also discrepancies worth mentioning in terms of sexual orientation. In 16 out of the 17 sentences of Table 3.2, lesbian/gay respondents had statistically significantly superior mean levels of agreement than heterosexuals and, sometimes, also in comparison to bisexual/pansexuals (in 10 sentences). At the same time, bisexual/pansexual respondents' mean level of agreement was also statistically significantly superior to the agreement of heterosexuals in 12 sentences. Some of the sentences in which both lesbian/gays and bisexual/pansexuals had significantly superior mean levels of agreement than heterosexuals include, but are not limited, to the cases of: 'I try to identify my sexual orientation in my profile on the mobile apps I use', 'I'm interested in trying to identify the sexual orientation on the profiles of people I follow/connect with online', 'I've been approached online because of my sexual orientation', 'I have been sexually harassed because of my sexual orientation' and 'I have been attacked online because of my sexual orientation'.

Regarding having kids or not, respondents who already have kids had statistically significantly superior mean levels of agreement than the respondents who do not have kids for 15 out of the 17 sentences. The only two questions in Table 3.2 where there were no statistically significant differences were 'I've been approached by someone because of my gender' and 'I've been approached online because of my sexual orientation'.

Table 3.3 details the mean level of agreement with 15 experiences regarding young adults' perceptions of digital content creation and sharing behaviours, both by themselves and others. Regarding gender differences, the range of mean levels of agreement ranged from the highest 3.61 mean level of women agreeing with the sentences 'I keep my profiles private' (this registering a statistically significant superiority to the 3.37 mean level of agreement of men) and 'I feel I can be myself on the mobile apps I choose to use'. The lowest mean level of gender agreement was 2.02 and it was registered by women in the sentence 'The person I am online doesn't match the real me' (statistically significantly inferior to the 2.41 mean level of agreement of men).

Regarding sexual orientation, the highest mean level of agreement was, like in Table 3.2, registered by lesbian/gay young adults, who averagely agreed 3.92 to the sentence 'I feel confident with what I post on social media', which was statistically significantly superior to the mean level of agreement of both heterosexuals (3.66) and bisexual/pansexuals (3.51). On the other hand, the lowest mean level of agreement considering respondents' sexual orientations consisted of the mean level of 2.17 of heterosexuals agreeing with the sentence 'The person I am online doesn't match the real me', which was statistically significantly inferior to the 2.40 mean level of agreement of bisexual/pansexuals of the sample.

As for the case of parenthood status, the highest mean level of agreement was 3.71 among respondents with kids for the sentence 'I feel confident with what I post on social media', although that mean level of agreement was very similar to the one of respondents without kids (3.62). The lowest mean level of agreement was registered by young adults who do not have kids for the affirmation 'The person I am online doesn't match the real me' (2.16), which was a mean level of agreement statistically significantly inferior to the one of respondents with kids (2.44).

Although not as common as in Table 3.2, there are several cases in Table 3.3, of statistically significant differences for gender, sexual orientation and having kids or not. Men had statistically significantly superior mean levels of agreement in 3 out of the 18 sentences, while women had statistically significantly superior mean levels of agreement in three different sentences. The affirmations where men registered those statistically significant superior mean levels of agreement were

'The person I am online doesn't match the real me', 'I don't care what others think of my posts' and 'I post content privately to avoid my family seeing it'. The three phrases where women had statistically significant superior mean levels of agreement were 'I keep my profiles private', 'I get anxious when I don't have my mobile phone' and 'In some apps, I feel like I can really be me'. This suggests that women stand mostly in both anxiety and privacy concerns, while men are in terms of being able to be totally true to themselves in their digital footprints.

In terms of sexual orientation, lesbian/gay respondents had statistically significantly superior mean levels of agreement in 9 out of the 18 sentences of Table 3.3, either in comparison to one or two sexual orientations. Some of those were, for example: 'I feel confident with what I post on social media', 'I get anxious when I don't have my mobile phone', 'I feel pressured to have social media accounts', 'I'm sure that my followers enjoy my content', 'I like to share my life on the Internet' and 'I post content privately to avoid my family seeing it'. Bisexual/pansexuals had statistically significant superior mean levels of agreement in six sentences. Those were the cases, although not limited, of the following: 'The person I am online doesn't match the real me', 'I use some platforms just to see what other people are posting', 'I post content privately to avoid my family seeing it' and 'The content I publish/share is different from one platform to another because of who follows me' (in this one, bisexual/pansexuals mean level of agreement was statistically significantly superior in comparison to both heterosexuals and lesbian/gay respondents). Heterosexual respondents answered with statistically significant superiority in one sentence, in comparison to bisexual/pansexuals, to the sentence 'I don't care what others think of my posts'.

There were seven cases in which young adults with kids had statistically significant mean levels of agreement in comparison to the respondents who do not have kids. The following examples may reveal a privacy concern of those young adults with kids, suggesting digital uses that create a type of semi-barrier between their true lives and their digital personas, although encompassing the digital technologies in their lives. Those examples include: 'The person I am online doesn't match the real me', 'I get anxious when I don't have my mobile phone', 'It disturbs me to see what people write about me in the comments', 'I don't care what others think of my posts' and 'I like to share my life on the Internet'.

Table 3.4 presents 18 sentences regarding respondents' agreement with digital interaction and socialisation experiences. In terms of gender, the highest mean level of agreement was 4.31, by women, for the sentence 'I don't see colours or races: all people are the same' (which was statistically significantly superior to the 4.01 mean level of agreement of men). On the opposite pole, the lowest mean level of agreement was 1.75 registered by women in the sentence 'I argue online with people who don't follow the norms and customs of my culture because they have different religious beliefs' (which was statistically significantly inferior to the mean level of agreement of men).

Regarding the range according to sexual orientations, the highest mean level of agreement was 4.46, registered by lesbian/gay sampled young adults for the phrase 'People are all different according to gender, race, ethnicity and social class and that's not a problem for me', with statistically significant superiority to both the mean levels of agreement of heterosexuals (3.99) and bisexual/pansexuals (4.16). The lowest mean level of agreement registered according to sexual orientation was 1.83, by the bisexual/pansexual respondents, for 'I don't accept people of other races or ethnicities assuming online that they have my nationality'.

Even for matters of having kids or not, the range of mean levels of agreement was similarly wide. The highest mean level was 4.19, registered by young adults who do not have kids, concerning the sentence 'I don't see colours or races: all people are the same'. As for the lowest mean level of agreement it was 1.89, by young adults who do not have kids, for the phrase 'I don't accept people of other races or ethnicities assuming online that they have my nationality' (which was statistically significantly inferior to the 2.19 mean level of agreement by respondents with kids).

The analysis of Table 3.4 reveals that some socio-demographic factors may produce more statistically significant differences than others. Regarding gender, the men had 7 out of 18 sentences with statistically significant superior mean levels of agreement. In comparison, our sampled women had other seven sentences with statistically significant superior mean levels of agreement. Some of the phrases where men registered those statistically significant superior mean levels of agreement were: 'I think it's ridiculous for people to publish photos of themselves on social media', 'When I don't like what I read or see, I leave criticising comments', 'I've insulted people on social media' and 'I argue online with people who don't follow the norms and customs of my culture because they have different religious beliefs'. Those sentences suggest higher comfort by men in showing their opinions towards others online. Nonetheless, one should highlight that between those seven sentences, the men's mean level of agreement never surpasses 2.89. As for the other seven sentences where women had higher mean levels of agreement, six of those seven range between 3.49 and 4.31 as their mean levels of agreement. Some of those sentences were: 'I don't accept friend requests on social media from people I don't know', 'I follow a lot of people because I like what they share', 'I feel inspired when I scroll through some people's profiles', 'I seek inspiration from social media' and 'People are all different according to gender, race, ethnicity and social class and that's not a problem for me'. Therefore, women seem more focused on a sense of their digital security while also revealing that social media platforms are more used by them to see other's content in a more passive form.

In the case of sexual orientation, lesbian/gay respondents had six sentences with statistically significant superior mean levels of agreement over the heterosexuals' agreement (with two of those also being statistically significantly superior to bisexual/pansexuals). Some of those were, for example: 'I seek inspiration from social media', 'People are all different according to gender, race, ethnicity and social class and that's not a problem for me', 'I spend many hours watching what others share about their lives', 'I use social media to find people in the same situation as me', 'I'm certain that the people I meet through social media are my friends'. The bisexual/pansexual respondents had five sentences from Table 3.4 where their mean level of agreement was statistically significantly higher than the men's. Those include: 'I follow a lot of people because I like what they share', 'I feel inspired when I scroll through some people's profile', 'I use social media to find people in the same situation as me' and 'I'm afraid of what people might think of me when I post or share something on social media'. Thus, non-heterosexuals seem to use the digital to find similar situations and, perhaps, construct communities.

More than the previous socio-demographic factors, having kids is the factor with more statistically significant differences in Table 3.4. Young adults with kids had statistically significantly superior mean levels of agreement in 11 sentences compared to the respondents without kids. Most of the sentences may indicate that young adults with kids privilege their privacy while they assume that the digital realm is still embedded in their lives. Although not limited to, those sentences include the following: 'I don't accept friend requests on social media from people I don't know', 'It annoys me to read what others post on social media', 'I spend many hours watching what others share about their lives' and 'I use social media to find people in the same situation as me'.

Table 3.5's sentences concern topics of digital intimacy and sexualisation, with an array of 10 sentences. Regarding gender differences, the range of mean levels of agreement ranged from the highest 4.27, by women for the phrase 'I block people who send me sexual messages', which was statistically significantly superior to the men's mean level of agreement of 3.41. As for the lowest gendered mean level of agreement, it was the women's 1.81 mean level of agreement to the sentence 'I like it when people share intimate photos/videos of me as long as I authorise it', which was statistically significantly inferior to the men's 2.43 mean level of agreement.

When the sample is separated by their sexual orientation, the range of mean levels of Table 3.5 is slightly shorter than the gender one, with the highest being the bisexual/pansexuals' agreement of 4.04 to the sentence 'I block people who send me sexual messages'. As for the lowest, it was the heterosexual respondents' mean level of agreement of 2.08 to the affirmation, 'I like it when people share intimate photos/videos of me as long as I authorise it'.

Similar to the range regarding sexual orientation is the case of parenthood status, with the highest mean level of agreement being 3.90 by respondents with kids for the phrase 'I block people who send me sexual messages'. The lowest mean level of agreement was 2.05, registered by young adults without kids, for the experience 'I like it when people share intimate photos/videos of me as long as I authorise it', which was statistically significantly inferior to the 2.40 mean level of agreement by young adults with kids.

Gender was a defining factor for finding statistically significant differences in Table 3.5, as between the 10 sentences, seven of those, the men had statistically significantly superior mean levels of agreement. In comparison, the remaining three sentences had the women having statistically significantly superior mean levels of agreement. Some of the sentences where men showed higher mean levels of agreement were: 'I've had relationships with people I've met online, and I felt good about it', 'I feel comfortable in sharing my intimate life on some apps', 'I follow people who share their intimate lives online', 'My partner likes to share our life online, I do not', 'People have shared intimate photos/videos of me and I felt really bad' and 'I send sexual messages to other people'. The three sentences with statistically significant superior mean levels of agreement by women were: 'I don't dare to use dating apps', 'I unfriend people who publish intimate content' and 'I block people who send me sexual messages' (with those three having particular high mean levels of agreement, ranging from 3.12 to 4.27). Thus, the sampled men seem particularly more comfortable in interacting with others in intimate and sexual manners, although particularly uncomfortable when their own intimacy and sexuality are shared by others. Accordingly, women revealed preoccupation even regarding who they engage with digitally, that only after could evolve to an intimate and sexual tone.

Results of Table 3.5 regarding sexual orientation reveal that heterosexuals had only one case of a sentence in which their mean level of agreement was statistically significantly superior (in that case, in comparison to bisexual/pansexuals). That sentence was 'I unfriend people who publish intimate content'. As for lesbian/gays there were three phrases where their mean level of agreement was statistically significantly superior (all three in comparison to heterosexuals, and one of those in comparison to bisexual/pansexuals). Those were: 'I've had relationships with people I've met online and I felt good about it', 'I feel comfortable in sharing my intimate life on some apps' and 'I send sexual messages to other people'. The samples' bisexual/pansexual young adults had statistically significantly superior mean levels of agreement in five of the questioned experiences, all just when compared to heterosexuals. Those five sentences were: 'I've had relationships with people I've met online and I felt good about it', 'I feel comfortable in sharing my intimate life on some apps', 'I follow people who share their intimate lives online', 'People have shared intimate photos/videos of me and I felt really bad' and 'I send sexual messages to other people'. Therefore, results suggest that non-heterosexuals are more comfortable in navigating their digital lives with intimate and sexual experiences.

As for the young adults' parenthood status, results from Table 3.5 reinforce the idea that the respondents with kids seem to favour a more private intimate (digital) life. Young adults with kids had statistically significant superior mean levels of agreement in 6 out of the 10 sentences, including: 'I don't dare to use dating apps', 'I feel comfortable in sharing my intimate life on some apps', 'People have shared intimate photos/videos of me and I felt really bad' and 'I unfriend people who publish intimate content'.

Conclusion

This chapter thoroughly examines young adults' digital experiences within the context of various socio-demographic factors. The study offers nuanced insights into their digital behaviours by employing a quantitative methodology and surveying a representative sample of young adults in Portugal. Through inferential statistical analysis, significant correlations emerged across gender, sexual orientation and parenthood status, shedding light on the multifaceted nature of digital engagement among this demographic.

The findings challenge conventional assumptions of generational homogeneity in digital usage patterns, revealing a complex interplay between socio-demographic variables and online behaviours. Gender emerged as a particularly salient factor, influencing attitudes towards online interactions, harassment and content creation. While men generally displayed higher levels of agreement in statements related to digital engagement, women exhibited more significant concern for privacy and security online, highlighting gender disparities in digital experiences.

Similarly, sexual orientation played a pivotal role in shaping digital behaviours, with non-heterosexual individuals demonstrating distinct patterns of engagement characterised by a greater comfort with intimate digital interactions. Lesbian, gay, bisexual and pansexual respondents exhibited higher levels of agreement with statements related to personal expression online, reflecting unique dynamics within digital spaces based on sexual orientation.

Furthermore, parenthood status emerged as a significant determinant of digital behaviours, with young adults with children expressing a preference for more private online interactions. This result suggests a heightened awareness of the potential implications of their digital presence on their families, indicating a need for tailored approaches to digital engagement based on parental responsibilities.

Overall, the study underscores the intricate relationship between socio-demographic factors and digital behaviours among young adults, emphasising the importance of nuanced approaches in understanding digital experiences within diverse populations. These findings contribute valuable insights to the broader discourse on digital culture, informing future research and policy interventions to foster safe and inclusive digital environments for all individuals.

References

Amaral, I., Reis, B., Lopes, P., & Quintas, C. (2017). Práticas e consumos dos jovens portugueses em ambientes digitais [Practices and consumption of Portuguese youth in digital environments]. *Estudos em Comunicação, 24*, 107–131.

Amaral, I., Santos, S. J., & Brites, M. J. (2020). Mapping intergenerational masculinities on Instagram. *Lecture Notes in Computer Science, 12209*, 3–16. https://doi.org/10.1007/978-3-030-50232-4_1

Amaral, I., Santos, S. J., Daniel, F., & Filipe, F. (2019). (In)visibilities of men and aging in the media: Discourses from Germany and Portugal. *Lecture Notes in Computer Science, 11593*, 20–32.

Antunes, E., Amaral, I., Simões, R. B., & Flores, A. M. M. (2023). Who are the young adults in Portugal? Daily usage of social media and mobile phones, in a no-kids and no-independent housing context—Results from a representative online survey. *Youth, 3*(4), 1101–1120. https://doi.org/10.3390/youth3040070

Baym, N. K. (2015). *Personal connections in the digital age*. John Wiley & Sons.

Bento, M., Martinez, L. M., & Martinez, L. F. (2018). Brand engagement and search for brands on social media: Comparing Generations X and Y in Portugal. *Journal of Retailing and Consumer Services, 43*, 234–241.

Boni, F. (2002). Framing media masculinities: Men's lifestyle magazines and the biopolitics of the male body. *European Journal of Communication, 17*(4), 465–478.
boyd, d. (2014). *It's complicated: The social lives of networked teens*. Yale University Press.
boyd, d. (2015). Social media: A phenomenon to be analyzed. *Social Media+ Society, 1*(1). https://doi.org/10.1177/2056305115580148
Butler, J. (2016). Gender trouble, feminist theory and psychoanalytic discourse. In L. McDowell & J. Sharp (Eds.), *Space, gender, knowledge: Feminist readings* (pp. 247–261). Routledge.
Chadwick, A. (2017). *The hybrid media system: Politics and power*. Oxford University Press.
Citron, D. K. (2014). *Hate crimes in cyberspace*. Harvard University Press.
Connell, R. W., & Messerschmidt, J. W. (2005). Hegemonic masculinity: Rethinking the concept. *Gender & Society, 19*(6), 829–859.
Daniels, J. (2019). Race and racism in internet studies: A review and critique. *New Media & Society, 21*(3), 719–739.
Döring, N., & Mohseni, M. R. (2020). Gendered hate speech in YouTube and YouNow comments: Results of two content analyses. *SCM Studies in Communication and Media, 9*(1), 62–88.
Duguay, S. (2017). Lesbian, gay, bisexual, trans, and queer visibility through selfies: Comparing platform mediators. *Social Media + Society, 3*(2). https://doi.org/10.1177/2056305116641975
Ellison, N. B., Hancock, J. T., & Toma, C. L. (2012). Profile as promise: A framework for conceptualizing veracity in online dating self-presentations. *New Media & Society, 14*(1), 45–62.
Fotopoulou, A., & O'Riordan, K. (2017). Training to self-care: Fitness tracking, biopedagogy and the healthy consumer. *Health Sociology Review, 26*(1), 54–68.
Hepp, A. (2013). *Cultures of mediatization*. John Wiley & Sons.
Herring, S. C. (2003). Gender and power in online communication. In J. Holmes & M. Meyerhoff (Eds.), *Handbook of language and gender* (pp. 202–228). Blackwell.
Jenkins, H. (2006). *Convergence culture: Where old and new media collide*. NYU Press.
Livingstone, S., Bober, M., & Helsper, E. J. (2005). Active participation or just more information? Young people's take-up of opportunities to act and interact on the Internet. *Information, Community & Society, 8*(3), 287–314.
Loos, E., Haddon, L., & Mante-Meijer, E. (2012). Introduction. In L. Haddon & E. Mante-Meijer (Eds.), *Generational use of new media* (E. Loos (Ed.); 1st ed.). Routledge. https://doi.org/10.4324/9781315584270
Nakamura, L. (2014). Queer female of color: The highest difficulty setting there is? Gaming rhetoric as gender capital. *Ada: A Journal of Gender, New Media, and Technology, 4*.
Pacheco, L., Torres da Silva, M., Brites, M. J., Henriques, S., & Damásio, M. J. (2017). Patterns of European youngsters' daily use of media. *Observatorio, 11*(4), 1–18.
Pinto, P. A., Antunes, M. J. L., & Almeida, A. M. P. (2021, June). Portuguese national health service on Instagram: University students' perception of@ sns_pt content in the COVID-19 pandemic. In *2021 16th Iberian conference on information systems and technologies (CISTI)* (pp. 1–6). IEEE.

Ranzini, G., & Lutz, C. (2017). Love at first swipe? Explaining Tinder self-presentation and motives. *Mobile Media & Communication*, 5(1), 80–101.

Santos, S. J., Amaral, I., Simões, R. B., & Brites, M. J. (2021). Debunking the #Manosphere: An exploratory analysis on patriarchy and ageism within the digital realm. *Lecture Notes in Computer Science*, *12786*, 420–429.

Schrøder, K. C. (2011). Audiences are inherently cross-media: Audience studies and the cross-media challenge. *CM Komunikacija i mediji*, 6(18), 5–27.

Silveira, P., & Amaral, I. (2018). Jovens e práticas de acesso e de consumo de notícias nos media sociais [Young people and news access and consumption practices on social media]. *Estudos em Comununicação*, *1*, 261–280.

Simões, R. B., & Amaral, I. (2022). Sexuality and self-tracking apps: Reshaping gender relations and sexual and reproductive practices. In E. Rees (Org.), *The Routledge companion to gender, sexuality and culture* (pp. 413–423). Routledge.

Simões, R. B., & Silveirinha, M. J. (2019). Framing street harassment: Legal developments and popular misogyny in social media. *Feminist Media Studies*, *22*(3), 621–637.

Tynes, B. M., Giang, M. T., Williams, D. R., & Thompson, G. N. (2008). Online racial discrimination and psychological adjustment among adolescents. *Journal of Adolescent Health*, *43*(6), 565–569.

Van Dijck, J. (2014). Datafication, dataism and dataveillance: Big data between scientific paradigm and ideology. *Surveillance and Society*, *12*(2), 197–208.

Vieira, J. (2018). Media and generations in Portugal. *Societies*, *8*(61). https://doi.org/10.3390/soc8030061

Vieira, J., & Sepúlveda, R. (2017). A autoapresentação dos portugueses na plataforma de online dating Tinder [The self-presentation of the Portuguese on the online dating platform Tinder]. *Observatório (OBS*)*, *11*(3), 153–185.

Wolak, J., Mitchell, K. J., & Finkelhor, D. (2007). Does online harassment constitute bullying? An exploration of online harassment by known peers and online-only contacts. *Journal of Adolescent Health*, *41*(6), S51–S58.

Zhang, J., Calabrese, C., Ding, J., Liu, M., & Zhang, B. (2018). Advantages and challenges in using mobile apps for field experiments: A systematic review and a case study. *Mobile Media & Communication*, *6*(2), 179–196.

Chapter 4

The Storefront of Gender in the Portuguese Google PlayStore

Ana Marta M. Flores[a], Sofia P. Caldeira[b] and Elena Pilipets[c]

[a]University of Coimbra, Portugal
[b]Lusófona University, Portugal
[c]University of Siegen, Germany

Abstract

Notions of gender and sexuality are much more complex than the traditional heteronormative system suggests in most Western societies. From a perspective that approaches gender as a social construction, the chapter focuses on how gender is constituted in the offer of Android apps in the Portuguese Google PlayStore. The authors propose two research questions: (*RQ1*) How do app icons and descriptions visually and textually express the gender spectra based on the search results for the terms mulher (woman), homem (man), agénero (agender), transgénero (transgender) and não-binário (non-binary)? (*RQ2*): Which apps are recommended across genders? Adopting an exploratory digital methods approach, the authors address these questions by combining different data points, ranging from the app publication date, rating, number of downloads, price, gender-based options, etc. The query design attends to different app typologies for everyday practices such as games, self-tracking, dating, fitness and social media. The analysis focuses on the app market in Portugal, allowing us to explore how collective narrative processes on app-based platforms enhance power relations by perpetuating hegemonic masculinities and femininities anchored upon heteronormativity. Employing a multi-modal approach, the authors' goal is to assess whether the app market challenges or replicates the standard heteronormative social behaviour. The results show a significant difference between the predominant genres, especially regarding the application's colour palettes, description and proposed uses.

Keywords: Gender mediations; sexuality; app ecosystem; digital methods; queer identities; digital inclusivity

Introduction: The Arena of Gendered App Cultures

Digital spaces have often been imagined as progressive spaces, particularly concerning gender. In the early years of the Internet, techno-utopian discourses proliferated in both academic and popular writings, seeing the digital as carrying the potential to disrupt existing hierarchical structures, including gender (van Zoonen, 2011). Earlier online experiences, predominantly text-based, were imagined as allowing for unprecedented identity and gender play, moving beyond the social and cultural constraints of 'real life' (e.g. Haraway, 1991; Turkle, 1995). Yet, as the Internet and digital technologies like mobile apps became evermore entrenched in everyday actions, these utopian narratives were abandoned mainly and supplanted by more critical, and even overtly negative, perspectives on how existing inequalities and narrow gendered views could be produced and reproduced by digital technologies (van Zoonen, 2011). Our current Internet culture occupies a contested space. On the one hand, contemporary digital environments are highly gendered, often reinforcing hegemonic gender norms, not only within the user-generated social media practices explored by van Zoonen (2011) and a lot of scholarship that followed her work but also within the underlying mobile apps' imaginaries (Simões & Amaral, 2022). On the other hand, digital spaces also offer possibilities to discover, explore and engage with diverse gender identities that may fall outside the normative binary (Szulc, 2020).

We understand gender as socially and culturally constructed rather than biologically grounded (Butler, 2006). As such, while individual actions reify gender, they reflect wider social structures and underlying power dynamics. Within particular socio-cultural contexts, certain conceptions of gender can thus emerge as normative and ideal, setting the standard of how people of a certain gender are expected to be and behave (West & Zimmerman, 1987). Within the heterosexual matrix that prevails in Western cultures, these dominant perceptions of gender are expanded to encompass expectations related to sex and sexual desire, reiterating a binary norm of women/men, feminine/masculine and heterosexual/homosexual that is assumed to neatly align (Butler, 2006). Yet, these rigid binaries do not reflect how people experience gender in their lives. Gender and sex (as assigned at birth) do not always necessarily align, as evidenced by the experiences of trans people (Keyes, 2021). Some people exist in the flow between different ends of the gender spectrum, such as non-binary or genderfluid people. And some might eschew gender at all, as with agender people (Szulc, 2020). As a culturally and temporally situated construct, gender is thus open to negotiations, resignifications and change. However, gender is not only performed by individuals but also produced through various technologies of gender (de Lauretis, 1987), which carry the symbolic power to mediate gender in particular ways.

Considering App Stores and their environment as an 'online curated marketplace' (Jansen & Bloemendal, 2013), digital stores play a pivotal role in shaping how individuals engage with mobile applications and shape societal norms, potentially perpetuating gender inequalities (Prescott & Bogg, 2014). As a prevalent and highly favoured form of technology, mobile apps actively contribute to the construction and configuration of human capabilities and desires, as articulated by Lupton (2014). These interactive artefacts are seamlessly integrated into daily societal life, extending their influence to digital artefact ecosystems and harbouring the potential to impact their users profoundly.

Even though digital cultures are now recognised as embedded in everyday life and broader socio-cultural structures (Markham, 2017), the gendered aspect of certain widely used technologies like mobile apps has often been overlooked (Simões & Amaral, 2022). Many existing apps focus on and address their users, as either men or women, embedding normative conceptions of masculinity and femininity in their design, data structures and affordances. Much like gender itself, the gendered dimension of mobile apps also has a political and disciplinary dimension, choosing to emphasise particular aspects and invisibilise others in ways that can reinforce and normalise specific conceptions of gender – most often binary and heteronormative ones (Simões & Amaral, 2022). The gendering of mobile apps can be linked to commercial interests, reducing people's multifaceted gender experiences to neat data points that can be used to create gender-based market segments for advertisers, in a clear example of the commodification of gender (Bivens, 2017). While many apps offer opportunities for users to select gender labels outside the binary (Szulc, 2020), others can condense this surface-level diversity back into a binary system at a back-office level without the knowledge or consent of its users so that this information can be sold to advertisers (Bivens, 2017). This chapter explores how gender is mediated by and reflected in a segment of mobile apps available on the Google PlayStore.

Methods and Data Collection

To explore multiple empirical perspectives, we adopted a mixed-method approach combining digital methods (Rogers, 2013) and qualitative analysis to answer the research questions: (*RQ1*) What are the app categories and their visual and textual expressions when searching for terms that define some of the gender spectra? and (*RQ2*) Which apps are common across the genders?

This approach draws on the existing scholarship addressing topics related to app ecosystems, digital inclusivity, gender and sexualities.

The empirical procedure was developed in three stages: (1) Query Design; (2) Scraping Data and (3) Analysis (see Fig. 4.1). Firstly, we defined the search terms and queried them using Google Play App Store's native search tool: 'homem' (man), 'mulher' (woman), 'agénero' (agender), 'transgénero' (transgender) and 'não-binário' (non-binary). In addition to setting our location to Portugal, these terms were queried in Portuguese, as our research sought to address gender issues in the Portuguese app market. Accordingly, the terminology reflects colloquial uses in Portuguese, for example, the choice to query for man and woman rather than male and female. Next, in the Scraping stage, we conducted a series of five

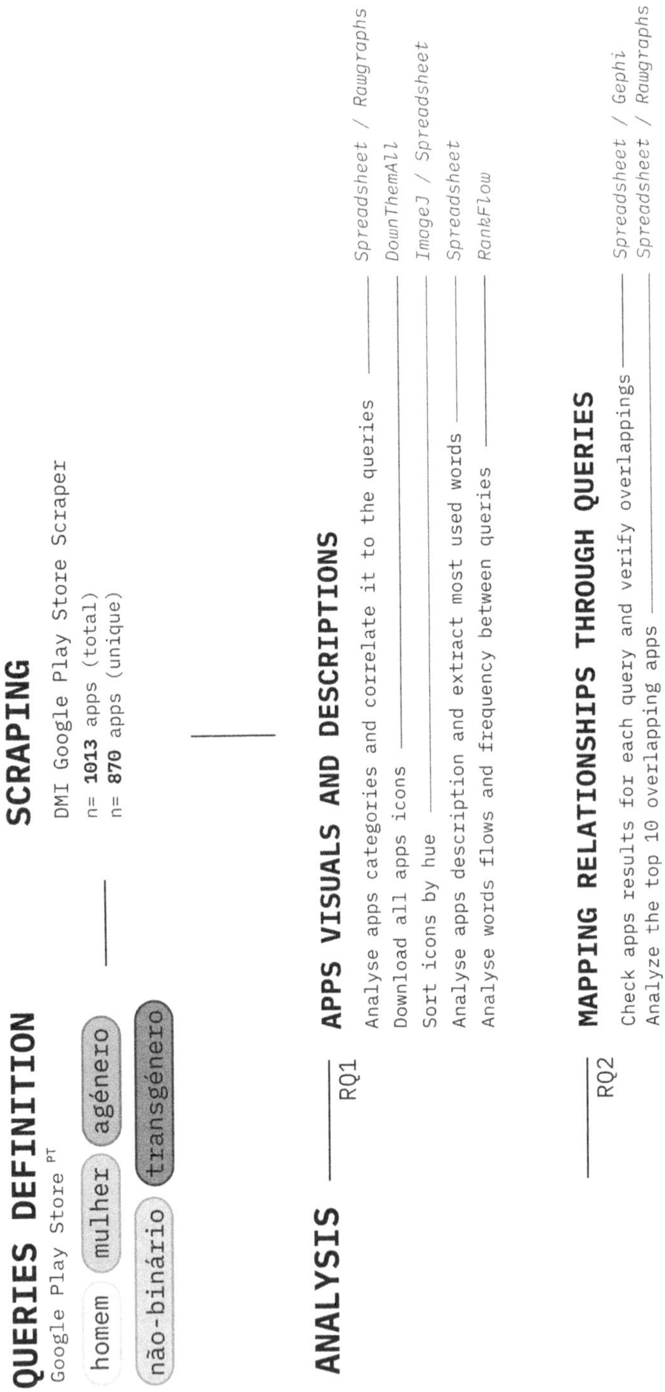

QUERIES DEFINITION
Google Play Store PT

- homem
- mulher
- agénero
- não-binário
- transgénero

SCRAPING
DMI Google Play Store Scraper

n= **1013** apps (total)
n= **870** apps (unique)

ANALYSIS

RQ1 — APPS VISUALS AND DESCRIPTIONS

Analyse apps categories and correlate it to the queries — *Spreadsheet / Rawgraphs*
Download all apps icons — *DownThemAll*
Sort icons by hue — *ImageJ / Spreadsheet*
Analyse apps description and extract most used words — *Spreadsheet*
Analyse words flows and frequency between queries — *RankFlow*

RQ2 — MAPPING RELATIONSHIPS THROUGH QUERIES

Check apps results for each query and verify overlappings — *Spreadsheet / Gephi*
Analyze the top 10 overlapping apps — *Spreadsheet / Rawgraphs*

Fig. 4.1. Visual Research Design. *Source:* Authors.

extractions (one for each keyword) using the Google Play Scraper (Digital Methods Initiative, 2019), developed by the Digital Methods Initiative and distributed under the MIT licence. The final dataset compiled 1,013 unique apps recommended by the platform.

In the Analysis stage, we segmented the focus of the study into two axes related to the research questions. The first phase analysed the visuals and descriptions of the apps using a combination of digital tools such as DownThemAll, ImageJ, Rankflow and RawGraphs. The second axis sought to understand the relationships between the apps resulting from the search for each term. We further integrate digital tools like Gephi, network analysis software and AppInspect to explore the apps' access requirements and permissions. This approach allowed us to explore the proposed research questions, generating a series of findings we explored in light of previous scientific production.

Findings and Discussion: Gender and Biases in the Portuguese Google PlayStore

To study how gender is constituted through app recommendations within the Portuguese Google PlayStore, we follow intersectional approaches to platform critique (Gipson et al., 2021). Seeking to expand beyond limited binary understandings, our analysis shows how the store curates and displays apps across various gender identities. The findings expose a complex interplay between the virtual store and the construction of gender within its app ecosystem. This section delves deeper into the results, highlighting the limitations of binary representation and the performative nature of gender identity in the digital sphere.

App Icons, Colour and Gendered Alignments

As visual digital objects that 'bring consistency and a cleaner look to Google Play' (Google Play Developers, n.d.), app icons share a unified shape, allowing users to focus on the artwork and surrounding information such as the title, ratings and price. Brand guidelines for designing Google Play icons emphasise the importance of providing better visual context for everyday app use (Google Play Developers, n.d.). An icon, in this sense, is less a representation but rather an 'operative image' (Farocki, 2004; Parikka, 2023) or a visual language 'for doing' that is designed with practices and not with interpretations in mind (Dieter et al., 2019). This operational function is characterised by the capacity of the icon to set in motion human activities that become part of the interface processes through app searching, selecting, installing, playing, etc. Every icon is designed to operate within a formation of similar icons, allowing researchers to explore how Google Play shapes associations between search results. From this perspective, icons link to the products that match the search query and activate relations between apps and their intended targeted audiences. Icon grids accessible through Google Play Search are visual collections of software items. Dieter et al. (2019) describe creating a seemingly coherent environment for downloading and purchasing apps. Raising questions about the reproduction of power and value under the order of platforms, Google Play enables data-intensive forms of 'controlled consumption' that apps facilitate by design (Andersen & Pold, 2018). A relational visual analysis of app icons according to the Google Play sorting logic, therefore, offers an entry point into the apps' intended use.

The montage method introduced below assists with exploring this logic from a systematic visual perspective (see Fig. 4.2). Arranging 1,013 app icons by colour similarity within each of the search queries – mulher (female), homem (male), agénero (agender), transgénero (transgender) and não-binário (non-binary) – , it provides a means for understanding the gendered and sexualised configurations of recommended apps. Through the strategic use of colours, app icons anchor and sustain prescriptive uses along established gender norms. This phenomenon is especially pronounced in the icon colour palettes of Google Play recommendations, where artwork design conveys implicit messages about gender and sexuality. Our analysis in Fig. 4.2 acknowledges how the intersection of icon design and app descriptions is utilised to capture user attention. Ultimately, we show how icons contribute to the potential perpetuation of stereotypes and underscore the importance of critically evaluating design decisions to challenge entrenched biases and promote inclusivity within digital platforms.

In visual and gender studies, colour has been used as a central methodological device for understanding affective ties and social connections. In their visual analysis of 'becoming smart' on Twitter, Gillian Rose and Alistair Willis (2019) conceptualise colour as an avenue for approaching the engaging territories of online platforms. Writing in the context of consumer culture, Xue et al. (2024) investigate the relationship between clothing colours and gender stereotyping. Our interpretation of app icons combines these perspectives, attending to the relations of fixity and flexibility in the gendered modalities through which apps intend to appeal to users. We arranged the images within each gender-specific 'style space' to analyse visual patterns using the image montage layout (Manovich, 2011). Displaying images side by side based on colour similarity, Fig. 4.2 separates our gendered search queries into distinct visual dimensions. Within each style, the colour intensity and tone range translate into the logic of proximity and distance between the icons. Visually similar icons are close; icons operationalising distinct colours appear further away.

Based on the varying persistence of colours across genders, the analysis reveals that different colours are associated with gender to a different extent. As Xue et al. (2024) elaborate, the prevalence of blue and pink tones in the male and female app audiences is unsurprising, given that normative colour perception and the development of gender stereotypes are closely intertwined. Blue tends to be associated with masculinity, whereas pink is considered a more feminine colour (Ishii et al., 2019). However, the practice of 'doing gender', as described by Judith Butler (1988), is evident not only in the visual patterns of heteronormative app store recommendations but also in the use of colours in queer app recommendations. Search results for the agender, transgender and non-binary queries showcase diverse colour schemes, challenging traditional norms. It's crucial to note how apps 'iconise' gender offers insight into the normative construction of associated use scenarios. Such scenarios require further contextualisation,

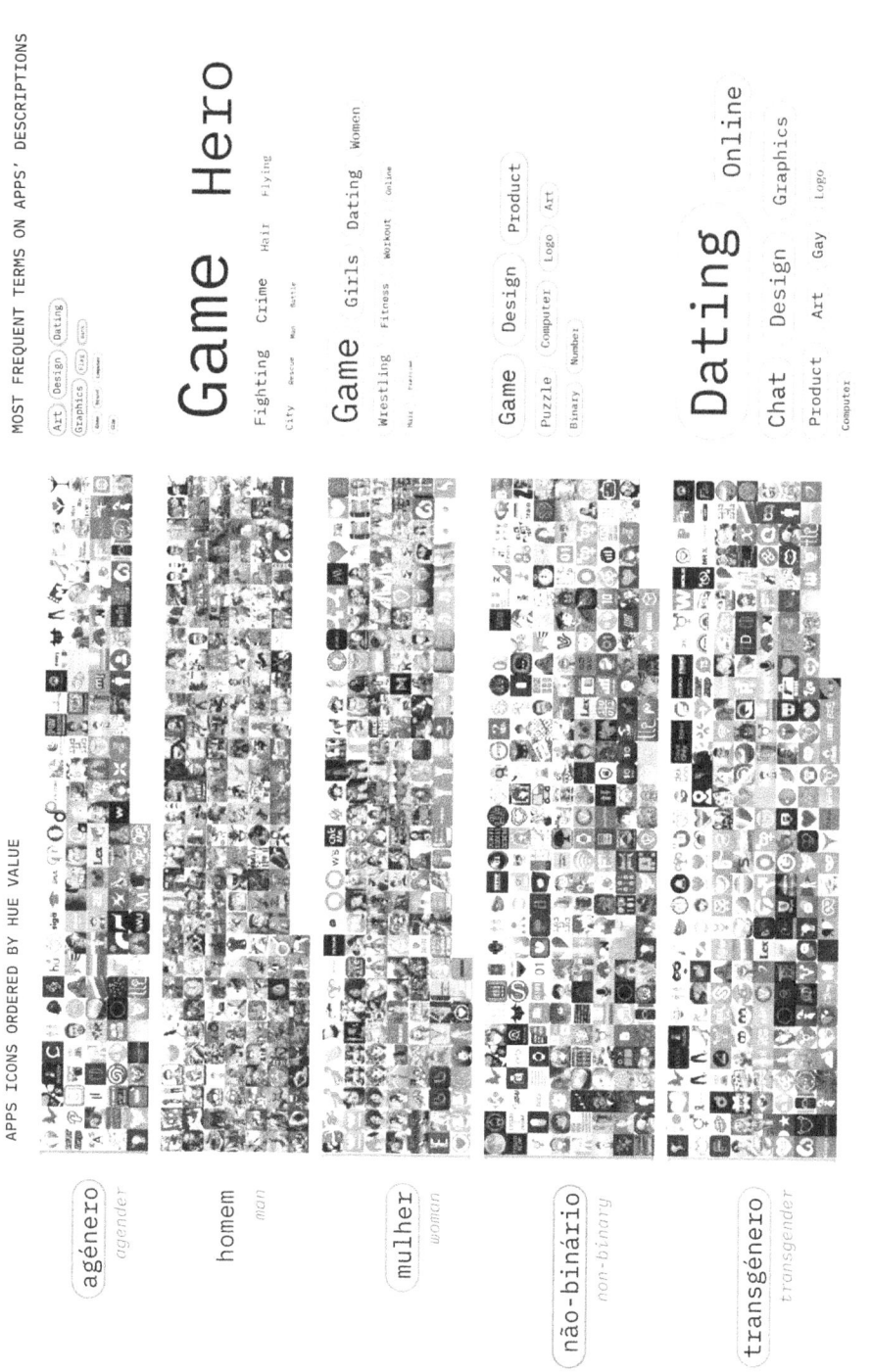

Storefront of Gender in the Portuguese Google PlayStore 63

Fig. 4.2. Visualisation of Combined App's Icons by Hue and Most Frequent Terms in Their Descriptions. *Source*: Authors.

which can be achieved by analysing frequently repeating terms in the app descriptions. The latter can be utilised to address how normative alignments of sexuality and sociality 'write themselves' into the strategically recommended categories of apps and associated user journeys.

Cross-reading repeating terms from the app descriptions within and across each gendered space, we can identify several trajectories of association intensified through colour: Apps tailored for men primarily use blue-coloured icons, focussing on gaming and superheroes. Female apps share the gamification aspect in the icons depicting wrestling, which appear visually close to fitness and workout apps. The abundance of pink-themed Bible apps 'for girls' may stem from ingrained gender stereotypes and societal expectations, linking Portuguese women with religious values. In a contrasting scenario, transgender app descriptions predominantly revolve around dating, lacking everyday-life topics like fitness or health. Similarly, agender and non-binary apps feature abstract, colourful game icons instead of body images, which suggests a focus on identity play and diverse self-expression rather than actual integration into society.

The Gendered Gaze: Reinforcing Societal Pressures on Women

Searches associated with 'mulher' (women) in the Google PlayStore paint a contrasting picture compared to results for other queried gender identities. The curated app selection presented by the Google PlayStore algorithm showcases a strong connection between notions of womanhood and concerns about body image and physical appearance. While lived femininities are necessarily plural, the culturally dominant ideals of normative femininity tend to be constructed concerning, and often oriented towards, the desires and interests of men (Connell, 1987). As such, normative femininity tends to be conflated with concerns about physical appearance and beauty (Dobson, 2015, p. 36). Pursuing idealised and ever-shifting femininity standards thus requires active construction through forms of aesthetic labour and feminine efforts (Elias et al., 2017) – such as fashion, beauty care, make-up, hairstyling, diets, exercise routines, etc. This feminine labour is also associated with aspirational consumption of goods and services that promise to approximate those who buy them from this ideal (McRobbie, 2007).

We can see these cultural norms play out (and perhaps be reinforced) in the sample of apps queried for 'women', as many focus on appearance aspects, such as fitness apps specifically directed at women. This alignment with existing societal pressures that prioritise female attractiveness reinforces a narrow and potentially limiting definition of femininity within the digital marketplace. However, the store recommendation ecosystem also offers possibilities that contribute to adding nuance to traditional gender structures. While the searcher for 'women' helps to highlight pressures to conform to limited beauty standards, the apps recommended by Google PlayStore exhibit a degree of porosity when it comes to these gendered social constructs. We can see these in the connections emerging between apps targeted at women and those geared towards 'queer' identities, primarily in the realm of dating. These connections suggest a potential for the category of women to navigate beyond its seemingly limited position in the heterosexual matrix (Butler, 2006) and seek platforms that might encourage a broader sense of self-definition. These connections indicate a space where women can explore identities that challenge the restrictive notions of femininity perpetuated by the curated app selection. In this case, the app ecosystem offers a glimmer of agency, inferring that women can potentially subvert societal expectations and embrace a more multifaceted understanding of womanhood. These porous breaches in the curated app landscape may offer possibilities for a 'female gaze', a critical response to the male gaze, aiming to empower female perspectives and challenge traditional gender representations (Fan, 2023; Xing, 2023; Yang, 2023).

This analysis reveals tensions within the Store and its user culture. On the one hand, the algorithmic curation reinforces a specific, narrow vision of femininity. On the other hand, the very structure of the app ecosystem, with its interconnectedness across gender categories, challenges those limitations. This observation underscores the complex interplay between technology and human agency. While algorithms can perpetuate bias, users also possess the ability to navigate the digital landscape in ways that defy these expectations. Ultimately, the app ecosystem becomes a playground where societal pressures and individual agency collide, offering users the potential to redefine the very nature of femininity within the digital sphere.

The Gender Binary: A Tale of Two Masculinities

The analysis of the Google PlayStore's app recommendations exposes a fascinating yet concerning portrayal of masculinity. 'Man' is often taken as the 'default setting' of humanity, a seemingly 'neutral' baseline against which all other genders must define themselves (de Beauvoir, 1956). This assumption is reflected in the sample of apps we analysed, as most apps queried for 'homem' (men) were not overtly gendered. Rather, they tended to be indirectly gendered by their relationship to hegemonic imaginaries of masculinity, for example, through genre, as noted in the dominance of fighting games that rely on stereotypical conceptions of masculinity. In stark contrast to the focus on appearance within the 'mulher' (women) category, searches associated with 'men' paint a distinct picture. While not always explicitly gendered, the app recommendations for men often rely heavily on stereotypical notions of masculinity. This is particularly evident in the abundance of fighting games, which reinforce the association of manhood with aggression and dominance. While masculinities, like all gendered conceptions, can be negotiated and contain multiple meanings (Farci & Scarcelli, 2023, p. 4), there are still culturally dominant expectations regarding what ideal masculinity is expected to be. These are not necessarily representative of the lived realities of most (if any) men but rather offer an ideal for men to position themselves with, providing widespread aspirational models and fantasies (Connell & Messerschmidt, 2005). These ideals can, of course, be resisted and shifted over time and according to cultural context.

While games were present across all gendered queries, we could see that this category is most visible in the 'men' query, thus fitting the common cultural association of masculinity with computer and game cultures (Farci & Scarcelli, 2023). This was noticeable in our coding of the app icons and in analysing the app descriptions. A simple frequency count of the most repeated words in the app descriptions highlights how the word 'games' and its variations, as well as related words such as superhero, were repeatedly used for the apps in this category, contrasting to other categories (like non-binary and agender) where these words show up only a couple of hundred of times.

However, we can understand normative masculinities not only by the characteristics they are expected to share but also by what they are not. Gender is relational, and normative masculinities are often culturally constructed in counterpoint to imaginaries of femininity (Connell & Messerschmidt, 2005, p. 848). Normative masculinities tend to distance themselves from the perceived otherness of the feminine and of forms of so-called 'subordinated' masculinities, such as queer masculinities and queerness in general, which are imagined as proximate to femininity (Budgeon, 2014, p. 322). This symbolic delineation of masculinity becomes apparent when we observe how distinct and detached the apps in the 'men' query are from the other queried categories. Not only do these apps have a much narrower focus on gaming, as seen above, but they also have distinct visualities that can fall into gendered patterns. In addition, when looking at the network of relations between the queried apps it becomes clear that the apps in the 'men' category share only three overlapping apps with the other queried categories. These include only one photo app that allows users to change the appearances of their photos, change hairstyles and add facial hair or make-up to 'change' one's gender between the two binary poles of man and woman. The other two apps connecting the 'men' query to the queer categories are gay dating apps, thus highlighting how sexuality can push masculinities across to a different quadrant of the sex–gender–sexuality system of the heterosexual matrix (Butler, 2006).

By contrast, apps explicitly gendered in their app name or description tended to focus on topics or practices that typically fall outside the scope of dominant masculinity, such as fitness *for men* or kegel exercises *for men*. This suggests a potential discomfort or may even reflect a form of algorithmic bias, in openly acknowledging men's engagement in activities that fall outside the rigid boundaries of stereotypical masculinity. The apps recommended for men often exist in a space largely detached from those targeted at other gender identities. This lack of connection between categories reinforces the concept of a separate sphere for men, potentially disconnected from areas like self-care or personal and emotional exploration, where apps geared towards other genders might be present. In essence, through its curation methods, the Google App Store can perpetuate a limited view of manhood, potentially alienating men who seek apps that cater to a broader range of interests and experiences. This observed binary in the portrayal of masculinity and femininity highlights the complex interplay between technology and societal norms. While the app store's algorithms might reinforce these stereotypes, it's crucial to acknowledge the potential for user agency.

The Performance of Identity: Play and Work

Drawing on research on queer identities in digital media which explores the intersection of LGBTQ+ experiences with technology, social platforms and data representation (Schimanski & Treharne, 2018; Weathington & Brubaker, 2023), it is also important to be attentive to how queer individuals navigate and are represented within digital spaces and the implications of these interactions for identity, community and visibility. Our analysis of the Google PlayStore environment brings forth links between the performance of gender and app usage. Role-playing games allow users to playfully explore and experiment with various gender identities in a safe, digitally mediated environment. However, gender is also continuously performed in everyday life, as the existence of apps specifically designed for tracking transitions, voice modulation, or hormone management helps to highlight. These apps exemplify how some queer experiences presuppose constant self-construction and negotiation. Parallels can be drawn with femininity, often framed as a state of perpetual 'work in progress', requiring constant attention to appearance and behaviour. Interestingly, the apps in this sample open space for non-normative femininities, as we can also observe some game apps that, at first sight, encroach into arenas traditionally imagined as masculine, like wrestling. While femininities incorporating seemingly masculine traits or interests are not uncommon (Budgeon, 2014, p. 326), we can see that many of the icons of these female wrestling game apps seem to emphasise the sexiness of the avatars shown, with many female figures combatting while wearing bikinis or revealing clothes. As such, the icons of these games seem to frame female wrestling through a lens that seeks to appeal to presumably heterosexual men's desires. We can also see a prevalence of dating apps amongst the apps in the 'women' category, thus highlighting the social and relational character of femininity. These dating apps also create a bridge between the apps in the 'women' and the queer categories (Fig. 4.3).

We can observe this on two levels. First, the analysis of the most repeated words in the app descriptions shows that the apps queried for 'women' share quite a few words with the gender-queer queries, including women, dating, singles and friends. Second, through the network of relations between the queried apps, which shows several dating apps connecting the 'women' and queer clusters. These observations highlight both the porosity of the app's ecosystem and potential disruptions to the heterosexual matrix (Butler, 2006), which refers to a social construct that aligns biological sex, gender identity and sexual orientation in a way that normalises heterosexuality and marginalises other identities.

Beyond Dating and Games: The Invisibility of Queerness in Everyday Life

The most striking finding lies in the analysis of apps associated with 'agênero' (agender), 'não-binário' (non-binary) and 'transgénero' (transgender) – collectively referred to as 'queer' for this discussion. Queer identity is a fluid and changing concept, allowing for diverse experiences and meanings, challenging heteronormativity and promoting fluidity in sexuality and gender practices

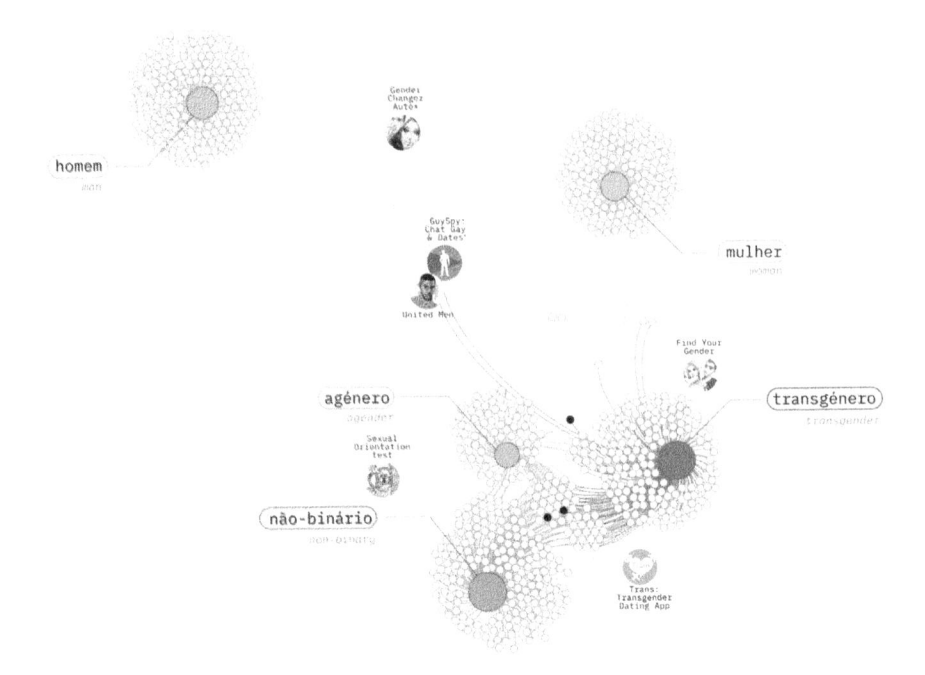

Fig. 4.3. Unique and Shared App Recommendations Network for the Five Gender Queries. *Source:* Authors, 2024.

(Peters, 2005). As Fig. 4.3 showcases, these queries reveal a significant overlap in the recommended apps, suggesting a shared space for these gender identities within the Google PlayStore, but also a potential flattening of the differences within these identities. Conversely, apps targeted at men exhibit almost no overlap with those aimed at other genders.

While queerness can be enmeshed with varied aspects of contemporary digital lives, from social media self-representational practices to online fandom or meme cultures (Duguay, 2022), within the studied Google Play ecosystem, we could observe a prevalence of dating apps for three queer queries. Dating has long been central to queer digital cultures (O'Riordan, 2020), creating new avenues for queer people to find or forge community while also prompting discussions about the potential sexualisation of these identities. Gay dating forums, for example, and to an even greater extent, locative dating applications, have always relied heavily on the construction of the ideal queer user as a point of reference, both online *and* offline (Light et al., 2008; Mowlabocus, 2010). Trans people have complex, sometimes contradictory relations to their use of mainstream digital technologies, which tend to accommodate trans bodies and sexualities only insofar as they cooperate with dominant norms (Gossett et al., 2019). Such construction of queer difference through alignments of gender and sexual practices is evident in the limited alternative app recommendations for trans, agender and non-binary communities. While queer genders are highly visible in the dating category, they are largely absent from other everyday domains represented on the Google PlayStore. For example, there's a notable absence of recommended apps for queer fitness, health or entertainment. This suggests a social and (infra)structural invisibility, underscoring that queer identities are not yet fully integrated into the app developers' ideas of everyday life.

Despite the relative novelty of the app development industry, a lack of diverse representation within the industry itself is likely reflected in the app landscape, pointing to a troubling conflation of queerness with sexuality. The abundance of dating and hook-up apps within the 'queer' category suggests a potential for viewing queer identities solely through a sexual lens. This mirrors the way femininity is often linked to dating and relationships. However, this association can lead to the 'adultification of the queer experience', neglecting the diversity within these identities. Furthermore, the potential deplatforming of sex-related apps (Tiidenberg & van der Nagel, 2020) might lead to the further invisibilisation of queer experiences, while 'normative' masculine and feminine apps can remain present in everyday life domains, thus creating a double standard for representation within the app ecosystem. In this light, the integration of queer identities through representation in art, media, and, as we see in this chapter, commercial app environment is crucial for combating marginalisation (Kesić, 2017). At the same time, capturing the nuances of queer identities in structured databases remains a significant challenge, highlighting the need for more inclusive and sensitive data practices.

Conclusion

This study provides a situated view of how gender is constituted and curated within the digital environment of the Portuguese Google PlayStore, reflecting on how its algorithmic labelling and recommendation practices can expose underlying biases. Moving beyond overly optimistic understandings of the Internet as a space for increased gendered experimentation, we have discussed how gender can be essentialised into easily quantifiable and commodifiable segments, which necessarily miss its complexity. Uncovering connections between gendered app recommendations, our analysis indicates both potential challenges to and reproductive dimensions of the dominant heterosexual framework (Butler, 2006). On the one hand, the Google PlayStore app ecosystem displays some flexibility, as apps targeted at 'women' and 'queer' identities intersect, especially within the category of dating. The widespread availability of role-playing games across gender queries also allows users to explore diverse gender identities, encouraging self-discovery and breaking away from normative expectations. On the other hand, however, our explorations show that the Google PlayStore emerges as a complex digital environment where different conceptions of gender perpetuate established hierarchies and co-exist in uneasy tensions.

Table 4.1. Gender Bias in Google PlayStore App Recommendations.

Gender	Most Frequent App Categories	Most Frequent Visual Representation	Store Bias Potential Impact
Homem (Men)	Fighting games, aggression	The design features a contrasting colour scheme (blue and red), an iconic comic book aesthetic, and an imposing physique with strong muscles or bearded faces	Reinforces hegemonic masculinity
Mulher (Women)	Fitness, beauty	Pink, floral and heart patterns or idealised bodies	Societal pressure on women's appearance
Agénero (Agender) Não-binário (Non-binary) Transgénero (Transgender)	Dating, social, simulation games & tools (e.g.: Voice modulation, hormone management)	Diverse colour palette, particularly incorporating rainbow hues, inclusive gender symbols, or flags representing different groups within the LGBTQIA+ community	The conflation of queerness with sexuality, limited representation and medicalisation of transgender experience

Our findings (summarised in the simplified matrix presented in Table 4.1) showcase the relationship between fixity and flexibility in this digital environment. For certain gendered queries, like those for 'men' or 'women', the apps suggested by the Store could be seen as playing on pre-existing narrow understandings of gender that continue to reproduce social inequalities. We could see this play out in the searches targeting 'men', which directed us to app ecosystems distinct from those aimed at other genders and reinforced hegemonic masculinities, emphasising fighting games as expressions of aggression and dominance (Connell, 2020).

The overrepresentation of certain app categories associated with particular gender identities raises questions about the cultural associations underlying these recommendations, as seen with the dominance of dating and hook-up apps within the 'queer' (and, to a lesser extent, 'women') categories. This abundance not only points to a conflation of femininity with dating but also suggests the potential for viewing queer identities solely through a sexual lens. This both risks the adultification of the queer experience and erases its multifaceted nature.

Similarly, within the 'women' category, we could see a normative emphasis on fitness and beauty, reinforcing societal pressures on women to conform to a limited beauty standard (Elias et al., 2017; Fredrickson & Roberts, 1997). Apps within the 'queer' categories are also linked to the relationship between the performance of performative gender and app usage, with an array of apps for tracking transitions, voice modulation, and hormone management that highlight the constant process of self-construction and negotiation of bodies who, much like femininity, seem to be framed in a state of perpetual 'work in progress' requiring constant attention to appearance and behaviour (Walkerdine, 1989).

While these findings are, necessarily, situated and may not reflect the experiences of all users within each category, the matrix helps to highlight potential areas for further investigation, such as how the Google PlayStore recommendation system reinforces (or disrupts) gender norms and how app discovery can be made more inclusive for all users regardless of gender identity.

As our chapter showcases, apps and their store environments can reproduce or reinforce hegemonic norms. They can be spaces for control or potential resistance and disruption, as users can negotiate, subvert or reject the gendered imaginaries advanced by app recommendations. As such, this study provides a first exploratory entry into this contested realm, calling for further research into how people engage with apps and app stores and how they navigate these gendered digital environments in their everyday lives.

References

Andersen, C. U., & Pold, S. B. (2018). *The metainterface: The art of platforms, cities, and clouds*. The MIT Press.
Bivens, R. (2017). The gender binary will not be deprogrammed: Ten years of coding gender on Facebook. *New Media & Society, 19*(6), 880–898.
Budgeon, S. (2014). The dynamics of gender hegemony: Femininities, masculinities and social change. *Sociology, 48*(2), 317–334.
Butler, J. (1988). Performative acts and gender constitution: An essay in phenomenology and feminist theory. *Theatre Journal, 40*(4), 519–531. https://doi.org/10.2307/3207893
Butler, J. (2006). *Gender trouble: Feminism and the subversion of identity*. Routledge.
Connell, R. W. (1987). *Gender and power: Society, the person, and sexual politics*. Stanford University Press.
Connell, R. W. (2020). *Masculinities*. Routledge.
Connell, R. W., & Messerschmidt, J. W. (2005). Hegemonic masculinity: Rethinking the concept. *Gender & Society, 19*(6), 829–859.
de Beauvoir, S. (1956). *The second sex*. Jonathan Cape.
de Lauretis, T. (1987). The female body and heterosexual presumption. *Semiotica, 67*(3–4), 259–279.

Dieter, M., Gerlitz, C., Helmond, A., Tkacz, N., van der Vlist, F. N., & Weltevrede, E. (2019). Multi-situated app studies: Methods and propositions. *Social Media + Society*, 5(2). https://doi.org/10.1177/2056305119846486

Digital Methods Initiative. (2019, v6.2.3). Google Play Store Scraper [Software]. https://tools.digitalmethods.net/app-scrapers

Dobson, A. S. (2015). *Postfeminist digital cultures: Femininity, social media, and self-representation*. Palgrave Macmillan.

Duguay, S. (2022). *Personal but not private: Queer women, sexuality, and identity modulation on digital platforms*. Oxford University Press.

Elias, A., Gill, R., & Scharff, C. (2017). *Aesthetic labour: Beauty politics in neoliberalism* (pp. 3–49). Palgrave Macmillan.

Fan, X. (2023). An analysis of the correct use of female gaze from the perspective of gaze theory – A case study of portrait of a lady on fire. *BCP Social Sciences & Humanities*. https://doi.org/10.54691/bcpssh.v21i.3458

Farci, M., & Scarcelli, C. M. (2023). Men have to be competent in something, women need to show their bodies. Gender, digital youth cultures and popularity. *Journal of Gender Studies*, 1–13. https://doi.org/10.1080/09589236.2023.2241857

Farocki, H. (2004). Phantom images. *Public*, 29. https://public.journals.yorku.ca/index.php/public/article/view/30354

Fredrickson, B. L., & Roberts, T.-A. (1997). Objectification theory: Toward understanding women's lived experiences and mental health risks. *Psychology of Women Quarterly*, 21(2), 173–206. https://doi.org/10.1111/j.1471-6402.1997.tb00108.x

Gipson, B., Corry, F., & Noble, S. U. (2021). In N. B. Thylstrup, D. Agostinho, A. Ring, C. D'Ignazio, & K. Veel. (Eds.), *Uncertain archives. Critical keywords for big data* (pp. 305–312). MIT Press.

Google Play Developer Documentation. (n.d.). Linking to Google Play. https://developer.android.com/distribute/marketing-tools/linking-to-google-play

Gossett, R., Stanley, E. A., & Burton, J. (2019). *Trap door: Trans cultural production and the politics of visibility*. MIT Press.

Haraway, D. (1991). A cyborg manifesto: Science, technology, and socialist-feminism in the late twentieth century. *Simians, Cyborgs and Women: The Reinvention of Nature*, 149–181.

Ishii, K., Numazaki, M., & Tado'oka, Y. (2019). The effect of pink/blue clothing on implicit and explicit gender-related self-cognition and attitudes among men. *Japanese Psychological Research*, 61, 123–132. https://doi.org/10.1111/jpr.12241

Jansen, S., & Bloemendal, E. (2013). Defining app stores: The role of curated marketplaces in software ecosystems. In G. Herzwurm & T. Margaria (Eds.), *Software business. From physical products to software services and solutions* (Vol. 150, pp. 195–206). Springer Berlin Heidelberg. https://doi.org/10.1007/978-3-642-39336-5_19

Kesić, S. (2017). Theory of queer identities: Representation in contemporary East-European art and culture. *AM Journal of Art and Media Studies*, 14, 123–131. https://doi.org/10.25038/am.v0i14.211

Keyes, O. (2021). (Mis)Gendering. In N. B. Thylstrup, D. Agostinho, A. Ring, C. D'Ignazio, & K. Veel. (Eds.), *Uncertain archives. Critical keywords for big data* (pp. 339–346). MIT Press.

Light, B. A., Fletcher, G., & Adam, A. E. (2008). Gay men, Gaydar and the commodification of difference. *Information Technology & People*, 21(3), 300–314.

Lupton, D. (2014). Self-tracking cultures: Towards a sociology of personal informatics. In *Proceedings of the 26th Australian computer-human interaction conference on designing futures: The future of design* (pp. 77–86). Association for Computing Machinery (ACM).

Manovich, L. (2011, August 4–6). Style Space: How to compare image sets and follow their evolution [Draft text]. http://manovich.net/content/04-projects/073-style-space/70_article_2011.pdf

Markham, A. N. (2017). Ethnography in the digital era: From fields to flow, descriptions to interventions. In N. Denzin & Y. Lincoln (Eds.), *The Sage handbook of qualitative research* (5th ed., pp. 650–668). SAGE Publications.

McRobbie, A. (2007). Top girls? Young women and the post-feminist sexual contract. *Cultural Studies, 21*(4–5), 718–737.

Mowlabocus, S. (2010). *Gaydar culture. Gay men, technology and embodiment in the digital age.* Routledge.

O'Riordan, K. (2020). Queer digital cultures. In S. Sommerville (Ed.), *The Cambridge companion to queer studies.* Cambridge University Press.

Parikka, J. (2023). *Operational images: From the visual to the invisual.* University of Minnesota Press.

Peters, W. (2005). *Queer identities: Rupturing identity categories and negotiating meanings of queer* (Vol. 24). Canadian Woman Studies.

Prescott, J., & Bogg, J. (2014). The experiences of women working in the computer games industry: An in-depth qualitative study. In *Gender considerations and influence in the digital media and gaming industry* (pp. 92–109). IGI Global.

Rogers, R. (2013). *Digital methods.* MIT Press.

Rose, G., & Willis, A. (2019). Seeing the smart city on Twitter: Colour and the affective territories of becoming smart. *Environment and Planning D: Society and Space, 37*(3), 411–427. https://doi.org/10.1177/0263775818771080

Schimanski, I., & Treharne, G. (2018). Extra marginalisation within the community: Queer individuals' perspectives on suicidality, discrimination and gay pride events. *Psychology & Sexuality, 10*, 31–44. https://doi.org/10.1080/19419899.2018.1524394

Simões, R. B., & Amaral, I. (2022). Sexuality and self-tracking apps: Reshaping gender relations and sexual and reproductive practices. In *The Routledge companion to gender, sexuality and culture* (pp. 413–423). Routledge.

Szulc, L. (2020). Digital gender disidentifications: Beyond the subversion versus hegemony dichotomy and toward everyday gender practices. *International Journal of Communication, 14*, 19.

Tiidenberg, K., & van der Nagel, E. (2020). *Sex and social media.* Emerald Publishing Limited.

Turkle, S. (1995). Ghosts in the machine. *Sciences, 35*(6), 36–39.

van Zoonen, L. (2011). The rise and fall of online feminism. In M. Christensen, A. Jansson, & C. Christensen (Eds.), *Online territories: Globalisation, mediated practice, and social space* (pp. 132–146). Peter Lang.

Walkerdine, V. (1989). Femininity as performance. *Oxford Review of Education, 15*(3), 267–279. https://doi.org/10.1080/0305498890150307

Weathington, K., & Brubaker, J. (2023). Queer identities, normative databases: Challenges to capturing queerness on Wikidata. *Proceedings of the ACM on Human-Computer Interaction, 7*, 1–26. https://doi.org/10.1145/3579517

West, C., & Zimmerman, D. H. (1987). Doing gender. *Gender & Society*, *1*(2), 125–151.

Xing, Y. (2023). The popularity of Ding Zhen: Female gaze, female power and public sphere. *Media and Communication Research*. https://doi.org/10.23977/mediacr.2023.040404

Xue, Z., Li, Q., Zhao, J., & Zeng, X. (2024). An investigation into the relationship between clothing colors and gender stereotyping in children. *Journal of Retailing and Consumer Services*, *76*, 103559.

Yang, L. (2023). A visual analysis of the female gaze in Korean pop culture. *Communications in Humanities Research*. https://doi.org/10.54254/2753-7064/4/20220482

Chapter 5

Young Adults' (Re)Negotiation of Gender and Sexual Identities Across Mobile Apps in Portugal

Rita Alcaire[a]*, Sofia José Santos*[b] *and Filipa Subtil*[c]

[a]University of Coimbra, Portugal
[b]Faculty of Economics and Centre for Social Studies, University of Coimbra, Portugal
[c]School of Communication and Media Studies, IPL – Politécnico de Lisboa, LIACOM and ICNOVA, Portugal

Abstract

Stemming from a critical approach towards technology (understood as a producer of meanings, subjectivity and agency, and, thus, shaped by power relations) and taking into account the role of broader societal norms and structures in technological uses and gratifications, this chapter explores the (re) negotiations of gender and sexual identities among Portuguese young adult app users. It focuses on if app usage allows these users to break hetero-cisnormativity and hegemonic notions of masculinity. For that purpose, the study conducted six focus groups involving 31 participants and 25 semi-structured interviews with young adults (18–30 years old). The scripts were designed to collect data about mobile app usage practices and what meanings interviewees attribute to used platforms, navigating through imaginaries, meanings, appropriations, incorporations and mostly negotiations. Analytically, this study contributes to an enhanced understanding of how apps might change young adult lives concerning gender and sexual identities and to challenging uses and gratifications theory, which, after almost 80 years since its first formulations, has gained new impetus with the ongoing digitisation process and the so-called interactive technologies that integrate it.

Keywords: Dating apps; young adults; sexual and gender identities; uses and gratifications; technology as an extension of the self; identity management

Introduction

Technology is much more than technical artefacts, and the implications of its usages include a dynamic of uses and gratification (UandG) that goes far beyond that equation. Technology – in its production and uses – is not neutral but embodies and produces subjectivities (Feenberg, 1991; Habermas, 2006; Pool, 1983). Mobile applications are no exception to this dynamic, nor is the realm of gender and sexualities a misfit of this logic amidst the multiple identities one holds.

In recent years, mobile applications have emerged as popular and essential platforms for (self-)exploration and expression of gender and sexual identities, particularly amidst still ingrained heteropatriarchal societies. Moreover, digital media have played a crucial role in orienting young LGBTQIA+ people's notions of 'community' around performances of identity and individuality (Pym et al., 2020). Digital interfaces also create spaces for connecting with other people who share common identities or interests, significantly impacting their sense of community and belonging. Online communities, forums and social media groups dedicated to specific genders and sexualities or sex education provide people who use them with a variety of resources and functionalities that they may not have access to or find these kinds of spaces and welcoming offline (Adkins et al., 2018; Jenzen, 2017; McConnell et al., 2017). At the same time, digital interfaces can also present challenges and risks for people with non-normative orientations and identities, especially those who prefer to keep them private in their daily lives or are still questioning them. Harassment, discrimination and misgendering (Mkhize et al., 2020; Scheuerman et al., 2018) also occur online, and sometimes more violently because there is no face-to-face contact, with accurate and significant impacts on the mental health and well-being of people in these spaces. In addition, digital spaces may not always accurately reflect the complexities and nuances of identities and sexualities and, therefore, reinforce negative stereotypes and norms that lead to exclusion.

The main aim of this chapter is to explore the (re)negotiations of gender and sexual identities among Portuguese young adult app users who participated in the MyGender project. Drawing from six focus groups involving 31 participants and 25 semi-structured individual interviews with young adults (18–30 years old), we analyse the major trends identified concerning uses, imaginaries, meanings, appropriations, incorporations and negotiations by young adults in Portugal, hence exploring how mobile app usage makes young adults subscribe to hegemonic gender norms concerning gender and sexual identities or contest, coopt or (re)negotiate them.

Challenging UandG: A Gendered Critical Overview of Technology

Technology is widespread in today's societies. Its usage and utility are not only seemingly universal but also make everyday tasks so much more effective in terms of time and effort that there is a trend to perceive it as a mere rational and objective tool devoid of ideological or subjective dimensions.

One of the theoretical attempts to make sense of how media affects society has been the UandG hypothesis – a liberal and individually focused approached that, while recognising the subjective dimension of technology, could not import to its epistemological and methodological spheres the structural conditions of society and how they influenced media and technology uses. The notion of 'use' in media studies emerged during the 1940s through the 'UandG' hypothesis. This hypothesis focused analytical attention on consumers' uses and choices, conjecturing that different individuals could use the same mass media sources for various purposes. By understanding consumers' needs for each medium, the hypothesis acknowledged that consumers' motives for their usage behaviours were to receive gratification. This research programme was a turning point concerning the first approaches (for example, the 'magic bullet theory' associated with the linear models of behaviourist psychology) to the relationship between the public and the media. The public was understood as a relatively passive entity that perceived messages and behaved more or less homogeneously, following the meaning of the information and culture transmitted by the media. The objective of knowing why individuals pay attention to specific media content and the gratification that could result from it made it possible to value the critical role of cognitive variables and subcultures, namely popular cultures. However, understanding media use by the consumer vector or the media vector can be, in some way, complementary, as each approach leads to a different type of explanation for media use behaviour. From a methodological point of view, the first approaches are under a 'structural' approach that highlights the media as a fundamental influence and focuses the analysis on media content and properties.

The UandG hypothesis follows a 'behavioural' approach, highlighting and studying individual needs and their reasons. This theoretical approach can be combined with another, of a 'socio-cultural' nature, which emphasises and studies the context in which each individual finds himself and how he chooses to face the diversity of the media (McQuail, 1994/1983, p. 390). The first studies on UandG had little theoretical coherence as well as an individualistic and descriptive bias, seeking to classify audience members' responses into meaningful categories. Criticisms of the initial hypothesis about UandG focused on the fact that (a) it relies heavily on self-assessments; (b) not be sophisticated about the social origin of the needs that audiences bring to the media; (c) maintains an overly uncritical position about the possible dysfunction, both for oneself and for society, of certain types of audience satisfaction; (d) being very much a prisoner of the supposed inventive diversity of audiences (Katz, 1987). More far-reaching criticisms regarding UandG's vision of media technologies and receivers can still be advanced. As for media technologies, the idea of various possible uses cannot be denied, as they tend to stimulate pre-defined practices. Concerning recipients, there is a liberal presumption in which individuals rationally calculate their acts based on the utility and satisfaction they can derive from them. Regardless of the criticism, the UandG approach has contributed to the statement that the nature of the involvement, role or dependence in which readers come into contact with the media conditions the uses, gratifications and potential effects.

However, changes in the media or the technological system, particularly at the turn of the 21st century with the advent of new media, will likely force us to rethink and even reevaluate the approaches briefly presented/listed before. The advent and dissemination of digital technologies, their increasing transformation into a basic technological infrastructure for information exchange and the role of algorithmic systems require considering uses in another theoretical and analytical light. This is not to call into question the idea of the potentially active and selective performance of consumers/users, nor to undermine the investigation of why individuals show interest in specific means or technologies and the compensations they can derive from them, much less neglect of sociocultural variables. This research heritage has every reason to exist. It is vital to discuss information technologies and their influence beyond the notions of 'behaviour', 'social utility' and 'choice'. Firstly, 'behaviour' is just a social research variable that does not cover other structural dimensions, which include technological, media and economic systems, among others; secondly, one of the structural constraints of societies lies in the power of current technologies, in particular, the algorithmic capacity and design of apps; finally, the emphasis on individuals' choices implies a liberal conception of the subject that would guide their conduct by preferences and satisfaction.

In terms of gender, although recognising a subjective dimension in uses and gratifications, this theory has shown less contribution in challenging patriarchy in the sense that it somehow dismisses its structural dimension.

To our understanding, critical technology studies have a significant contribution here. As Santos summarises, although there are different critical approaches to technology, they equally share a dialectical approach towards technology – works both in favour of the status quo and to challenge dominant power structures, and the recognition of the subjectivity – the 'locus of enunciation' to use Mignolo's expression (1999) – of the production and use of technology (Santos, 2021, pp. 195–200).

As technology is human-created and unfolds in a particular social context, it depends on the subjectivities of the actors who create and use it and the (power) structures in which these actors are integrated (e.g. Brock, 2011; Santos, 2021). The use given to a specific technology is, thus, limited by the design and possibilities allowed by those who created it and reflects the ideological and functional context within which it was made, therefore embodying the broader logic of power and how it influences social modelling and political action. According to Brock (2011, p. 1088), although the online realm is a place in itself, they somehow stick to the offline realm, i.e. the technological structures of the digital realm reflect 'offline ideological patterns and preferences' (Brock, 2011, p. 1088) and are, thus, an expression of 'technocultural' dominant beliefs – being them capitalism, racism, sexist, liberal orders, authoritarian orders, etc. The example of the BlackBird browser is illustrative of this.[1] Technological structures apart, technological crafts also allow the generation

---

[1] See: https://blackbirdhome.com/moreinfo/

and dissemination of narratives while hindering the propagation of many others. Although virtually everyone can speak online, it does not mean everyone is listened to similarly. Here, once again, online and offline realms converge. As Santos claims: 'The power of each subject in a given configuration of forces determines the influence and scope of what they say. If dominant narratives about the internet tend to create a universal equivalence of access and voice, denying the asymmetry of access and amplification that upstream inequalities create (Feagin and Elias, 2012), the truth is that it is impossible to dissociate the control of narratives from the control of the structure itself and that the online space takes place in a space of already constituted hegemonic power, which amplifies or reduces certain voices and interactions' (Santos, 2021, p. 200).[2]

Gender-wise, societies have organised themselves in heteropatriarchal structures – even at times shifting. In other words, there is an 'institutionalization of male dominance in vertical structures, with very high correlations between position and gender, legitimized by the culture (e.g., in religion and culture), and often emerging as direct violence with males as subjects and females as objects' (Galtung, 1996, p. 40). The heteropatriarchal system operates through a complex interplay of power dynamics and asymmetrical relationships (Butler, 1990; Connell, 2005). At its core, it upholds the dominance of heterosexual, cisgender White men over other genders and sexual orientations. This system is perpetuated through various means, including institutional structures, cultural norms and interpersonal interactions in which power is concentrated in the hands of those who conform to traditional masculine ideals.

In contrast, others, particularly women, non-binary individuals and LGBTQIA+ people, are marginalised and disenfranchised (Hooks, 2000). Therefore, the impact of the cisheteropatriarchal system extends beyond the gender binary and not only reinforces the subjugation of women but also enforces rigid gender roles and expectations that limit the freedom and expression of all individuals. Non-binary and transgender individuals face additional challenges as they navigate a society that often fails to recognise or validate their identities when intersecting forms of oppression based on race, class, sexuality (Collins, 2000; Crenshaw, 1989), and other social categories. In this sense, individuals who do not conform to hegemonic ideals of being, behaving and expressing themselves

---

[2]Original quote, in Portuguese: 'O alcance do que cada sujeito diz depende, em grande medida, da posição que esse sujeito ocupa na rede (online, offline e, sobretudo, uma simbiose dessas duas esferas) e da forma como essa posição é calibrada em cada momento. A internet é um espaço de múltiplas vozes, mas também de múltiplos e constitutivos lugares de enunciação. O poder de cada sujeito numa determinada configuração de forças determina a influência e o alcance do que diz. Se as narrativas dominantes sobre a internet tendem a criar uma equivalência universal de acesso e de voz, negando a assimetria de acesso e de amplificação que desigualdades a montante criam (Feagin e Elias, 2012), a verdade é que há uma impossibilidade de se dissociar o controlo das narrativas do controlo da própria estrutura e que o espaço online acontece num espaço de poder hegemónico já constituído, que amplifica ou reduz determinadas vozes e interações' (Santos, 2021, p. 200).

as either feminine or masculine tend to feel excluded. Various literature has pointed out a mutual formation of gender and technology (van Zoonen, 2002; Wajcman, 2007).

As far as gender and sexual diversity are concerned, challenging UandG of technology involve leveraging technology to address and challenge issues relating to sexual orientation and gender expression and identity, provide support and promote inclusivity and representation. Uncovering the specific UandG of mobile apps used by non-normative people requires a deeper understanding of the confluence of different aspects such as place, space, technology and communication behaviours of LGBTQIA+ people. From a dialectical perspective, there is a need to analyse how these apps may facilitate the breakdown of boundaries between online and offline, public and private and heteronormative and non-normative individuals and communities. Indeed, technology also allows individuals to rewrite the original scripts of technology. In this sense, enquiring how individuals engage with the apps they use and, most importantly, how they comply with or challenge gender scripts while using different apps is paramount.

Methodology

This research draws on qualitative data from semi-structured interviews and focus groups within the scope of the MyGender project.[3] Twenty-five in-depth semi-structured interviews were carried out between May and October 2022 with 16 (self-identified) women and nine (self-identified) men in Portugal who considered themselves frequent users of mobile apps. The call-out was issued through public calls and invitations, and we also used snowballing techniques. While challenges were encountered in diversifying the sample, efforts were made to include individuals with varying social backgrounds and identities. Nevertheless, the sample is predominantly urban, educated and middle class. Participants were geographically dispersed, and the option was to interview them via Zoom, facilitating reliable audio and video recordings, with participants expressing written and verbal consent. Data supporting this chapter are also drawn from six focus groups conducted between July 2021 and April 2022. Due to the COVID-19 pandemic, the focus groups were conducted remotely via Zoom. Each meeting

---

[3] MyGender is the first-ever study in Portugal aimed to investigate how young adults (18–30 years old) engage with the technicity and imaginaries of mobile applications, incorporating them into their daily lives, embodying them in their everyday practices and using them to (re)negotiate their gender and sexual identities. This age group's conceptualisation diverges from conventional studies that often encompass a broader age range, combining children, adolescents and adults. Challenging research focused either on the risks and opportunities or the uses and gratifications of digital practices, MyGender assumes an understanding of technology as producing meaning, subjectivity and agency shaped by power relations. Adopting a critical perspective of contemporary digital media, the project analysed mobile app affordances, grammar, platform politics, content and their uses, appropriations and embodiment to understand how they shape hegemonic normativity and change young adulthood lives.

gathered between four to six people (31 people in total) and had an average duration of 60 minutes. In addition to age as a selection criterion, the participants were all undergraduate or Master's students from several Portuguese public universities in distinct areas of expertise. In total, 16 participants identified as women, 14 as men and one as non-binary. The researcher who conducted the focus groups mediated through questions and comments, always seeking to promote interaction between all participants with the least interference possible. The focus groups were audio and video recorded with the participants' informed consent. Focus groups and interviews were conducted in Portuguese. Excerpts presented here were translated into English, respecting how people spoke as much as possible.

In analysing our empirical data, we adopted the critical thematic analysis proposed by Lawless and Chen (2019). This approach is well-suited for understanding the role of power in shaping the social construction of shared realities. Following the framework outlined by these authors (p. 96), we identified patterns in interpreting individual practices within social media mobile apps. This exploration illuminated the interplay of power relations embedded in app affordances, user practices and the broader sociocultural context.

Discussion

To understand how apps contribute to (re)shaping hegemonic normativity and are intertwining with young adulthood lives, our analysis is structured around three main clusters: Technology as an Extension of Daily Lives (to understand how pervasive apps are in everyday reality and, subsequently, in the construction of everyday identities); Identity management (to explore how (re)negotiation unfolds) and Dating apps (understood as a pivotal realm where gender identities and sexual orientation are expressed).

Technology as an Extension of Daily Lives

Mobile applications have seamlessly woven into the fabric of daily life for young adults in Portugal, evolving into indispensable tools that influence diverse aspects of their existence. This assimilation goes beyond mere utility, shaping central facets of their identity, such as communication habits and daily routines. The integration of technology as an extension of their daily lives was further underscored by examining digital diaries crafted by participants in another phase of the MyGender project (see Alcaire et al., 2024). Maintaining connections with acquaintances, immediate or extended family and close or past friends and colleagues is the primary motivation for engaging in activities and investing time in the lifeworld through mobile social media. Facilitated by smartphones, these activities, particularly on Instagram and Facebook, manifest as ongoing embodied engagements prioritising authentic connection and interaction on specific social platforms (Simões et al., 2023). This stance contrasts with the early digital interactions where users were inclined to connect with unfamiliar individuals and explore fictional identities (Papacharissi, 2002).

Almost everyone who participated in the focus groups or was interviewed stated they could go without a smartphone for an hour, a day or longer. Still, throughout the conversation, they reported using apps for various functions such as contacting other people, making home banking transactions, booking healthcare services and researching content on subjects they were interested in, from DIY tutorials and lifestyle inspiration to social causes they were involved in, access to streaming or other entertainment outlets and to get news updates and information concerning their academic study daily. Instant messaging services like WhatsApp or Facebook Messenger reportedly permitted respondents to create or be part of groups related to family, fellow students or work and interact with a usually restricted number of people who are not bound due to geographical constraints. By reporting their use of apps, interviewees clarified that technology is a bridge connecting them with family, friends, colleagues and like-minded people.

Social media platforms, email and instant messaging have become channels for nurturing close relationships and strengthening bonds. As this 21-year-old male interviewee explains, his use of mobile apps is mainly 'To communicate with friends or family, and so. To see content and get some clarification, something like that, like getting more into a certain subject from other perspectives'. For this 26-year-old female, the use of mobile apps is mainly '[...] for research, I use it a lot to access, for example, the bank, payments, now it's all MBWay, we don't use cash so much anymore, oh, but honestly I have no idea, just opening it here to see.[4] [...] I think I spend more time on WhatsApp than Instagram because I have work groups, I have family groups, I have groups for everything and something else'.

Mobile apps also provide a safe space (sometimes safer and more accessible than offline) for people to express their sexuality and sexual orientation. Discussing this topic, this 24-year-old male interviewee refers to that possibility, not neglecting the ambivalence of using certain apps:

> Clearly, the ability to meet people in the community. Sometimes it's difficult, there ends up being a bit of an openness at a social level for people to be there and open up and talk, but there are still a lot of people who unfortunately hide. [...] Disadvantages, we are exposed to the worst that the community has to offer, I think, at least from the LGBT community's point of view, sometimes there are outrageous things that are seen, that are said, that are done in apps. [...] That's why I reiterate that they have immense potential, but you need to be very careful about the people you choose.

---

[4]MBWay is an app that offers an interbank solution for immediate purchases and transfers via a smartphone or tablet.

In other words, constant connectivity is perceived as a prerequisite for engaging in everyday life. Even when they do not use a specific app, they consider using it (or installing it) to be integrated into their social networks. Other interviewees articulated experiencing peer pressure to participate in social media to be part of something: a group, a trend, or an activity – showcasing how existing structures might condition everyone's experiences. They highlight the challenge of relinquishing their current usage or considering alternatives without jeopardising complete integration in specific groups or realities. For instance, a 21-year-old male participant emphasised this sentiment: 'If you're not there, if you don't post on social media, you don't exist'.

Identity Management

One of the most relevant aspects for discussing the perception and negotiation of sexual and gender identities in the MyGender research – also reflected in the academic literature – is the concept of 'self-representation'. In digital spaces, there is the possibility of curating your online persona and presenting oneself in the way you choose, which can align (or not) with your identity. This possibility also creates the space for individuals to stretch the plethora and horizon of gender identities made possible in that technological realm, which can include selecting the username, the profile photos and the description they prepare that reflects how they want to be seen, the pronouns they use and other aspects of their identity. In the testimony that we share next, a 26-year-old female participant addresses how she navigates this subject, a choice that echoes the concerns of others in the research:

> I'm a little reserved about most of the things I do... [...] I hardly share my things, and when I share them, it's mostly using "stories", because they stay on for 24 hours and then disappear, so we are not marked by them, and sometimes if it's something very personal, I limit it to mutual or close friends, but I'm not much of a sharer.

When it comes to the virtual representation of an individual in the digital world, many participants address that they tend to approach most shared aspects of their lives with a reserved demeanour and are quite selective about what they choose to share and with whom. Consequently, they also carefully manage (and negotiate in their own terms) their gender and sexuality performances on social media. To do this, they use privacy and security controls, monitor their self-expression, manage friendship networks, create multiple accounts, select and edit personal photographs and restrict content related to specific issues – feminist and LGBTQIA+ issues, for example. This management becomes very clear in the following statement by a 24-year-old male participant:

> It depends on the social network. On Grindr, for example, I don't like it; it's a photo of mine that's there, but it's a photo where you

can't see my face because I like to have a minimum of criteria, like, in terms of showing it. Now, other social networks obviously, yes, because how will people know? Facebook has it [a photo], Instagram has it, and all the others have it. Grindr only has a photo from the neck down. Still, if it's someone I want to continue talking to, I quickly send a photo of my face, too, because I think it's important to know who we're talking to. Not for the sake of making some kind of judgment based on physical appearance or anything like that; it's for the sake of associating a face with the person.

Displaying an actual photo on social media and dating apps can be a deeply personal decision, laden with various considerations and implications. For many, it is a deliberate act of self-representation, offering a glimpse into their identity and personality. A profile picture serves as a digital introduction, conveying not only physical appearance but also aspects of character and style. However, this seemingly simple gesture carries weighty implications, particularly in the realm of online dating, where first impressions are paramount. Sharing one's face can evoke feelings of vulnerability, as it invites judgement and scrutiny from potential matches. Yet, it also fosters authenticity and transparency, laying the foundation for genuine connections based on mutual attraction and compatibility. Moreover, for individuals belonging to LGBTQIA+ communities or ethnic minorities, displaying their faces can carry additional risks, including discrimination and harassment. Despite these complexities, the decision to showcase a real photo reflects a desire for connection and validation in the digital age, where identity is both constructed and perceived through pixels and profiles.

boyd (2002) recognised that managing these different facets is particularly challenging in social media, where specific dimensions and nuances are eliminated, and platforms may not adequately differentiate between audiences, which has been described as 'context collapse'. Subsequent work (e.g. Marwick & boyd, 2011) highlights how specific social media platforms, such as Twitter, remove context, making it more difficult for an individual to manage their identity selectively and effectively. More recently, Kerrigan and Hart (2016) have drawn on Turner's (1960, 1974) dramaturgical approach to describe how digital personhood is carefully assembled, portrayed and mobilised through social media. At the centre of his work is Turner's (1960) concept of 'liminality', referring to the transitional state of being 'betwixt and between'. Kerrigan and Hart (2016) identified evidence of 'multiple temporal selves', in which account holders attempt to link their activities within specific platforms to manage different states. However, the availability of performances of past identities on social media means that past selves can coexist with present selves despite the transition to a new state. Thus, sometimes performances are interrupted due to what they call a 'social media leakage', in which attempts to keep different digital identities separate from each other fail.

In their work on managing LGBTQ+ identities in social media, Talbot et al. (2022) adapt the performance theories of Morgenroth and Ryan (2020) to interpret the digital performances of gender and sexuality of LGBTQ+ students in their transition to university. They use the term 'identity management' to refer to a person's intentional and unconscious strategies to adapt their public performances, that is, the behaviour they know the public is watching (Goffman, 1959). Unlike their heterosexual and cisgender peers, LGBTQ+ people face unique challenges in consciously and consistently disclosing their gender and/or sexual identity (Guittar & Rayburn, 2016). Instead, Orne (2011) argues that LGBTQ+ people evaluate specific social situations before determining whether to disclose an LGBTQ+ identity, applying a strategic approach, that is, an ongoing and contextual management of their sexual identity. Brumbaugh-Johnson and Hull (2019) highlight how this selective and strategic revealing is also relevant for gender-diverse individuals who continually make strategic decisions based on their social context. Thomas et al. (2017) found that it is widespread for students to use the period before starting university to curate their digital selves, sometimes removing photographs of pets and family members and replacing these records with pictures of parties. In subsequent work (Thomas et al., 2020), they observed that students who hid their previous online identities during the transition to university were more likely to experience loneliness. Yang et al. (2018) described these difficulties as 'identity disturbance', relating them to an individual's inability to reconcile different aspects of themselves into a coherent whole. Such findings are highly relevant to students who may find it more challenging to present their LGBTQ+ identities when starting university, who may use specific social media platforms in their presentations and who may also experience forms of identity distress as they struggle to manage their injunctions.

Dating Apps

As mentioned at the beginning of this analysis, most participants said that they could spend hours or days without their smartphones or access to the internet. Still, throughout the conversations, they revealed that they found it challenging to imagine daily routines without mobile apps, considering social media a necessary inclusion in social activities and peer interactions. However, their narratives also unveil the ambiguous impact of apps on their social relations. While the apps enable them to sustain and cultivate relationships, they concurrently contribute to heightened anxiety associated with time-wasting and accountability. Notably, how users navigate this tension gives rise to diverse gender performances deeply rooted in hegemonic gender scripts.

Dating app narratives illustrate the pervasive influence of gender norms on the lives of Portuguese young adults interviewed for this research. Many female participants refrained from fully engaging in these platforms, viewing apps like Tinder or Bumble as primary spaces for casual encounters (as shown by Simões et al., 2023, when analysing scripted gender practices in apps in Portugal). These apps are often perceived as arenas where individuals, particularly women, encounter unwanted advances and harassment from strangers. They are also very critical of 'authenticity' in dating apps, how others manage their identity, what they choose to reveal and how that can influence your perceived notions of safety. A minority of female participants who mentioned having profiles on Tinder stated that they use the platform to make initial contact with individuals they do not know, with whom they may exchange private messages. However, they prefer not to engage on Tinder itself due to the high risk of receiving unsolicited sexual images and experiencing harassment. Instead, they opt for supposedly more mainstream social media platforms like Facebook, where they are less likely to dismiss someone solely based on physical appearance. A 27-year-old female participant explained this approach: 'It is a way of checking whether people are really who they say they are. In other words, Tinder is very volatile; it's only good for [knowing new people], and that's it. Then we only want to get the hell out of there'.

The importance of authenticity was further stressed by this 28-year-old female participant when she stated that: 'On Tinder if you don't post a real photo, you're a piece of shit. Sorry, but [if you do that] you're really playing with me. As I have repeated for the hundredth time, it's a site, a dating app, right? So please, post your [actual] photo. Now, on YouTube, no. On YouTube, you could [choose to] not post your photo. Because, after all, you can also invent an alter ego when you add content, so it can be used in a very creative way. So I don't think it's necessary. On Tinder, yes'. Also reflecting on internet authenticity and on whether the feeling of safety is contrasting for different genders, a 26-year-old female interviewee mentioned that she believes there is a difference: '(...) because, unfortunately, in the society we live in, based on patriarchy, I believe that we [women] can more easily be subjected to comments that we don't want to hear or photos that we don't them to sent us. Unfortunately, I think a lot of this is taken for granted that we [women] have to always be available for this'.

These testimonies align with academic literature, which has highlighted that in an attempt to present an ideal but authentic self (Ward, 2017), women are more likely than men to use enhanced photos and emphasise their youth and physical attractiveness (Abramova et al., 2016). Consistent with traditional gender scripts, women are less likely than men to initiate a conversation through private messaging and seem more reluctant to move on to face-to-face encounters (Carpenter & McEwan, 2016; Sharabi & Dykstra-DeVette, 2019). Men report a greater tendency towards casual sex or short-term relationships than women (Sumter & Vandenbosch, 2019). This tendency persists even in dating apps that call themselves feminist, such as Bumble, as there remains a lack of adequate responses when hegemonic masculinity or a solid reaction to rejection arises (MacLeod & McArthur, 2018; Pruchniewska, 2020). Research on the subject also shows that, in heterosexual dating app contexts, women seem to experience higher levels of negotiation with traditional scripts (Albright & Carter, 2019; Eaton et al., 2016). The predominant script that emerges from the best known app for relationships between men, Grindr, is the search for a one-night stand supported by geolocation (Licoppe et al., 2017).

Reflecting on these tensions, a female 30-year-old interviewee described how many of her friends fall into this trap:

> The negative side is the social expectation that is created in relation to what people expose on social media, which, in reality, is a cut-out of their lives. I really try not to go that way; I don't follow influencers; I am terrified of these things [...] It is a

stimulus to unbridled consumption; it is a stimulus that may reverberate in a charge on a personal level to satisfy an expectation that the person thinks she has to meet because that starts to be placed for her as something to be achieved and desired.

These behaviours go unnoticed in the accounts provided by participants who identify as male regarding their experiences and perspectives about dating apps and dating in general. This perspective reflects the patriarchal notion of passive–submissive femininity, reinforcing traditional gender roles outlined in the 'heterosexual script' (Kim et al., 2007), which dictates distinct behaviours for men and women in romantic and sexual relationships. While young men commonly discuss their involvement with these apps without stigma, viewing them as tools to overcome logistical barriers in meeting potential partners, women express concerns about authenticity and disappointment. Female interviewees highlight the disparity in intentions between genders (referring to men and women), noting that women are more inclined to seek genuine connections. In contrast, men often prioritise casual sexual encounters. Overall, for many women, experiences with dating apps are characterised by superficiality and the frustration of encountering individuals with conflicting intentions, as stated by this 24-year-old male interviewee:

> Afraid, yes, afraid of judgment. [...] People who talk, people who look at the physique, you send a message, people look at the physique and if they don't speak negatively about the physique so directly... like the person sends a photo of themselves and sends something or says something and sometimes we are directly insulted, sometimes we are blocked out of nowhere, people become uninhibited to a point where they are cruel sometimes, this is obviously a disadvantage. For someone who is unsure of themselves and unsure of their self-image, apps have the potential to exacerbate this. And once again, that's why I reiterate, criteria, criteria, criteria, a person has to be very careful with the people they are talking to.

In his research into the uses of Grindr in the Portuguese context, Santos (2020) concludes that this platform is a 'space for exploring and experimenting with the affectivity and homoeroticism that runs through contemporary gay culture' (p. 26).[5] But beyond the possibility of meaningful connections with other people with similar identities, the author identified Grindr as a multifaceted digital space of exclusion, most evident in three specific aspects: gender expression, normative physical standards, and age. Concerning gender expression, those who do not follow (or do not want to follow) the recognisable format of normative

---

[5] Original in Portuguese: '(...) é um espaço de exploração e experimentação da afetividade e do homoerotismo que atravessa a cultura *gay* contemporânea' (p. 26).

masculinity are excluded from any kind of interaction and are derogatorily referred to as 'faggots' ('bichas').[6] About normative male body standards, Santos' research has shown a constant valorisation of a muscular body and the rejection of all those who do not meet this prerequisite. Having a body that is (considered) overweight makes the subject predisposed to different forms of bullying expressed by users on the platform itself. Age is also an exclusionary factor in this app, with younger subjects being valued. Based on the work of Stoer and Magalhães (2005), Santos (2020) points out that these dimensions of exclusion on Grindr are three of the significant factors of exclusion in contemporary post-capitalist societies, as they represent the major niches through which the market logic is articulated. According to Rob Cover (2012), 'what homonormative queer culture does is produce a set of exclusions that are used to police the boundaries of the queer community in ways that seem plausible, desirable and profitable for wider neoliberal sociability' (p. 124).

Conclusion

The findings from the MyGender project underscore the profound impact of mobile applications on the daily lives and self-presentation of young adults in Portugal, particularly concerning the power dynamics of gender identity and expression, as well as those concerning sexual orientation. Within the technological landscape painted by these testimonies, smartphones cease to be mere devices and evolve into extensions of the self, reflecting a generation deeply intertwined with technology.

Social media platforms, like Instagram and Facebook, play pivotal roles in fostering genuine connections and a sense of community among users. Yet, they also exert pressure on individuals to maintain a constant online presence and engagement. While these platforms offer safe spaces for those with nonnormative gender identities and sexual orientations to connect with like-minded individuals, they simultaneously present challenges such as (creating) a constant fear of missing out and the pressure to uphold carefully curated online personas. While young people employ diverse strategies to manage this online persona, nonnormative individuals encounter distinct obstacles. They must navigate the disclosure of their sexual orientation or gender identity strategically, all while contending with the potential for online harassment or discrimination.

Therefore, the MyGender study reinforces that technology – both its design and its usage – is not detached from mainstream cishetero societal norms but rather co-creates and perpetuates them. In the context of Portugal's heteropatriarchal framework, mobile applications often reinforce hegemonic understandings of gender and sexuality, compelling users to conform to binary cisheteronormative ideals. Female participants, for instance, express reluctance to

---

[6]"Bichas' is a derogatory that equates male homosexuality with certain characteristics that are attributed to effeminate behaviour.

fully engage with certain apps due to concerns about harassment, highlighting the pervasive influence of sexism on app usage.

The analysed data also reveal a dynamic interplay between young adults and mobile applications, illustrating their adaptability to the nuances and trends of each platform. Moreover, it underscores their ability to shape the interactional norms within these digital spaces to align with their own preferences, expectations and desires. The possibility of making choices highlights the considerable agency wielded by users in moulding the technological landscape to suit their needs while also challenging prevailing gender norms. Furthermore, the study findings indicate that apps serve as catalysts for the exploration and expansion of gender identities, offering individuals the opportunity to navigate and redefine traditional constructs within the digital realm. Participants in the focus groups and interviews demonstrate a nuanced approach to managing their gender and sexuality performances and presentations across various apps. They engage in a continuous negotiation process that reflects the ongoing co-construction of gender norms, technology and individual identity. Recognising the significance of social media in shaping identity formation is crucial. These platforms provide individuals with a platform to construct a meticulously curated self, incorporating elements of gender identity, sexual orientation and personal beliefs.

The findings also underscore the significant impact of hegemonic gender norms on online dating dynamics, revealing distinct approaches adopted by the women and men in our sample. Women typically prioritise safety, authenticity and seeking meaningful connections, whereas men may lean towards more casual encounters. These contrasting preferences echo broader mainstream societal norms surrounding masculinity and femininity, which persist even within the digital sphere. Technology has emerged as a formidable force shaping the lives of young adults in Portugal, offering indispensable tools for communication, connection and self-expression. However, alongside its benefits, it is essential to acknowledge the potential drawbacks of constant connectivity and the pressures associated with managing one's online identity. Achieving a balance between harnessing the benefits of technology and mitigating its potential drawbacks is essential for effectively navigating the digital landscape.

References

Abramova, O., Baumann, A., Krasnova, H., & Buxmann, P. (2016). Gender differences in online dating: What do we know so far? A systematic literature review. In T. X. Bui & R. H. SpragueJr. (Eds.), *Proceedings of the 49th annual Hawaii International conference on system sciences* (pp. 3858–3867). IEEE. https://doi.org/10.1109/HICSS.2016.481

Adkins, V., Masters, E., Shumer, D., & Selkie, E. (2018). Exploring transgender adolescents' use of social media for support and health information seeking. *Journal of Adolescent Health, 62*(3), S44. https://doi.org/10.1016/j.jadohealth.2017.11.087

Albright, J. M., & Carter, S. (2019). The myth of the Siren's song: Gendered courtship and sexual scripts in online dating. In A. Hetsroni & M. Tuncez (Eds.), *It happened on Tinder: Reflections and studies on internet-infused dating* (pp. 10–30). INC.

Alcaire, R., Flores, A. M. M., & Antunes, E. (2024). Beyond words: Tapping the potential of digital diaries while exploring young adults' experiences on apps. *Societies, 14*, 40. https://doi.org/10.3390/soc14030040

boyd, d. (2002). *Faceted ID/entity: Managing representation in a digital world*. Dissertação de mestrado. Massachusetts Institute of Technology.

Brock, A. (2011). Beyond the pale: The Blackbird web browser's critical reception. *New Media & Society, 13*(7), 1085–1103.

Brumbaugh-Johnson, S. M., & Hull, K. E. (2019). Coming out as transgender: Navigating the social implications of a transgender identity. *Journal of Homosexuality, 66*(8), 1148–1177. https://doi.org/10.1080/00918369.2018.1493253

Butler, J. (1990). *Gender trouble: Feminism and the subversion of identity*. Routledge.

Carpenter, C. J., & McEwan, B. (2016). The players of micro-dating: Individual and gender differences in goal orientations toward micro-dating apps. *First Monday, 21*(5). https://doi.org/10.5210/fm.v21i5.6187

Collins, P. H. (2000). *Black feminist thought: Knowledge, consciousness, and the politics of empowerment*. Routledge.

Connell, R. W. (2005). *Masculinities* (2nd ed.). University of California Press.

Cover, R. (2012). *Queer youth suicide, culture and identity unliveable lives?* Ashgate.

Crenshaw, K. (1989). *Demarginalizing the intersection of race and sex: A black feminist critique of antidiscrimination doctrine, feminist theory and antiracist politics*. University of Chicago Legal Forum.

Eaton, A. A., Rose, S. M., Interligi, C., Fernandez, K., & McHugh, M. (2016). Gender and ethnicity in dating, hanging out, and hooking up. *The Journal of Sex Research, 53*(7), 788–804. https://doi.org/10.1080/00224499.2015.1065954

Feenberg, A. (1991). *Critical theory of technology*. Oxford University Press.

Galtung, J. (1996). *Peace by peaceful means: Peace and conflict, development and civilization*. International Peace Research Institute, Oslo. Sage. ISBN: 9780857022813. http://digital.casalini.it/9780857022813

Goffman, E. (1959). *The presentation of self in everyday life*. Doubleday.

Guittar, N. A., & Rayburn, R. L. (2016). Coming out: The career management of one's sexuality. *Sexuality & Culture, 20*, 336–357.

Habermas, J. (2006). *Técnica e Ciência como Ideologia*. Edições 70.

Hooks, B. (2000). *Feminism is for everybody: Passionate politics*. South End Press.

Jenzen, O. (2017). Trans youth and social media: Moving between counterpublics and the wider web. *Gender, Place & Culture: A Journal of Feminist Geography, 24*(11), 1626–1641. https://doi.org/10.1080/0966369X.2017.1396204

Katz, E. (1987). *Communication research since Lazarsfeld*. University of Pennsylvania ScholarlyCommons.

Kerrigan, F., & Hart, A. (2016). Theorising digital personhood: A dramaturgical approach. *Journal of Marketing Management, 32*(17–18), 1701–1721.

Kim, J. L., Sorsoli, C. L., Collins, K., Zylbergold, B. A., Schooler, D., & Tolman, D. L. (2007). From sex to sexuality: Exposing the heterosexual script on primetime network television. *The Journal of Sex Research, 44*, 145–157.

Lawless, B., & Chen, Y. W. (2019). Developing a method of critical thematic analysis for qualitative communication inquiry. *Howard Journal of Communications*, *30*(1), 92–106. https://doi.org/10.1080/10646175.2018.1439423

Licoppe, C., Rivière, C. A., & Morel, J. (2017). Proximity awareness and the privatization of sexual encounters with strangers. In C. Marvin, S. H. Hong, & B. Zelizer (Eds.), *Space and place and mediated communication* (pp. 57–77). Routledge.

MacLeod, C., & McArthur, V. (2018). The construction of gender in dating apps. *Feminist Media Studies*, *19*(6), 822–840. https://doi.org/10.1080/14680777.2018.1494618

Marwick, A. E., & boyd, d. (2011). I tweet honestly, I tweet passionately: Twitter users, context collapse, and the imagined audience. *New Media & Society*, *13*(1), 114–133.

McConnell, E. A., Clifford, A., Korpak, A. K., Phillips, G., & Birkett, M. (2017). Identity, victimization, and support: Facebook experiences and mental health among LGBTQ youth. *Computers in Human Behavior*, *76*, 237–244. https://doi.org/10.1016/j.chb.2017.07.026

McQuail, D. (1994/1983). *Mass communication theory. An introduction*. Sage.

Mignolo, W. D. (1999). I am where I think: Epistemology and the colonial difference. *Journal of Latin American Cultural Studies: Travesia*, *8*(2), 235–245.

Mkhize, S., Nunlall, R., & Gopal, N. (2020). An examination of social media as a platform for cyberviolence against the LGBT+ population. *Agenda*, *34*(1), 23–33. https://doi.org/10.1080/10130950.2019.1704485

Morgenroth, T., & Ryan, M. K. (2020). The effects of gender trouble: An integrative theoretical framework of the perpetuation and disruption of the gender/sex binary. *Perspectives on Psychological Science*, *6*(16), 1113–1142. https://doi.org/10.1177/1745691620902442

Orne, J. (2011). 'You will always have to "out" yourself': Reconsidering coming out through strategic outness. *Sexualities*, *14*(6), 681–703. https://doi.org/10.1177/1363460711420462

Papacharissi, Z. (2002). The presentation of the self in virtual life, characteristic of home pages. *Journalism & Mass Communication Quarterly*, *79*(3), 643–660.

Pool, I. D. S. (1983). *Technologies of freedom*. Belknap Press.

Pruchniewska, U. (2020). "I like that it's my choice a couple different times": Gender, affordances, and user experience on bumble dating. *International Journal of Communication*, *14*, 2422–2439.

Pym, T., Byron, P., & Albury, K. (2020). 'I still want to know they're not terrible people': Negotiating 'queer community' on dating apps. *International Journal of Cultural Studies*, *24*(3), 398–413. https://doi.org/10.1177/1367877920959332

Santos, H. (2020). "Só masculinos, bichas abstenham-se". O Grindr como espaço de (re)produção de homonormatividade. *Sociologia Online*, (22), 11–29. https://doi.org/10.30553/sociologiaonline.2020.22.1

Santos, S. J. (2021). Admirável mundo velho: Os (e-)continuuns de poder nas Relações Internacionais da era digital. In J. M. Pureza & M. F. Ferreira (Eds.), *Emancipar o mundo: Teoria Crítica e Relações Internacionais* (pp. 187–212). Almedina.

Scheuerman, M. K., Branham, S. M., & Hamidi, F. (2018). Safe spaces and safe places: Unpacking technology-mediated experiences of safety and harm with transgender people. In K. Karahalios, A. Monroy-Hernández, A. Lampinen, & G.

Fitzpatrick (Eds.), *Proceedings of the ACM on human-computer interaction* (Vol. 2, pp. 1–27). Association for Computing Machinery. https://doi.org/10.1145/3274424

Sharabi, L. L., & Dykstra-DeVette, T. A. (2019). From first email to first date: Strategies for initiating relationships in online dating. *Journal of Social and Personal Relationships*, *36*(11–12), 33893407. https://doi.org/10.1177/0265407518822780

Simões, R. B., Amaral, I., Flores, A. M. M., & Antunes, E. (2023). Scripted gender practices: Young adults' social media app uses in Portugal. *Social Media + Society*, *9*(3). https://doi.org/10.1177/20563051231196561

Stoer, S., & Magalhães, A. (2005). *'A diferença somos nós'. A gestão da mudança social e as políticas educativas e sociais*. Edições Afrontamento.

Sumter, S. R., & Vandenbosch, L. (2019). Dating gone mobile: Demographic and personality based correlates of using smartphone-based dating applications among emerging adults. *New Media & Society*, *21*(3), 655–673. https://doi.org/10.1177/1461444818804773

Talbot, C. V., Talbot, A., Roe, D., & Briggs, P. (2022). The management of LGBTQ+ identities on social media: A student perspective. *New Media & Society*, *24*, 1729–1750. https://doi.org/10.1177/1461444820981009

Thomas, L., Briggs, P., Hart, A., & Kerrigan, F. (2017). Understanding social media and identity work in young people transitioning to university. *Computers in Human Behavior*, *76*, 541–553. https://doi.org/10.1016/j.chb.2017.08.021

Thomas, L., Orme, E., & Kerrigan, F. (2020). Student loneliness: The role of social media through life transitions. *Computers & Education*, *146*, 103754. https://doi.org/10.1016/j.compedu.2019.103754

Turner, V. W. (1960). *Rite of passage*. Routledge.

Turner, V. W. (1974). *Drama fields and metaphors: Symbolic action in human society*. Cornell University Press.

van Zoonen, L. (2002). Gendering the internet. *European Journal of Communication*, *17*(1), 5–23. https://doi.org/10.1177/0267323102017001605

Wajcman, J. (2007). From women and technology to gendered technoscience. *Information, Communication & Society*, *10*(3), 287–298. https://doi.org/10.1080/13691180701409770

Ward, J. (2017). What are you doing on Tinder? Impression management on a matchmaking mobile app. *Information, Communication & Society*, *20*(11), 1644–1659. https://doi.org/10.1080/1369118X.2016.125241

Yang, C., Holden, S. M., Carter, M. D., & Webb, J. (2018). Social media comparison and identity distress at the college transition: A dual-path model. *Journal of Adolescence*, *69*, 92–102. https://doi.org/10.1016/j.adolescence.2018.09.007

Chapter 6

Fostering Intimacy in a Digital Environment: Couples, Mobile Apps and Romantic Relationships

Rita Sepúlveda

ICNOVA, Instituto de Comunicação da NOVA. Faculdade de Ciências Sociais e Humanas, Universidade Nova de Lisboa, Portugal

Abstract

This chapter provides a mapping of the so-called couple apps, i.e. apps that generically promise to promote connectivity in several areas among the members of a romantic relationship. We focus on Apple's App Store offering and analyse all the available relevant apps: their year of release, the different categories, the apps' developers, the apps' presentation through its icon and description and the profile creation process. If couples' communication and behaviours have an impact on romantic relationship satisfaction and users' well-being, we question how such apps are characterised. We reveal that these apps try to respond to couples' needs related to several romantic relationship topics through a variety of approaches and methods. Nevertheless, such apps are governed by private companies with a commercial objective and through their design and affordances promote behaviours of a one-size-fits-all approach. As such, they seem not to promote diversity or spontaneity. Among these apps, heteronormativity regarding gender, roles, sexual orientation and romantic relationship format is to be assumed as the norm. As an effect, traditional views of what a couple is and related behaviours are transmitted, impacting how apps are understood and appropriated by users and having consequences on practices.

Keywords: Digital stores; couple; apps; apps studies; mediated intimacy

Introduction

The attention given to technology usage regarding romantic relationships has accompanied technological evolution, with a growing body of research focused on those specific solutions that relate to digital environments. The way people appropriate and incorporate digital technologies in the various stages of their romantic relationships is heterogeneous and diverse and has its dynamics. Studies have reported on the use of mobile applications (apps), social networks and messenger services through which to start, construct, maintain or even break up a relationship (Gershon, 2012; Nadel et al., 2021; Sepúlveda, 2023; Timmermans & De Caluwé, 2017).

Research has shown that sociocultural meanings given to digital technologies have an impact on practices and the diversity of personal experiences in romantic relationships (Gershon, 2010; Sharabi & Hopkins, 2022). Homogeneous representations of the technology adoption process in the context of romantic relationships and the meanings attributed to them (e.g. dating apps are only for sex; social media networks have a negative impact on romantic relationships) assume that people's needs, within the scope of their relationships, are similar. They also presuppose that couples are identical about their values, age, sexual orientation, gender or the type of relationship they are looking for. These assumptions contribute to homogeneity, and consequently prejudice, and to the supporting of behaviours and attached roles depending on the characteristics of the members involved in a loving relationship (Pennington, 2009). How a couple is composed, the needs inherent to each of its members or the couple as a whole and how digital technologies can be used to satisfy them cannot be seen in a generalised way.

Several factors can impact the process and dynamism of romantic relationships, taking into account that they go through different stages, whether in their construction or in their dissolution (Knapp, 1978). A common narrative points not only to communication as a necessary process for a healthy relationship but also to the desire for clear and effective communication (Arikewuyo et al., 2022; Gottman, 1994; Gottman & Gottman, 1999) as a way to achieve it.

Taking into account the above, this chapter starts from the understanding that apps are adopted as a means by which couples resort to satisfy specific needs about their relationship. Bearing in mind that apps, by posing as couple communication mediators, have an impact on how the relationship is lived, they must therefore be inclusive about couples' needs and representations. Additionally, they cannot be restrictive given the type of couple and type of romantic relationship.

Drawing from multi-situated app studies (Dieter et al., 2019, 2021), this contribution complements a growing body of literature that has focused on digital technologies as a way to meet someone with whom to develop a relationship and contrasts with the contributions that mainly point to digital platforms as relationship problem causers and don't consider them as relationship bonders. Its objective is to map the offer of apps for couples and analyse how it is characterised.

The emergence of smartphones brought with it the proliferation of the app industry and app stores. Over the years, a growing and varied number of apps have been made available. Currently, through such software, various activities, of different levels of complexity and from different areas of everyday life, are performed. As so it is interesting to understand which solutions are available and are presented in terms of couples' needs underlying romantic relationships. Thus, the research question that guides this chapter is: 'How are couple apps characterised?'

Romantic Couples and Mobile Apps: A Communication Mediator

Romantic relationships encompass relevant aspects of individual lives once they could be a source of gratification and well-being (Miller, 2018). In the pursuit of a fulfilling romantic relationship, couples face the challenge of communicating clearly and effectively between them. Couple communication is understood as an essential part of romantic relationships playing a vital role in their sustainability (Lavner et al., 2016; Yoo et al., 2014).

The lack of communication, miscommunication or ineffectiveness, which can unfold in different aspects, is at the origin of several problems, conflicts or feelings having the power to negatively influence the quality of the relationship, impacting also the well-being of the members of the couple (De Netto et al., 2021; Körner & Schütz, 2021). We understand that the term communication, in the context of couples, encompasses different relational experiences. It usually refers to the sharing of information between members of a romantic relationship. More specifically, it includes the sharing of emotions, feelings, desires, needs or wants.

Once communication plays a key role at the heart of the development of romantic relationships and their quality, partners must be able to know when, where and how to communicate with the other to achieve the desired and intended goals (Arikewuyo et al., 2022), both for the relationship and at the individual level.

According to the theory of relational dialectics, which exposes the communication pattern adopted by individuals in a relationship (Baxter, 2004), differences in characteristics and communication skills between individuals in a relationship can lead to tensions and conflicts. As such, communication styles are an important factor in a couple's adaptability.

However, it is necessary to consider social and cultural variables in the context of romantic relationships as they can influence the way couple members communicate and how relationships are experienced (Jerves et al., 2022); they can also lead to romantic relationships based on assumptions that may turn to fractures.

In such a context, it is important to take into consideration the impact that gender stereotypes can have on how roles are performed and romantic relationships are lived (De Meyer et al., 2017; Minowa et al., 2019; Tolman et al., 2016). Considering couple composition, conventional norms and values are challenged: as romantic relationships and intimate scenarios diversify, critiques regarding the normalisation of monogamous, heterosexual relationships emerge (Braida et al., 2023; Brown, 2020).

Despite the heterogeneity with which the romantic relationship can be lived, throughout its life cycle, as well as throughout the person's life cycle, individuals face a series of events and subjects that can be challenging when it comes to communicating about them with their partner (e.g. parenting, finances, emotional or physical intimacy). The lack of or poor communication can lead to relationship dissatisfaction.

As a solution, individuals may seek out friends or family members to help resolve divergent points of view or conflicts. To these is added a range of professionals (Jones et al., 2018) with their own methods and strategies, and whose objective is to help make communication as clear and rich as possible and, consequently, make romantic relationships healthy and pleasurable. Many of these options are available digitally. As such, digital technology is positioned as a mediator through which people can seek solutions to improve communication. In this context, the role assigned to smartphones is undeniable: not only do they dialectically influence the daily lives of individuals through the set of possibilities offered by the device (Sela et al., 2022), but they also impact how romantic relationships are experienced (Lapierre & Custer, 2021).

Among the functional possibilities of smartphones, individuals can download apps from app stores according to their objectives and to satisfy their needs. App domestication reflects a set of communicative affordances of mobile media – portability, availability, locatability and multimediality (Schrock, 2015) – that impact social and cultural practices and dynamics within the scope of romantic relationships. For instance, dating apps are used to find romantic partners, messaging and video call apps are adopted by partners to communicate, and social networks are employed for sharing commitment stages and related events (Nadel et al., 2021; Sepúlveda, 2023; Sharabi & Hopkins, 2022; Timmermans & De Caluwé, 2017).

App stores are the main site for accessing, downloading and distributing apps, with Apple App Store and Google Play dominating the market (Statcounter, 2023). As gatekeepers between app developers and users, they set up the norms for app creation, classification and distribution, ensuring app exposure to potential customers (Dieter et al., 2019).

As a way of organising and helping users to discover apps, these are classified by stores according to pre-established categories based on the adequacy, positioning or functioning of the app and algorithmic logic (App Store, n.d.a; Dieter et al., 2019, 2021). Categories differ among stores and include dimensions as diverse as games, entertainment, utilities, social or health and well-being, among others.

Apps are strongly present in different sectors of everyday life and everyday practices, insinuating themselves into users' routines and habits and becoming a culturally important object (Gerlitz et al., 2019). As non-neutral technologies, through their design, affordances, norms and rules, they impose behaviours. As a result, users' experiences are conditioned, namely concerning gender-related expression (Lopes & Vogel, 2019; Sepúlveda & Vieira, 2019; Shahin et al., 2023). In response, criticisms arise indicating that apps are embedded in cultural stereotypes and are not inclusive (Lopes & Vogel, 2020). This is of particular interest when it comes to apps aimed at couples, which can lead to non-binary persons and same-sex couples being unrecognised and invalidated (Shahin et al., 2023) and thus feeling excluded.

The recourse to digital environments for facilitating communication and interactions shapes society and personal relationships in unique ways (see, for example, the impact of dating apps on romantic relationships). Apps, by positioning themselves as intermediaries, facilitate or impose practices on users, thus impacting social and cultural dynamics (Dieter et al., 2019; Gerlitz et al., 2019), including in the context of romantic relationships.

On the relationship spectrum, dating apps have received attention from academia; however, just as romantic relationships follow different stages, different apps are domesticated for managing relationships, satisfying needs and facing challenges during those stages. To this end, a group of so-called apps for couples has emerged (McVeigh-Schultz & Baym, 2015; Pandya, 2022).[1] If a couple's communication and behaviours are a predictor of relationship satisfaction (Lavner et al., 2016), such apps promise to promote connectivity between the members of a romantic relationship. However, little is known about this specific group of apps. Following the conceptualisation that certain social sectors of life are being transformed by the rise and adoption of digital platforms (van Dijck et al., 2018), there is a need to focus on the apps for couples available.

Method and Data Collection

This study focuses on apps available in the Apple App Store. Data collection took place in April 2023 and was carried out using a store scraper, specifically the 'search' module which simulates the store search field.[2] Since it was intended to obtain apps for couples, the search was operated by the term 'couple'. The following data collection parameters were established: $n = 1,000$ apps, language 'en' (default) and country 'US' (default). First, an exploratory analysis using a qualitative–quantitative approach took place, considering data such as the date of app launch, app category and developers. The objective was to describe the existing offer to characterise it. Second, to assess app positioning, we analysed how apps present themselves. For this, a qualitative content analysis (Hsieh & Shannon, 2005) of the app's presentation (icon and description) was performed, grouping them thematically. Third, to look particularly at the range of choices regarding gender, sexual orientation and type of relationship, the 10 apps with the highest rating were analysed by using the walkthrough method. This is defined as 'a way of engaging directly with an app's interface to examine its technological mechanisms and embedded cultural references to understand how it guides users and shapes their experience' (Light et al., 2018, p. 882). We specifically focused on the profile creation process.

Couples' Apps: Characterisation

Data collection originated a dataset with 507 unique apps in a CSV file with a set of details and data for each of the apps (e.g. category, date of release, developers, descriptions, icons, screenshots, among others). In what follows, the results from our analysis of the 'couple' apps in the Apple App Store (iOS) are presented.

Date of Release, Categories and Actor Type

We first analysed the app distribution in our dataset according to the date of release, categories and the actors involved in their production. Fig. 6.1 shows the distribution

---

[1] https://fueled.com/blog/8-best-apps-for-couples/
[2] The app tool used, 'store scraper', was developed by the App Studies and Digital Methods Initiatives and is available at https://tools.digitalmethods.net/app-scrapers/

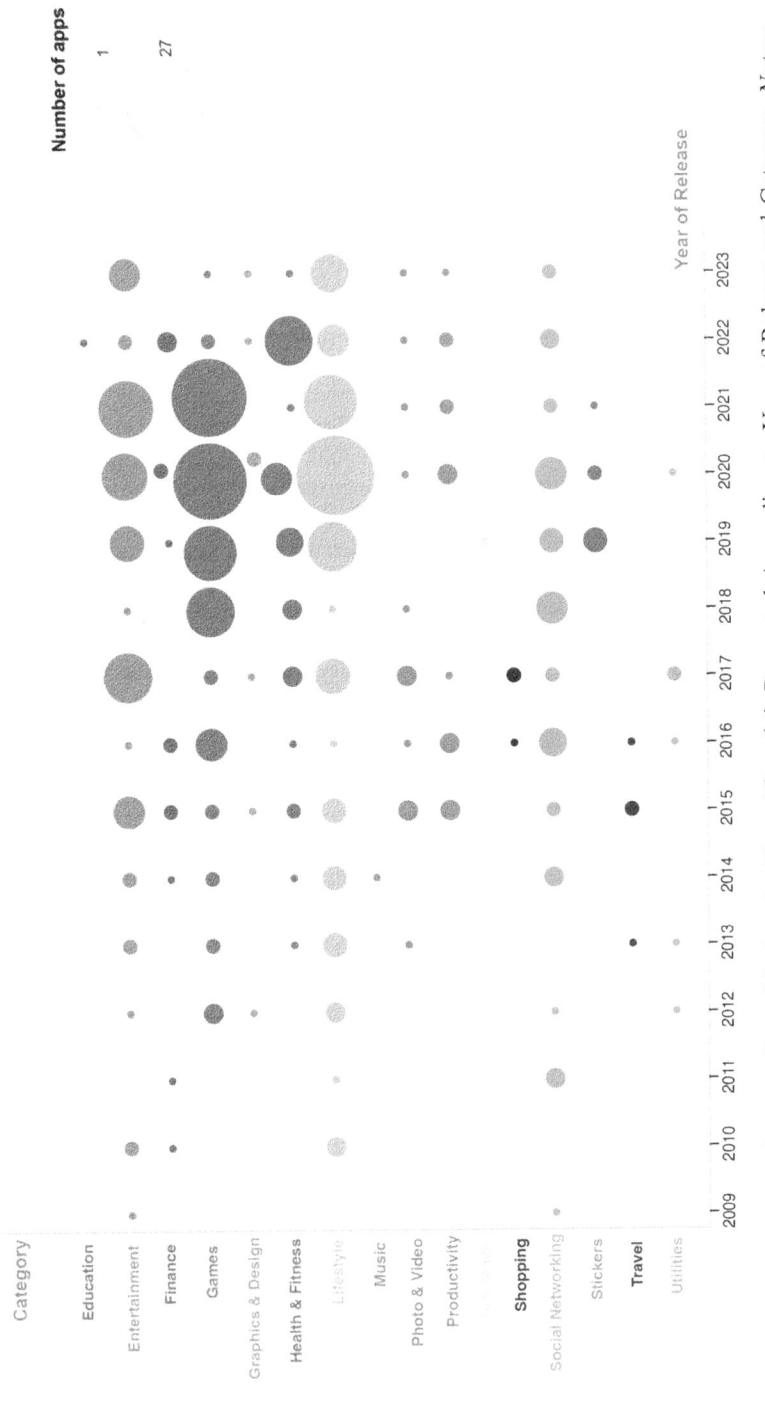

Fig. 6.1. Available Apps Found Using the Term 'Couple', Presented According to Year of Release and Category. *Notes*: Note that the year 2023 comprises only 4 months of data. Circumference size reflects the number of apps. *Source*: Author (2024).

of couple apps according to date and related category. Data are colour-coded by category.

Regarding the distribution according to the date of release, the number of apps available associated with the term 'couple' has increased. This growth highlights a growing trend in terms of the number of apps on Apple's App Store, which was launched in July 2008 with 500 apps. Today, the offer encompasses 2.18 million apps (Ceci, 2023). The trend also follows the growth in users' appropriation of apps to perform everyday tasks. In 2022, 148 billion apps were downloaded worldwide, and those in the romantic relationship spectrum were no exception in the growing trend (Nadel et al., 2021; Sepúlveda, 2023; Sharabi & Hopkins, 2022).

Data indicate that the largest number of couple-related apps available was concentrated in the years 2020 ($n = 86$; 16.96%), 2021 ($n = 71$; 14%) and 2022 ($n = 69$; 13.61%). These years were strongly marked by the COVID-19 pandemic which challenged communication, sociability and everyday life activities in general. As a response, individuals turned to digital platforms as a solution for facing successive lockdowns and their inherent restrictions. During these years, romantic relationships were particularly challenged. On the one hand, cohabiting couples spent more time together, with studies indicating that the dynamics imposed by COVID-19 led to an increase in relationship conflict, and poor well-being among romantic partners (Luetke et al., 2020). On the other hand, those in a relationship but not cohabiting, or who were forced to be physically separated, including those in long-distance relationships, spent more time alone. Thus, couples' apps may also have emerged as a response to needs or relational problems caused by the pandemic restrictions.

Games, Lifestyle, Entertainment and More

In the Apple App Store, apps are grouped according to categories established and defined by the store. The developer can choose between 27 different categories (App Store, n.d.a). Although apps could be indexed to more than one category, one must be indicated as primary. Looking at apps' distribution according to their primary category (Fig. 6.1), the three most frequent were 'Games' ($n = 133$; 26.23%), followed by 'Lifestyle' ($n = 113$; 22.29%) and 'Entertainment' ($n = 105$; 20.71%). When compared with the ranking of the most popular Apple App Store categories (Ceci, 2022), only 'Games' was common; 'Lifestyle' and 'Entertainment' categories occupied, on such ranking, respectively the fifth and eleventh positions. The second and third places on the ranking of the most popular Apple App Store categories, 'Business' and 'Education', were absent, in case of 'Business', and residual, in the case of 'Education' ($n = 1$; 0.20%), from our results. Additionally, of the 507 apps, 85.6% ($n = 434$) were associated with more than one category.

Another result is the variety of categories. Our sample comprised 16 different categories among the 27 existing ones. When analysing the absent, some of them (e.g. Weather or Navigation) might not be seen as relevant given the research topic, although others (e.g. Food & Drink, Books or Sports) might be more questionable since they could be related to activities that can be developed by couples or with content aimed at couples.

Such findings led us to state that, in general, apps for couples were not among the most popular categories and made us reflect on which categories couples apps were primarily associated with and if they were associated with secondary ones. A developer's choice, however, is limited since it is restricted to the options previously made available by the Apple App Store. Since such a choice aims to help users discover apps in their searches, or to be positioned as suggestions in searches through similar apps (App Store, n.d.a), associating the app with a certain category(ies) may reflect a developer's strategy to improve app visibility and increase conversion rate. Developers balance between relevance – by choosing the category that relates to the app – and competition – by choosing the category with fewer competitors when the app fits more than one (Fishman, 2020). As a result, similar apps can be found in different categories (Sepúlveda, 2020). It also relates to the operational mechanisms of the Store, which are based on recommendation logic and editing (Dieter et al., 2019, 2021), suggesting apps to users according to those that they have already downloaded.

From the Private Sector

There is great heterogeneity with regard to the composition of actors developing 'couple' apps that are available in the Apple App Store. Among the 507 apps, 397 actors were identified. However, about typology, these were entirely from private companies offering commercial solutions. Not only did such private companies position themselves as key actors on the topic by proposing services related to couple dynamics, but the topics that make up the ecosystem of romantic relationships are seen as commercially appellative. Although Apple's App Store is smaller in number of apps and users, when compared to Google Play, it remains responsible for the majority of app consumer spending (Curry, 2023). Additionally, studies have pointed to how capitalism has shaped romantic relationships in a digital context, leading to emotions being treated as commodities (Illouz, 2017). Although these studies mostly focus on dating apps, our results indicate that other stages of romantic relationships are also shaped by economic principles.

Considering that the quality of relationships has an impact on well-being, it is interesting to question why apps from public health institutions, health authorities or government-related ones did not appear in the results. One hypothesis is that the apps were developed by private companies or adopted by governmental institutions (Dieter et al., 2021). Apps have been progressively recommended by health professionals and adopted by patients as a way, for example, to monitor health (Wired, 2023). In the context of romantic relationships, apps could be promoted by governments, alone or in collaboration with companies, as tools for counselling or therapy.

The fact that private companies dominate the market about offering apps for couples also raises questions regarding users' data, pointing to issues related to privacy, namely about data collection, storage and usage. Apps, including those related to romantic relationships have been involved in critiques of the treatment and usage of user's data and have been targets of data leaks resulting in unauthorised releases of personal data with harmful consequences for users (Doffman, 2020). Additionally, it also reinforces the concept of datafication of intimacy, exploring it beyond dating apps (De Ridder, 2021).

Discursive Positioning of Couple Apps
Hearts and Bodies in a Red Spectrum

An app's icon constitutes the app's unique image, appearing in the store and on smartphone screens and app lists (Apple, n.d.b). Analysis showed elements such as letters, words, animals, flowers, calendars, geometric symbols and objects used as icons.

Nevertheless, two types of elements stood out due to their greater frequency, dominating among the existing variety: (1) Heart ($n = 105$; 20.7%). This could be just one heart, complete or not, alone or combined with other hearts or elements such as a hand, a speech balloon, an arrow, or with symbols such as gender. It could stand alone as a main element or be part of an app name. Although not exclusive, heart symbols were quite common among apps from Lifestyle or Social Networking categories; and (2) Human representation ($n = 101$; 19.92%), that is, drawings, illustrations or emojis that simulate a person. These could be part of a person's body (e.g. hand, foot, mouth), a person alone (e.g. smiling figures, holding a finger in front of the mouth asking to keep a secret, blindfolded) or two persons (e.g. embracing, whispering in the ear, holding hands, kissing or exercising).

Looking in more detail at such human representations revealed heteronormativity and heterosexuality as the norm regarding couples since they were composed of always a male and female figure, and never more than two persons. Since the typology of romantic relationships has diversified (Braida et al., 2023; Brown, 2020), traditional representations can lead users to feel excluded from apps for couples.

Additionally, female figures were presented in a context that sexually objectified the body (Szymanski et al., 2011). They did so through poses that could be considered provocative, highlighting aspects of their bodies such as their breasts or referring to sexualised behaviours such as sucking a finger. These representations play an important role in gender inequality, could lead to women's self-objectification and have the potential to shape users' perceptions of apps.

When looking at the app icon colours, red, pink and purple were dominant. We speculate that the use of such colours is related to the research topic since their use is symbolically associated with romance, passion, excitement or sex (Cerrato, 2012).

App presentation is an element of media ideology construction. This happens through cultural messages or even cultural ideologies embedded in the symbols, names or colours used. As such, and regarding those aimed towards couples, gender representations, colours and objects associated can be of particular importance. Although, according to the Apple App Store, an app icon must follow a set of best practices (Apple, n.d.b), none of those listed mentioned gender inclusiveness. Such results reinforce critiques that point to apps as not being inclusive regarding gender (Lopes & Vogel, 2020) and highlight users' argument of being ashamed of opening apps in public due to the symbols and colours attributed (Epstein et al., 2017).

Dating and Mingle

Our search using the term 'couple' retrieved apps that position themselves for dating and mingling (e.g. among Lifestyle, Social Networking and Games categories). They were dating apps targeting singles and distinguished among themselves according to their positioning (e.g. sexual preferences, religion, women's taking initiative), functioning (e.g. to video chat or send voice clips) or targeting users of a specific gender or sexual orientation (e.g. non-binary, transgender, queer, gay, lesbian, bisexual, pansexual). These apps, rather than being for couples, were apps for forming couples. Dating apps have been progressively adopted and classified by users as a valid way to meet other people with whom to engage in a romantic relationship, in addition to traditional solutions (Sepúlveda, 2023).

Those dating apps specifically aimed at couples were mostly for connecting those looking for swing or threesome experiences. Such couples were commonly referred to, in the app description, as kinky, open-minded or pursuing an open relationships lifestyle. This is a construction that, from a media ideology perspective, can impact how such apps are perceived and classified by users (Gershon, 2010), influenced by whom and how they are adopted and the resulting practices. Such an offer highlights app developers' awareness of different types of romantic relationship possibilities, namely consensual non-monogamy.

Fostering Emotional and Physical Intimacy in Pursuing a Healthy Relationship

According to the Apple App Store's offer (e.g. Health and Fitness, Lifestyle, Social Networking, Games and Finance categories), healthier relationships could be achieved through apps which promise to improve couples' communication and boost emotional and physical intimacy. To achieve long-lasting relationships, apps present strategies including teaching couples to communicate better, more effectively or deeply, providing techniques on how to deal with or manage conflict and suggesting ideas for what to do on dates or what to talk about. For this, formats such as exercises (physical or not), quizzes for doing alone or with the partner(s), answering pre-written questions, engaging with daily affirmations, monitoring emotions or journaling relationships by keeping a romantic diary were suggested. Since couples communication can be challenging and since poor communication may be the cause of conflicts or non-resolution (Arikewuyo et al., 2022), mobile apps seem to map such evidence, presenting different options that can satisfy users' needs, and encouraging them to download and engage with the app. The general promise is that by using such apps, users can achieve efficient couple communication, an essential key for the relationship itself as also for the well-being of each member of the couple (De Netto et al., 2021; Körner & Schütz, 2021; Lavner et al., 2016).

As a possible way to make the apps appealing to users, app descriptions referenced experts (e.g. licensed therapists, coaches, specialists in relationships), methods (e.g. using behavioural science, relying on scientific research from different fields) and/or results (e.g. with results proven, number of users, referenced in the media). The number of apps available is high and as competition increases, apps must be distinctive and offer added value to their potential users (van Heerde et al., 2019) making credible promises seems to be a strategy for doing so.

Apps propose to help users deal with communication on concrete topics such as parenting – giving tips on how to raise happy children; personal finances – helping users keep track of expenses, engaging in conversation about finances, habits, and goals; or with issues related to sexual intimacy and intimate health. Physical intimacy is considered one of the main components in a relationship and the means through which individuals assess its quality (Moss & Schwebel, 1993).

Apps regarding physical intimacy included tips on how to boost sexual confidence, suggestions for sexual positions, sexy audio stories to listen to and ideas on how to spice up sexual encounters. Apps to pair with body-wearable smart objects (e.g. bracelets to feel each other's heartbeat; app-controlled vibrator) were also present among the results. During the COVID-19 pandemic, couples resorted to digital technologies to find innovative ways to keep the romantic connection from a healthy perspective, which also contemplates physical intimacy. Data shows that the demand for sexual toys and those controlled by distance have risen in response to the needs of couples due to the imposed pandemic restrictions (Arafat & Kar, 2021). Fostering physical intimacy was also proposed entertainingly in some apps, encouraging couples to approach sexual life in a more adventurous, fun or exciting way. For this approach, apps from the 'Games' category were common.

Finally, specific apps such as trackers for monitoring intimate health, sexual activity or the fertility cycle were also part of the results. While specific apps aimed directly at women (e.g. period trackers) or men (e.g. track and improve sexual health), references to the LGBTQIA+ community and specification of non-heterosexual orientations in app descriptions were poor. The term 'LGBT' only appeared in the description of nine apps. Studies suggest that apps should be more inclusive regarding, for example, gender or sexual orientation, and should follow a set of strategies to this end. For instance, reviews of apps should be taken into consideration during app development, and gender bias fazed out by incorporating more women in tech industries (Shahin et al., 2023).

Organising and Keeping Up With Events and Friends

In different app categories (e.g. Productivity, Utilities, Social networking, Lifestyle or Travel), couple bonding was approached as a matter of organisation. For this, calendars, planners and countdowns were presented. The aim was for couples to plan their lives, organise family activities, delegate tasks, combine events, plan trips or share wishes. They also aimed to ensure that important dates such as the couple's anniversary, birthdays or the amount of time since they were together were not forgotten. The argument was that organisation and inherent management help couples to be aware of their responsibilities as well of the other's needs or wishes. Some couples' conflict topics are related to a lack of responsibility or with the non-division of tasks (Meyer & Sledge, 2022). Accordingly, couple apps that offer a calendar to set tasks could be a way to avoid such conflicts.

From the perspective of 'keeping up', apps to stay in touch or to keep and track relationship memories were presented as a way for couples to strengthen their relationships. In general, this type of app's main promise was closing the distance between loved ones through voice, video calls or text messages. As a way to make chat more fun or to spice up textual conversations, emojis or stickers were suggested.

Finally, couples' sociability and activities with friends were also taken into consideration as a way for couples to connect. These apps positioned themselves to be used by couples with friends on different occasions such as parties or dinners. They highlighted the importance of having couples' friends and the impact that friendships can have on relationships (Pelley, 2021).

Gendering Couples

Our analysis of app logos and self-descriptions already gave us clues to understanding how the gender topic was approached, showing several limitations towards gender inclusiveness and pointing to heteronormative relationships as the norm. Since some apps restrain users' profile creation, namely in gender expression (Sepúlveda & Vieira, 2019), we decided to explore this process among the top 10 apps ranked by user rating scores.

From the analysis carried out, it was possible to conclude that, in the process of login and profile creation, data regarding sex, gender, identity and sexual orientation or type of relationship (monogamous or not) were not always requested. In general, the apps seemed to ignore such information, giving the idea that it was not important in the context of their performance as also not a relevant variable in the case of a couple's communication, connection or bonding. However, from our point of view, ignoring the existence of diverse gender identities does not make apps inclusive.

Observation of the first screen of the apps (referring to the login page or the first step of profile creation) revealed not only a reinforcement of monogamous relationships, since couples were presented as two people, but also heteronormative relationships since couples were exclusively represented by the figure of a man and a woman. This aspect was even more questionable when observed in an app that presented itself as being for pride celebration.

The analysis also did not locate the use of established gender-neutral personal pronouns such as 'they', 'them' and 'theirs' or specific references to LGBTQIA+ communities.

The posing of such a representation as a norm, while reinforcing traditional conceptualisations, points to romantic relationship restraints. As such, couples that do not identify with the traditionally established norms may feel excluded from these apps. As a response, they may find mechanisms to circumvent app impositions, a practice that has already been registered in other apps (De Ridder, 2021).

Conclusion

Mobile applications, among a variety of possibilities, present themselves as technologies to keep couples connected in several ways and for different purposes. As part of their users' practices, as they use them to carry out everyday activities within the relationship, they impact them in different ways, shaping how the relationship is experienced. They do so through their positioning.

In this chapter, we have demonstrated and discussed how a specific type of app – those associated with the search term 'couple' in one of the market's major players in app industries, the Apple App Store – is posing as couples' romantic relationship mediators. We observed distinctive methods of approaching the topic either through the type of apps on offer, their positioning, by whom they were developed or how they presented themselves.

Regarding the challenges that couples face throughout their relationship, which can be of various origins and heterogeneous, the apps presented solutions that promise to help couples to communicate more efficiently and through which couples can foster emotional and physical intimacy. Such apps may belong to heterogeneous categories, resort to diversified strategies such as games, quizzes or trackers, be designed through multiple approaches such as asking questions, sending phrases for reflection or benefit from expert input and knowledge from science. They can be designed to be used individually, by each member of the couple, together or even with third parties (e.g. friends) and have a more educational, serious or playful approach.

However, these apps were developed by private companies with a focus on commercial conversion, either through the data they collect from their users, or through business models that require payment of monthly fees or in-app purchases. This fact refers not only to a datafication of intimacy, in various stages and dimensions of romantic relationships, but also to the inclusion of capitalist principles in which users and the emotional aspects related to their romantic relationships are seen as a commercial currency.

Considering the diversified offer and its scope, within the context of mobile apps for couples, it is important to situate supply and demand temporally and contextually, since events classified by users as turning points (Caetano, 2018) can justify an app's appropriation. These encompass events on a micro level, related to the life stages of the members of the couple (e.g. getting a new job; leaving the parents' home) and stages of the relationship (e.g. engagement, parenting), but also on a macro level and relative to events over which individuals have no control (e.g. COVID-19 pandemic, economic crisis).

While couple apps could be generally understood by couples to help with aspects of their romantic relationship regardless of gender, sexual orientation or relationship format and choices, in general, such apps choose to position themselves as non-inclusive. This occurs through the icons chosen to represent them, their self-description, or by ignoring relevant aspects of users during the profile creation process. Once the apps are used by younger people, they can reject them when they don't see their gender identities, sexual choices or type of relationship being equated only with the traditional gender roles presented in the apps. These constructions have consequences on how the media ideology of couple apps is formed, reflecting considerations about who uses them and the resulting practices.

This study aimed to map the Apple App Store offer to search results using the term 'couple' and to carry out an exploratory analysis. It is presented as an important research contribution to a specific type of app that mediates such a relevant dimension of people's lives. Its findings may benefit from including Google Play Store apps, by looking at other countries either alone or comparatively, by conducting interviews with users to discover how these apps are appropriated and incorporated into the dynamics of the romantic relationship, by conducting interviews with developers aiming to address how gender-related topics are thought about and incorporated, by analysing reviews of apps or by applying the walkthrough method more fully. Thus, this study can be seen as a starting point for others.

Although app studies are recent, they are necessary and important when such software is so commonly present in the lives of its users, shaping their practices and experiences. Focusing attention on apps that position themselves in the context of romantic relationships allows for assessing the impact of their adoption on a specific dimension of social life that has repercussions on people's well-being.

References

App Store. (n.d.a). Choosing a category. App Store. https://developer.apple.com/app-store/categories/

Apple. (n.d.b). App icons. App Store. https://developer.apple.com/design/human-interface-guidelines/app-icons

Arafat, S. M. Y., & Kar, S. K. (2021). Sex during pandemic: Panic buying of sex toys during COVID-19 lockdown. *Journal of Psychosexual Health*, 3(2), 175–177. https://doi.org/10.1177/26318318211013347

Arikewuyo, A. O., Lasisi, T. T., Abdulbaqi, S. S., Omoloso, A. I., & Arikewuyo, H. O. (2022). Evaluating the use of social media in escalating conflicts in romantic relationships. *Journal of Public Affairs*, 22, e2331. https://doi.org/10.1002/pa.2331

Baxter, L. (2004). A tale of two voices: Relational dialectics theory. *Journal of Family Communication*, 4(3-4), 181–192. https://doi.org/10.1080/15267431.2004.9670130

Braida, N., Matta, E., & Paccagnella, L. (2023). Loving in consensual non-monogamies: Challenging the validity of Sternberg's Triangular Love Scale. *Sexuality & Culture*, 27, 1828–1847. https://doi.org/10.1007/s12119-023-10092-0

Brown, J. (2020). 'Non-monogamy is the hardest thing to disclose': Expressions of gender, sexuality, and relationships on the university campus. *Women's Studies Journal*, 34, 107–115. ISSN 1173-6615.

Caetano, A. (2018). O léxico das crises biográficas. *Análise Social*, 53(226), 88–111. https://doi.org/10.31447/as00032573.2018226.04

Ceci, L. (2022). *Most popular Apple App Store categories as of 3rd quarter 2022, by share of available apps*. Statista. https://www.statista.com/statistics/270291/popular-categories-in-the-app-store/

Ceci, L. (2023). *Number of available apps in the Apple App Store from 2008 to July 2022*. Statista. https://www.statista.com/statistics/268251/number-of-apps-in-the-itunes-app-store-since-2008/

Cerrato, H. (2012). *The meaning of colors*. The Graphic Designer.

Curry, D. (2023, May 16). Apple App Store Statistics (2023). Business of Apps. https://www.businessofapps.com/data/apple-app-store-statistics/

De Meyer, S., Kågesten, A., Mmari, K., McEachran, J., Chilet-Rosell, E., Kabiru, C., & Michielsen, K. (2017). «Boys should have the courage to ask a girl out»: Gender norms in early adolescent romantic relationships. *Journal of Adolescent Health*, *61*(4), 42–47. https://doi.org/10.1016/j.jadohealth.2017.03.007

De Netto, P. M., Quek, K. F., & Golden, K. J. (2021). Communication, the heart of a relationship: Examining capitalization, accommodation, and self-construal on relationship satisfaction. *Frontiers in Psychology*, *12*, 767908. https://doi.org/10.3389/fpsyg.2021.767908

De Ridder, S. (2021). The datafication of intimacy: Mobile dating apps, dependency, and everyday life. *Television & New Media*, 1–17. https://doi.org/10.1177/15274764211052660

Dieter, M., Gerlitz, C., Helmond, A., Nathaniel Tkacz, N., van der Vlist, F., & Weltevrede, E. (2019). Multi-situated app studies: Methods and propositions. *Social Media + Society*, *5*(2), 1–15. https://doi.org/10.1177/2056305119846486

Dieter, M., Helmond, A., Tkacz, N., van der Vlist, F., & Weltevrede, E. (2021). Pandemic platform governance: Mapping the global ecosystem of COVID-19 response apps. *Internet Policy Review*, *10*(3), 1–228. https://doi.org/10.14763/2021.3.1568

Doffman, Z. (2020, February 1). Ashley Madison hack returns to 'haunt' its victims: 32 million users now watch and wait. *Forbes*. https://www.forbes.com/sites/zakdoffman/2020/02/01/ashley-madison-hack-returns-to-haunt-its-victims-32-million-users-now-have-to-watch-and-wait/?sh=1106c8756770

Epstein, D., Lee, N., Kang, J., Agapie, E., Schroeder, J., Pina, L., Fogarty, J., Kientz, J., & Munson, S. (2017). Examining menstrual tracking to inform the design of personal informatics tools. In *CHI'17: Proceedings of the 2017 CHI Conference on Human Factors in Computing Systems* (pp. 6876–6888). https://doi.org/10.1145/3025453.3025635

Fishman, J. (2020). Choosing the right app category (and how it relates to ASO). *Storemaven*. www.storemaven.com/academy/how-to-choose-an-app-category

Gerlitz, C., Helmond, A., Nieborg, D., & van der Vlist, F. (2019). Apps and infrastructures – A research agenda. *Computational Culture*, *7*. http://computationalculture.net/apps-and-infrastructures-a-research-agenda

Gershon, I. (2010). Media ideologies: An introduction. *Journal of Linguistic Anthropology*, *20*, 283–293. https://doi.org/10.1111/j.1548-1395.2010.01070.x

Gershon, I. (2012). *The breakup 2.0: Disconnecting over new media*. Cornell University Press.

Gottman, J. M. (1994). *What predicts divorce? The relationship between marital processes and marital outcomes*. Lawrence Erlbaum Associates, Inc.

Gottman, J. M., & Gottman, J. S. (1999). The marriage survival kit: A research-based marital therapy. In R. Berger & M. T. Hannah (Eds.), *Preventive approaches in couples therapy* (pp. 304–330). Brunner/Mazel.

Hsieh, H.-F., & Shannon, S. E. (2005). Three approaches to qualitative content analysis. *Qualitative Health Research*, *15*(9), 1277–1288. https://doi.org/10.1177/1049732305276687

Illouz, E. (2017). *Emotions as commodities*. Taylor and Francis.

Jerves, E. M., Cevallos-Neira, A., De Haene, L., & Rober, P. (2022). Traditional gender roles translating into behaviors within adolescents' romantic relationships. *Revista Latinoamericana de Ciencias Sociales, Niñez y Juventud*, *20*(3), 1692–1715. https://doi.org/10.11600/rlcsnj.20.3.4727

Jones, A., Lucero, R., & Morris, N. (2018). Development and validation of the couple communication satisfaction scale. *American Journal of Family Therapy*, 46(5), 505–524. https://doi.org/10.1080/01926187.2019.1566874

Knapp, M. (1978). *Social intercourse: From greeting to goodbye*. Allyn and Bacon.

Körner, R., & Schütz, A. (2021). Power in romantic relationships: How positional and experienced power are associated with relationship quality. *Journal of Social and Personal Relationships*, 38(9), 2653–2677. https://doi.org/10.1177/02654075211017670

Lapierre, M. A., & Custer, B. E. (2021). Testing relationships between smartphone engagement, romantic partner communication, and relationship satisfaction. *Mobile Media & Communication*, 9(2), 155–176. https://doi.org/10.1177/2050157920935163

Lavner, J., Karney, B., & Bradbury, T. (2016). Does couples' communication predict marital satisfaction, or does marital satisfaction predict communication? *Journal of Marriage and Family*, 78(3), 680–694. https://doi.org/10.1111/jomf.12301

Light, B., Burgess, J., & Duguay, S. (2018). The walkthrough method: An approach to the study of apps. *New Media & Society*, 20(3), 881–900. https://doi.org/10.1177/1461444816675438

Lopes, M. R., & Vogel, C. (2019). Gender differences in online dating experiences. In A. Hetsroni & M. Tuncez (Eds.), *It happened on Tinder: Reflections and studies on internet-infused dating* (pp. 31–47). Institute of Network Cultures.

Lopes, M. R., & Vogel, C. (2020). Gender effects in mobile application development. In *2020 IEEE International Conference on Human-Machine Systems (ICHMS)*, Rome, Italy (pp. 1–6). https://doi.org/10.1109/ICHMS49158.2020.9209325

Luetke, M., Hensel, D., Herbenick, D., & Rosenberg, M. (2020). Romantic relationship conflict due to the COVID-19 pandemic and changes in intimate and sexual behaviors in a nationally representative sample of American adults. *Journal of Sex & Marital Therapy*, 46(8), 747–762. https://doi.org/10.1080/0092623X.2020.1810185

McVeigh-Schultz, J., & Baym, N. (2015). Thinking of you: Vernacular affordance in the context of the microsocial relationship app, couple. *Social Media + Society*, 1–13. https://doi.org/10.1177/2056305115604649

Meyer, D., & Sledge, R. (2022). The relationship between conflict topics and romantic relationship dynamics. *Journal of Family Issues*, 43(2), 306–323. https://doi.org/10.1177/0192513X21993856

Miller, R. (2018). *Intimate relationships* (8th ed.). McGraw-Hill Education.

Minowa, Y., Maclaran, P., & Stevens, L. (2019). The femme fatale in Vogue: Femininity ideologies in Fin-de-siècle America. *Journal of Macromarketing*, 39(3), 270–286. https://doi.org/10.1177/0276146719847748

Moss, B., & Schwebel, A. (1993). Defining intimacy in romantic relationships. *Family Relations*, 42(1), 31–37. https://doi.org/10.2307/584918

Nadel, H., Einav, G., & Galily, Y. (2021). Let's WhatsApp! Generation X couples' online and offline relationship patterns in the digital age. *New Media & Society*. https://doi.org/10.1177/14614448211043192

Pandya, S. (2022). In 50s and married for the first time: Examining the effectiveness of spirituality app and relationship counseling app in improving marital satisfaction and dyadic adjustment of very late first-marriage couples. *Marriage & Family Review*, 58(5), 413–443. https://doi.org/10.1080/01494929.2021.2015047

Pelley, V. (2021). The profound importance of having "couples friends". *Fatherly*. https://www.fatherly.com/love-money/the-profound-importance-of-having-couples-friends

Pennington, S. (2009). Bisexuals "doing gender" in romantic relationships. *Journal of Bisexuality*, *9*(1), 33–69. https://doi.org/10.1080/15299710802660029

Schrock, A. (2015). Communicative affordances of mobile media: Portability, availability, locatability, and multimediality. *International Journal of Communication*, *9*, 1229–1246.

Sela, A., Rozenboim, N., & Ben-Gal, H. C. (2022). Smartphone use behavior and quality of life: What is the role of awareness? *PLoS One*, *17*(3), e0260637. https://doi.org/10.1371/journal.pone.0260637

Sepúlveda, R. (2020). *Conhecer pessoas, namoro e sexo: as respostas da App Store*. MediaLab. https://medialab.iscte-iul.pt/conhecer-pessoas-namoro-e-sexo-as-respostas-da-app-store-2/

Sepúlveda, R. (2023). *Swipe, match, date*. Penguin Random House.

Sepúlveda, R., & Vieira, J. (2019). Lógicas de funcionamento do Tinder. Uma análise da aplicação e das perceções dos utilizadores. *Teknokultura*, *16*(1), 75–91. https://doi.org/10.5209/TEKN.62054

Shahin, M., Zahedi, M., Khalajzadeh, H., & Nasab, A. (2023). A study of gender discussions in mobile apps. In *IEEE/ACM 20th International Conference on Mining Software Repositories (MSR)*. https://doi.org/10.48550/arXiv.2303.09808

Sharabi, L., & Hopkins, A. (2022). Picture perfect? Examining associations between relationship quality, attention to alternatives, and couples' activities on Instagram. *Journal of Social and Personal Relationships*, *8*(12), 3518–3542. https://doi.org/10.1177/0265407521991662

Statcounter. (2023). *Mobile operating system market share. Worldwide. Apr 2022–Apr 2023*. Statcounter. Global Stats. https://gs.statcounter.com/os-market-share/mobile

Szymanski, D., Moffitt, L., & Carr, E. (2011). Sexual objectification of women: Advances to theory and research. *The Counseling Psychologist*, *39*(1), 6–38. https://doi.org/10.1177/0011000010378402

Timmermans, E., & De Caluwé, E. (2017). To Tinder or not to Tinder, that's the question: An individual differences perspective to Tinder use and motives. *Personality and Individual Differences*, *110*, 74–79. https://doi.org/10.1016/j.paid.2017.01.026

Tolman, D. L., Davis, B. R., & Bowman, C. P. (2016). «That's just how it is» A gendered analysis of masculinity and femininity ideologies in adolescent girls' and boys' heterosexual relationships. *Journal of Adolescent Research*, *31*(1), 3–31. https://doi.org/10.1177/0743558415587325

van Dijck, J., Poell, T., & de Waal, M. (2018). *The platform society: Public values in a connective world*. University Press.

van Heerde, H., Dinner, I., & Neslin, S. (2019). Engaging the unengaged customer: The value of a retailer mobile app. *International Journal of Research in Marketing*, *36*(3), 420–438. https://doi.org/10.1016/j.ijresmar.2019.03.003

Wired. (2023, July). Wired Health Special: The future of health, 64–75.

Yoo, H., Bartle-Haring, S., Day, R., & Gangamma, R. (2014). Couple communication, emotional and sexual intimacy, and relationship satisfaction. *Journal of Sex & Marital Therapy*, *40*(4), 275–293. https://doi.org/10.1080/0092623X.2012.751072

Chapter 7

Monitoring Bodies and Selves: Unveiling Menstrual Tracking Apps Under Foucault's Concepts

Juliana Alcantara

University of Coimbra, Portugal

Abstract

This chapter discusses the control of women's bodies and minds through the daily practices of menstrual control apps. Based on Michel Foucault's concepts (2003, 2006, 2013), the research is based on women's relationship with their own bodies. Still, it is wider than the body per se since the central theme is the construction of subjectivities. This paper embraces power modalities and explores disciplinary and discursive practices and regimes of truth, biopower, biopolitics and governance. The paper frames the fundamental points of Michel Foucault's analysis of power and how they are associated with strategies used for menstrual tracking apps. It looks at how apps act on the subjectivity of being a woman, shaping ways of thinking and acting. It looks at how disciplinary practices, knowledge–power and surveillance, as Foucault tells us, relate to themselves and medicine. The text highlights that monitoring data and corporate surveillance by menstrual apps poses unprecedented challenges to feminist politics. Therefore, we argue that the technology of menstrual tracking apps acts subtly and uninterruptedly to docilise female bodies and make them useful. Trying to find new paths and solutions from a feminist and critical perspective, we offer suggestions for further research on the topic, disregarding liberal approaches which rely on media literacy exclusively rather than a holistic comprehension of technology and women's rights.

Keywords: Female body; women's health; privacy; algorithmic governance; mobile technology; communication studies

Introduction

How users engage with mobile apps to self-monitor and improve health and fitness has recently attracted scholarly attention. Resorted from a user and design perspective, much research has been concentrated on women's use of pregnancy and parenting apps, showing at least two positive impacts: on emotional support and access to medical care information (Goetz et al., 2017; Lupton, 2017; Lupton & Pedersen, 2016). Other studies have focused on women's use of menstrual-tracking apps, pointing to their equally positive role in knowing the body better and in birth control (Alcantara, 2023; Epstein et al., 2017; Levy & Romo-Avilés, 2019). On the other hand, critical research on digital surveillance and self-tracking apps has been more concerned with how apps impact the broader sociocultural context. Research from this perspective has been questioning how these digital tools relate to power relations and reproduce or defy hegemonic normativity (Lupton, 2015a, 2015b; Megarry, 2018; Karlsson, 2019).

This article intends to relate Michel Foucault's concepts with the daily practices in our society, more specifically, to deal with issues related to the female body in contemporary times. Although Foucault has not contemplated the gender perspective in his analyses, it is possible to draw lines of thought that meet his ideas and encompass the modalities of power. This essay argues that mobile technology, specifically period tracking apps, involves power through disciplinary, discursive practices and regimes of truth, biopower, biopolitics and governance. According to Foucault, power does not only act on the consciousness; power acts on the body. To understand how this logic is installed and associated with algorithmic governance, we explore concepts in line with the fundamental points of Foucault's power analytics. Therefore, we associate it with the context of mobile apps that track and measure the menstrual cycle.

From a feminist framework, 'there is no form of surveillance that is innocent' (Nakamura, 2015, p. 221). As Lisa Nakamura (2015, p. 221) contends, surveillance technologies have always performed two functions: 'to regulate, define, and control populations; and to create new gendered, racialised, and abled or disabled bodies through digital means'. However, the new forms of data monitoring and mining and their implications for corporate and government surveillance pose unprecedented challenges to feminist politics.

Departing from a feminist and critical digital perspective (Lupton, 2019, 2020), this paper concerns how period trackers position and transform the body. In brief, this essay is structured in four sections. The initial sheds light on privacy issues, data commodification and the influence of algorithms on societal structures. The second one looks at the functions and strategies employed by menstrual tracking apps, focusing on Flo as an example. It also explores privacy concerns surrounding these apps, including data compromise and user privacy risks. The following discusses the intricate relationship between subjectivities and surveillance, drawing from Michel Foucault's conceptual framework. It highlights how algorithms and self-tracking apps are tools for establishing power through the governance of the body and feminine subjectivities. Finally, the fourth section intends to distinguish the dynamics of self-care and self-control in the context of surveillance. It underscores how period tracking apps shape women's minds, choices, body perceptions and desires, even when individuals believe they are in control. It explores the complex interplay of power, surveillance and individual agency. This paper argues that self-tracking makes invisible control of the female body and subjectivity to docilise their bodies and make them useful.

Algorithms and Power Dynamics

Research on privacy issues has reported that 61% (sixty-one percent) of 36 (thirty-six) menstrual control apps transfer data to Facebook automatically without consent.[1] Thus, whenever users open the app, their data are transferred to the social network, whether or not she is logged on to the social network. Indeed, the computational performance of the last few decades has realised the advertising dream: to segment and reach the target audience in particular. It was only possible due to social network's transformation of sociability – friendships, disagreements, interests and disinterests – into online data. Moreover, 'human beings shape the algorithms and are simultaneously "shaped" by them' (Latour *apud* Ramos, 2017, p. 78). Lastly, data on pregnant women are considered particularly valuable for advertisers since potential parents are consumers who will probably change their purchasing habits. These new forms of data monitoring and corporate surveillance implications pose unprecedented challenges to feminist politics. Not only because app technologies compromise personal data and users' privacy but also because the algorithmic governance fosters symbolic and material powers within the logic 'the body is yours, but the data is ours'.

The digital environment is numerical, encrypted and mediated by human beings. It opens to questions about who dictates the rules on the Internet. Being the Big Data 'socio-cultural artefacts' (Lupton *apud* in Karlsson, 2019, p. 111), it is not surprising that patriarchal logic is at its construction, context and purpose. That is to say, a new form of exercise of power emerges, one that unravels from existing structures in our society. Algorithmic governance is critical within multiple relationships of the social order: actors, mechanisms, institutions, and authorities are presented at different levels, often decentralised of the State and subject to private initiative. As Deborah Lupton and others contend, algorithmic governance does not come from the algorithm but through it (Castro, 2018; Lupton, 2016; Just & Latzer *apud* Katzenbach & Ulbricht, 2019).

> Beyond thinking critically about the nature of algorithms, there is also a need to consider their work, effects and power. Just as algorithms are not neutral, impartial expressions of knowledge, their work is not impassive and apolitical. Algorithms search, collate, sort, categorise, group, match, analyse, profile, model,

---

[1] A British non-governmental organization. Research report available at: https://privacyinternational.org/long-read/3196/no-bodys-business-mine-how-menstruation-apps-are-sharing-your-data

simulate, visualise and regulate people, processes and places. They shape how we understand the world and they do work in and make the world through their execution as software, with profound consequences. (Kitchin & Dodge *apud* Kitchin, 2017, p. 18)

Mobile platforms also play a role when it comes to safety in big cities, as in the case of Sensafety in Berlin, Germany (Rodriguez Garzon & Deva, 2019), and the case of OTT – Onde Tem Tiroteio (in English, Where There's Shooting) in Rio de Janeiro, Brazil (Grupillo et al., 2023). At the centre of these apps is trust, whereby users, by reporting crimes and sharing information about emergency cases, help people feel safer in their daily lives. However, it is not new that technology reinforces racial stereotypes in the identification of criminal suspects from surveillance images as a tool of the justice system (Buolamwini, 2023; Perkowitz, 2021), jeopardising not only privacy issues but also human rights and social justice. Academics have already problematised that 'machines' not only reinforce but also create sexist and racist behaviour (Noble, 2018; Velkova & Kaun, 2021) in control exercised at the level of the architecture of the digital ecosystem. Software, hardware, and network connectivity, then, give rise to forms of domination called digital colonialism (Kayser-Bril, 2020; Kwet, 2019). It is in this degree of decision over the body that racism is inscribed, as it emerges from biopower and is fundamental to its functioning. Foucault (2006, p. 271) points out: 'The qualification of certain races as good and others, on the contrary, as inferior, all this will be a way of fragmenting this biological field (...), of unlevelling some groups in relation to others, within the population'.

Power dynamics in the technological environment echo our platform society with rules imposed by algorithms that escape the perception of ordinary citizens. If we consider the broader systems and their effects on the deterioration and instability of democracy and digital capitalism, exemplified by the polarisation of public discourse (Habgood-Coote, 2019), echo chambers (Terren & Borge-Bravo, 2021), data surveillance (van Dijck, 2014), digital populism (Cesarino, 2021), distrust of traditional media (Bennett & Livingston, 2018; Donovan & boyd, 2021), trust in social networks and the big tech companies that mediate them (boyd, 2017, 2018; van Dijck, 2014), and other ramifications of the digital ecosystem that are certainly not mentioned, we will see many challenging issues unfold in various spheres of public and private life. For women in particular, it concerns a scenario of online hatred and hostility (Jones, 2021; Lewis et al., 2020; Nechushtai, 2023; Simões et al., 2022), which receives little or no attention from the legal, governmental, and regulatory spheres. In the field of media studies, research shows that misogynistic comments on online profiles raise extensive audience metrics in strategic harmony with tech companies that facilitate the practice and continuation of harassment and intimidation against women (Jatmiko et al., 2020; Posetti et al., 2020; UN Women, 2020). By intersecting the female gender with other identity layers, the most attention from abuse is over black women (Miller, 2023), those with public visibility (Stahel & Schoen, 2020) and those who are feminists (Ging & Siapera, 2019).

During the COVID-19 pandemic, algorithms validate disinformation narratives. Some examples involve anti-vax theories, which claim that the coronavirus vaccine is magnetised and contains 5G surveillance chips from China (Ahmed et al., 2020; Das & Ahmed, 2022), as well as causing irreversible side effects, cases of autism and genetic alteration (Das & Ahmed, 2022; Savolainen, 2021). Similarly, the prevented use of facial masks would not be necessary and could cause suffocation due to lack of oxygenation (Grimes, 2021). Also, physical distancing and quarantine would be pointless (Allcott et al., 2020; Ceron et al., 2021). In the same vein, content shared freely on social media called for the use of medicines considered to be miraculous, such as chloroquine, azithromycin and ivermectin (Alcantara & Ferreira, 2020; Covid Report, 2020).

Regarding health risk perception, as Paul Slovic (1993) points out, controversies over accepting or denying the measures imposed to minimise risk are not due to individuals' ignorance. Still, they are instead secondary effects of the form of democratic participation, which are amplified by technological and social changes that systematically undermine trust in the institutions responsible for risk management. Indeed, socioeconomic, and political dynamics can both influence the feeling of being at risk and the feeling of being safe and, therefore, shape human behaviour in dangerous situations (Dryhurst et al., 2020; Gerhold, 2020; Ju & You, 2022; Motta Zanin et al., 2020).

Menstrual Tracking App Functions and Strategies

Flo, Clue and My Calendar apps have more than 160 million downloads.[2] Taking the first app as an example, the Flo is meant to help women at each stage of their reproductive cycle. As with other mobile calendars for menstrual self-monitoring and birth control, it tracks menstruation, cycle prediction, preparation for conception, pregnancy and early motherhood, and gynaecological health. In addition, users must provide data about their health and habits to be better served by the technology. Information such as body weight, mood changes, premenstrual symptoms and visits to the doctor/gynaecologist is thus requested.

Likewise, users are invited to register their habits, such as physical exercise, cigarettes and alcohol consumption, as well as sexual life, including intercourse frequency, libido, whether or not they are sexually active during the menstrual period and their type of relationships. The app uses a notification strategy to remember and encourage users to fill the data with information about the cycle and feelings. It also strongly encourages the insertion of data about consumption habits. For example, 'which product is most often used – tampons, pads, menstrual cups?' and 'which contraceptive method do you use – hormonal contraceptives, condoms, IUDs?' if the user has already undergone some cosmetic surgery, being encouraged soon after to take care of her own body and appearance.

---

[2] According to Play Store on June 2023.

It offers content in the form of articles, chats and blogs. All content (texts and images) focuses on the young female body despite the promise to help women at each stage of their reproductive cycle. Texts reproduce patterns of hegemonic values, such as the invisibility of ageing women. The discursive strategies are simple, easy, and quick to read, highlighting female self-control and self-care. Interestingly, while the app requests data about sexual life, no articles accessed between July and December 2020 focused on this topic, at least in free access content. The 'practical guide to sexuality' the app offers is only accessible on paid access. Besides, there is no topic related to mental health. The menstruation theme is directed at women who use the app to get pregnant and avoid pregnancy. One of the articles addressed a discharge issue and did not indicate what an abnormal discharge would be, how the discharge varies according to the phases of the menstrual cycle, or which diseases are correlated to an abnormal discharge. Regarding health care and hormone issues, the content of the articles was directed to the reader, creating an atmosphere of complicity.

Together with these themes, there were calls to the reader out of curiosity, for instance: 'did you know that the temperature of water affects the speed at which the body absorbs it?'. Besides content with newsworthiness aspects linked to curiosity in a discursive strategy, some articles highlighted pathological aspects and health risks, such as: 'the lack or excess of testosterone leads to negative consequences', 'going to bed after 4 a.m. can cause metabolic imbalances, hormonal imbalances, weight gain, insulin resistance and increased vascular risk'. As for the theme of contraception, articles identified as such recognised women's diverse and possible choices. However, only heterosexual women were targeted. One more example involves sterilisation surgery, which is presented as a possibility for both women and men. The piece empowered women to know their own bodies, especially in non-hormonal contraception. At the same time, the Flo app reinforces the need to self-track the menstrual cycle and, thus, to use the technology it offers. As one of the articles suggests: 'this method will be effective only if the woman closely monitors her menstrual cycle'.

It is essential to highlight that there were no mentions of the specialists by their names. Credits are given to bodies of medical competence – for instance, the European Board & College of Obstetrics and Gynaecology. In mentioning medical societies, it guarantees the information's credibility and does not personalise texts as medical attendance. Another strategy was found in the use of the imperative verb tense – as with 'consult your doctor', 'inform your doctor', or 'consult a specialist'. It reaffirms medical knowledge and authority without taking power from the app. Curiously, the content does not rank medical knowledge when texts approach nutrition and exercise. On the contrary, using the verb 'we recommend' in the first-person plural impersonalises the message.

In sum, the Flo app content information is directly addressed to the reader, guiding women to make their own choices regarding their bodies. However, Flo, like other self-tracking apps, abled and disabled bodies and habitus, regulating and defining ways of being, ways of feeling and behaving, often reifying traditional gender roles and heteronormativity. The discursive strategies suggest that controlling the reproductive cycle and deciding to get pregnant is literally in women's hands. Finally, it should not be forgotten that this app is one of many that compromise personal data and users' privacy.

Subjectivities and Surveillance

Despite criticisms of Foucault from a gendered perspective, as already expressed in this work, the concepts worked on by the philosopher at the end of the 20th century are not only an inspiration but a basis for this research. The challenge in this essay resides in explaining some of the Foucauldian concepts that communicate with each other and trying to isolate certain concepts to form a structured explanation of how algorithms and self-tracking apps act as tools for power to establish itself through the governance of the body and feminine subjectivities, influencing ways of thinking and acting. Indeed, multiple power forces are exercised subtly in female bodies and minds.

For Foucault, for the control to be established and perpetuated, two factors need to come in sync: (1) the existence of docile bodies that are easy to control and easy to perform what is expected to, and (2) the categorisation of the data that these docile bodies produce. For him, disciplinary power hierarchises, segments and makes bodies useful and docile. When it involves women's bodies, it is important to note that the relations of domination addressed by Foucault are sustained by 'heterosexual and phallic cultural conventions' (Butler *apud* Narvaz & Nardi, 2007, p. 58) and that discipline acts on women's bodies in a different and domesticated way to men's bodies (Diamond & Quinby *apud* Narvaz & Nardi, 2007).

> A docile body is one that can be subjected, that can be used, that can be transformed and perfected. (...) It is not a question of taking care of the body, en masse, wholesale, as if it were an inseparable unit, but of working on it in detail; it is a question of exercising subtle coercion over it, of ensuring control at the very level of mechanics – movements, gestures, attitudes, speed: infinitesimal power over the active body. (...) These methods that allow for the minute control of the body's operations, that ensure the constant subjection of its forces and impose on them a relationship of docility, can be called "disciplines". (Foucault, 2006, pp. 158 e 159)

Once the docility of bodies has been instituted, the 'political anatomy' is born, which is also a 'mechanics of power' (Foucault, 2006, p. 160). In other words, since power is exercised in the 'political anatomy of details' (Guillen, 2004, p. 128), it constitutes micro-powers that perpetuate themselves uninterruptedly. Therefore, Foucault's central theme is not power per se, but the subject.

Foucault did not consider gender differences and subjugations. Nonetheless, the author was concerned with issues related to freedom by uncovering relations of knowledge and power, interconnecting bodies and selves to discipline and control them (Narvaz & Nardi, 2007). Looking at technology trust and the allowance for data-free permission is framed in a process that Jose van Dijk (2017, p. 41) explained as 'dataism'. This understanding clarifies that a 'widespread belief in the objective quantification and potential monitoring of all kinds of human behaviour (...) also involves trust in the (institutional) agents that collect, interpret and share the (meta)data'. As algorithmic governance, algorithmic governmentality – a neologism in line with Foucault's concept – expresses notions of panoptic surveillance (Machado, 2018). Foucault (2003, p. 303) explains governmentality as a 'set made up of the institutions, procedures, analyses and reflections, calculations and tactics that make it possible to exercise this very specific, very complex form of power, whose main target is the population'. The Foucauldian neologism that combines the words 'government' and 'mentality' points to the idea of government over oneself and government over others (Candiotto, 2012; Castro, 2018) in a process that leads to the development of a series of knowledge (Foucault, 2013). The meaning of 'govern' takes on the notion of leading, modelling, and structuring. Thus, it is possible to say that algorithmic governance not only administers a reality but also manages it.

Self-Care or Self-Control

Period tracking apps shape minds, choices, body perceptions and desires so that even the woman has no idea how her subjectivity is being reformulated, even if she thinks she is in control. Knowledge and control of one's own body have always been the desire of feminists. It is from this subjective knowledge that Foucault speaks, which goes far beyond the body per se. Power is exercised in the body and the soul as an 'effect and instrument of a political anatomy' (Foucault, 2013, p. 37). Power, therefore, operates in the body by recreating behaviours and subjectivities.

Foucault brings Socrates' 'know thyself' closer to the Greek semantics of 'care', 'take care of thyself' and disassociates the meaning from the Christian tradition, which is based on a narcissistic and selfish culture and a need to renounce oneself to achieve the desired place in paradise. For the Greeks, self-construction occurred through meditation, self-writing and physical exercises (Foucault, 1990, 1994; Fischer, 1999; Rago, 2006). Knowing oneself and caring for oneself complement each other and distance themselves from purification through pastoral confession. The Art of Living, as envisaged by the Greeks and spoken of by Foucault, encompasses friendship. In other words, when a person wants to share information about their life, they seek to 'listen' and not 'judge'. Therefore, there is no real empowerment when surveillance is practised. In the case of mobile phone apps, empowerment is even more distant since personal data is used for purposes beyond the initial intention, which would be monitoring the menstrual cycle. What is generated through self-government and knowledge of one's intimate data becomes a bargaining chip and a commercial space.

The feminist slogan 'The personal is political' makes sense in this context, where the public and private are blurred. There is a fine line that creates tension between feminist thinking, which seeks freedom, and the State's inaction when it fails to regulate the protection of personal data. At the same time, as women develop an awareness of their own bodies and the need to preserve them, they freely give away information about their intimacy without worrying about how this information will be used. That is to say, when a woman uses the menstrual tracking app to help her with self-knowledge, to help her get to know how her own body and to predict, somehow, the fertile period in a process that can be used to prevent pregnancy or to avoid it, she is at the same time being controlled by the app which keeps warning her when she is more likely to experience cramps, for example. Note: What political and economic links are presented? Wouldn't predicting that she will have cramps at a particular moment be a way of suggesting to this woman the need to buy painkillers preventively? To what extent can the political and economic actions of the self-tracking apps influence women's feelings?

The Panoptic metaphor is a useful concept to understand how a disciplinary tool acts on the anatomy of individuals. To introduce the idea of surveillance, Foucault uses Bentham's Panopticon, an architectural structure built to control prisons in the 18th century. The aspect of the tower in the centre of a circular building let to see without being seen. Without knowing for sure if anyone is actually watching them, control over the minds and bodies of prisoners (or the insane in the case of psychiatric hospitals and not prisons) is established. The Panopticon is a disciplinary tool that acts on the anatomy of individuals and is also an analogy of the relationships created in the online sphere. It begins in command for the body, when posting and when 'scrolls' are done. Thus, it is reached at the level of the mind. The control acts on the body and the minds of the people being watched, provided by social networks designed and conducted in vigilant continuous actions. In Foucault's words (2013, pp. 255 and 256), 'disciplines characterise, classify, specialise; they distribute by scale, distribute around a norm, reciprocally hierarchise individuals and, at the limit, disqualify and invalidate'.

Punishment is easy to see in factories, schools, and prisons. A fault, a delay or bad behaviour is charged individually but publicly or in a way that lets many people know, as a punishment that also serves as an example to others. The punishment in the case studied lies in the fact that if the self-tracking app does not meet the expectation – to warn about the fertile period when a woman wants to get pregnant or to warn to take contraception when a woman wants to avoid pregnancy. The menstrual mobile app fulfils the user's expectations better if she uses all or most features accurately. Otherwise, the punishment is real: 'losing' the chances that arise on fertile days or getting pregnant when she does not wish to. The punishment is individualised and makes the user responsible, placing the 'power of choice' in her hands.

This prism functions as a continuation of Foucault's work, which did not consider gender differences and subjugation. Still, it is undoubtedly clear that the author was concerned with issues related to freedom by uncovering relationships of knowledge and power. These are the connections of bodies and consciences to discipline and control them (Narvaz & Nardi, 2007).

For Foucault, surveillance does not constitute the construction of the self but instead a subjection to something. Foucault emphasises subjectivation, that is, forming a free, temperate and ethical individual (Rago, 2006). So, is self-care a kind of practice of empowerment? Yes, because it moves towards self-knowledge. Despite this, there is no real empowerment when surveillance practices exist. Since the intimate data are used to escape a personal purpose, what is generated through the governance of herself and the knowledge of her own body – her intimate data – becomes an exchange currency in a business area. It is only possible because our bodies have become a disciplinary instrument. Docile bodies are those that are easy to shape, submit and use. Through surveillance, normalisation and standardisation end up homogenising behaviours, while an individualising process occurs simultaneously (Guillen, 2004).

Power is exercised through a multiplicity of relationships which, as we have seen in the user-application context, include women, technology and inevitably the social body. Notably, different forces are constantly influencing each other. They act on subjectivity and bodies and are constructed by discursive practices and power-knowledge. From a feminist perspective of biomedical contexts, Margareth Rago (2006) exposes that modern gynaecology defines women's identity by dictating rules, such as how they should sit or even when and how they should become pregnant. Gynaecological medicine has created 'truths' that have spread beyond health centres and hospitals. These 'truths' have taken root in subjectivities and can be seen in the details of attitudes, choices, and actions. Undoubtedly, it echoes women's social roles, as if 'being a mother' and 'being a wife' were predictable paths. For centuries, scientific research excluded female samples and considered men's bodies the standard (Shock et al., 1984; White, 2002); when women started to be included in biomedical research, they were seen as inferior, being their bodies outlined to the sense of shelter a foetus.

In turn, biopolitics acts on the collective and its assumptions focus on controlling the population (examples are vaccination campaigns, large-scale public health decisions, births and mortality statistics). These processes and activities permit the installation of biopower, which is nothing more than a form of power exercised individually, in its 'experiential dimension' (Souza, 2010, p. 208) and whose product and purpose is the fate of individuals. In Foucauldian genealogy, the 'killing' of the sovereign gives way to 'letting live'. Notwithstanding, 'letting live' is conceived and planned in detail, as also manifested in the 'how to live' perspective. This practice is directly linked to disciplinary control and surveillance and is considered indispensable for the development of capitalism (Boyer, 2012; Souza, 2010).

> The technological dimension of surveillance, the spread of security devices and the bioregulation of human life still articulate local controls and networks, amplify the effects of disciplinary mechanisms, as well as pointing to a society in which the security apparatus is expanding in proportion to the threats to life and liberty. (Souza, 2010, p. 214)

Conclusion and Final Critical Remarks

Throughout the text, we examine women's self-care as empowerment, which, in the case under review, raises the question: 'What do you do with what you know about me?' This is one of the most concerning interrogations about self-care and apps where privacy is not guaranteed. It discussed the claims against the regulations of the female body and how algorithms are mechanisms for the practice of power to spread precisely because algorithms exist from a patriarchal logic. In this sense, the construction of subjectivities, through the discursive practice and in the relationships of knowledge-power, shape gynaecological and sexual practices.

It is crucial to analyse algorithms from various angles, including technical, computational, mathematical, political, cultural, economic, contextual, material, philosophical and ethical perspectives. When critically assessing algorithms' development and impact, it is vital to acknowledge the presence of power dynamics. Algorithms are far from neutral or impartial; they are inherently political and carry inherent biases and values (Kitchin, 2017).

Despite some scholars addressing media literacy as a universal solution (Blanco-Alfonso et al., 2022; Camarero et al., 2022; Jones-Jang et al., 2019) relying on a liberal perspective and focusing on individual decisions and not regulatory measures combined with individual daily life, feminist critique approaches media literacy standards problematising the political-economic context that guides capital interests (boyd, 2017), and locating the subjectivities more broadly in the decision processes rejecting the subject as 'unified and rational'. As Rosalind Gill (2012, p. 740) points out:

> The implicit idea seems to be that if someone is media literate, that is to say if they can discourse critically on the aims and techniques that comprise an image or text, they will somehow be 'innoculated' or protected against its otherwise harmful effects. It relies upon the idea of subjectivity as coherent, rather than split or contradictory, with the assumption that affect follows knowledge in rather a neat and obedient manner.

Therefore, future research directions should promote holistic and critical thinking about apps that work exclusively by accepting commitments restricting women's rights. From a feminist critical perspective, further research may try to understand how women perceive intimate and private issues and what motivates app users to produce and give away their data. More specifically, in this case, to give up data related to the menstrual cycle diary. It is part of tech media education to recognise which and who the market players are, how the algorithms work and frame their subjectivities within capitalist and patriarchal logic. We have seen that women's bodies and minds are used for commercial purposes in the context examined. By thinking critically about this issue, we believe women will find strategies to protect themselves from malicious situations and create their own technology based on ethical and egalitarian principles.

References

Ahmed, W., Vidal-Alaball, J., Downing, J., & Seguí, F. L. (2020). COVID-19 and the 5G conspiracy theory: Social network analysis of Twitter data. *Journal of Medical Internet Research, 22*(5), e19458.

Alcantara, J. (2023). Corpos datados e eus quantificados. In *Feminismo en la línea del tiempo, desde las (in) visibilidades al concepto de felicidad* (pp. 1131–1148). Dykinson.

Alcantara, J., & Ferreira, R. R. (2020). A infodemia da "gripezinha": uma análise sobre desinformação e coronavírus no Brasil. *Chasqui – Revista Latinoamericana de Comunicacion, 145*, 137–162.

Allcott, H., Boxell, L., Conway, J. C., Gentzkow, M., Thaler, M., & Yang, D. Y. (2020). *Polarisation and public health: Partisan differences in social distancing during the coronavirus pandemic*. National Bureau of Economic Research. https://www.nber.org/papers/w26946

Bennett, W. L., & Livingston, S. (2018). The disinformation order: Disruptive communication and the decline of democratic institutions. *European Journal of Communication, 33*(2), 122–139.

Blanco-Alfonso, I., Rodríguez-Fernández, L., & Arce-García, S. (2022). Polarización y discurso de odio con sesgo de género asociado a la política: Análisis de las interacciones en Twitter. *Revista de Comunicación, 21*(2), 33–50.

boyd, d. (2017). Did media literacy backfire? *Journal of Applied Youth Studies, 1*(4), 83–89.

boyd, d. (2018). You think you want media literacy… do you? https://medium.com/datasociety-points/you-think-you-want-media-literacy-do-you-7cad6af18ec2

Boyer, A. (2012). Biopolítica y filosofía feminista. *Revista de Estudios Sociales*, (43), 131–138.

Buolamwini, J. (2023). *Unmasking AI: My mission to protect what is human in a world of machines*. Random House.

Camarero, E., Herrero-Diz, P., & Varona-Aramburu, D. (2022). Desinformación de género en Honduras: Medios de comunicación y jóvenes frente a las noticias sobre violencia contra las mujeres. *Revista Estudios sobre el Mensaje Periodístico*, 41–52.

Candiotto, C. (2012). A governamentalidade em Foucault: da analítica do poder à ética da subjetivação. *O que nos faz pensar, 21*(31), 91–108.

Castro, J. C. L. (2018). Redes sociais como modelo de governança algorítmica. *MATRIZes, 12*(2), 165–191.

Ceron, W., Gruszynski Sanseverino, G., de-Lima-Santos, M. F., & Quiles, M. G. (2021). COVID-19 fake news diffusion across Latin America. *Social Network Analysis and Mining, 11*(1), 47.

Cesarino, L. (2021). Pós-verdade e a crise do sistema de peritos: uma explicação cibernética. *Ilha – Revista de Antropologia, 23*(1), 73–96.

Covid Report. (2020). *Infodemic Covid-19 in Europe: A visual analysis of disinformation*. A fact-checking report by AFP, CORRECTIV, Pagella Politica/Facta, Full Fact and Maldita.es. https://covidinfodemiceurope.com/report/covid_report.pdf

Das, R., & Ahmed, W. (2022). Rethinking fake news: Disinformation and ideology during the time of COVID-19 global pandemic. *IIM Kozhikode Society & Management Review, 11*(1), 146–159.

Donovan, J., & boyd, d. (2021). Stop the presses? Moving from strategic silence to strategic amplification in a networked media ecosystem. *American Behavioral Scientist*, 65(2), 333–350.

Dryhurst, S., Schneider, C. R., Kerr, J., Freeman, A. L. J., Recchia, G., van der Bles, A. M., Spiegelhalter, D., & van der Linden, S. (2020). Risk perceptions of COVID-19 around the world. *Journal of Risk Research*, 23(7–8), 994–1006.

Epstein, D. A., Lee, N. B., Kang, J. H., Agapie, E., Schroeder, J., Pina, L. R., Fogarty, J., Kientz, J. A., & Munson, S. (2017). Examining menstrual tracking to inform the design of personal informatics tools. In *Proceedings of the Conference on Human Factors in Computing Systems*, Denver (pp. 6876–6888).

Fischer, R. M. B. (1999). Foucault e o Desejável Conhecimento do Sujeito. *Educação & Realidade*, 24(1), 39–59.

Foucault, M. (1990). *Tecnologías del yo*. Ediciones Paidós Ibérica.

Foucault, M. (1994). *Hermenéutica del Sujeito*. Las Ediciones de la Piqueta.

Foucault, M. (2003). *Estratégia, poder-saber: Ditos e escritos IV*. Forense Universitária.

Foucault, M. (2006). *É Preciso Defender a Sociedade*. Livros do Brasil.

Foucault, M. (2013). *Vigiar e Punir. Nascimento da Prisão*. Edições 70.

Gerhold, L. (2020). *COVID-19: Risk perception and coping strategies*. Interdisciplinary Security Research Group, Freie Universität Berlin. PsyArXiv preprint: xmpk4.

Gill, R. (2012). Media, empowerment and the 'sexualisation of culture' debates. *Sex Roles*, 66, 736–745.

Ging, D., & Siapera, E. (Eds.). (2019). *Gender hate online: Understanding the new antifeminism*. Springer.

Goetz, M., Müller, M., Matthies, L. M., Hansen, J., Doster, A., Szabo, A., Pauluschke-Fröhlich, J., Abele, H., Sohn, C., Wallwiener, M., & Wallwiener, S. (2017). Perceptions of patient engagement applications during pregnancy: A qualitative assessment of the patient's perspective. *JMIR Mhealth Uhealth*, 5(5), 73.

Grimes, D. R. (2021). Medical disinformation and the unviable nature of COVID-19 conspiracy theories. *PLoS One*, 16(3), e0245900.

Grupillo, A., Melo, P., & Serra, J. (2023). Construção de confiança em apps colaborativos e desafios para o jornalismo: estudo sobre o OTT. *Chasqui: Revista Latinoamericana de Comunicación*, 154, 69–91.

Guillen, N. P. (2004). Relaciones de poder: leyendo a Foucault desde la perspectiva de género. *Revista de Ciencias Sociales (Cr)*, 4(106), 123–141.

Habgood-Coote, J. (2019). Stop talking about fake news. *Inquiry*, 62(9–10), 1033–1065.

Jatmiko, M. I., Syukron, M., & Mekarsari, Y. (2020). Covid-19, harassment and social media: A study of gender-based violence facilitated by technology during the pandemic. *The Journal of Society and Media*, 4(2), 319–347.

Jones, M. O. (2021). State-aligned misogynistic disinformation on Arabic Twitter: The attempted silencing of an Al Jazeera journalist. *Open Information Science*, 5(1), 278–297.

Jones-Jang, S., Mortensen, T., & Liu, J. (2019). Does media literacy help identification of fake news? Information literacy helps, but other literacies don't. *American Behavioral Scientist*, 65(2), 371–388.

Ju, Y., & You, M. (2022). It's politics, isn't it? Investigating direct and indirect influences of political orientation on risk perception of COVID-19. *Risk Analysis*, *42*(1), 56–68.

Karlsson, A. (2019). A room of one's own?: Using period trackers to escape menstrual stigma. *Nordicom Review*, *40*(s1), 111–123.

Katzenbach, C., & Ulbricht, L. (2019). Algorithmic governance. *Internet Policy Review*, *8*(4), 1–18.

Kayser-Bril, N. (17 de setembro de 2020). https://algorithmwatch.org/en/google-translate-gender-bias/

Kitchin, R. (2017). Thinking critically about and researching algorithms. *Information, Communication & Society*, *20*(1), 14–29.

Kwet, M. (2019). Digital colonialism: US empire and the new imperialism in the global south. *Race & Class*, *60*(4), 3–26.

Levy, J., & Romo-Avilés, N. (2019). "A good little tool to get to know yourself a bit better": A qualitative study on users' experiences of app-supported menstrual tracking in Europe. *BMC Public Health*, *19*, 1–11.

Lewis, S. C., Zamith, R., & Coddington, M. (2020). Online harassment and its implications for the journalist–audience relationship. *Digital Journalism*, *8*(8), 1047–1067.

Lupton, D. (2015a). *Digital sociology*. Routledge.

Lupton, D. (2015b). Quantified sex: A critical analysis of sexual and reproductive self-tracking using apps. *Culture, Health and Sexuality*, *17*(4), 440–453.

Lupton, D. (2016). The diverse domains of quantified selves: Self-tracking modes and dataveillance. *Economy and Society*, *45*(1), 101–122.

Lupton, D. (2017). 'It just gives me a bit of peace of mind': Australian women's use of digital media for pregnancy and early motherhood. *Societies*, *7*(3), 1–13.

Lupton, D. (2019). 'It's made me a lot more aware': A new materialist analysis of health self-tracking. *Media International Australia*, *171*(1), 66–79.

Lupton, D. (2020). Data mattering and self-tracking: What can personal data do? *Continuum*, *34*(1), 1–13.

Lupton, D., & Pedersen, S. (2016). An Australian survey of women's use of pregnancy and parenting apps. *Women and Birth*, *29*(4), 368–374.

Machado, H. F. S. (2018). Algoritmos, regulação e governança: uma revisão de literatura. *Journal of Law and Regulation*, *4*(1), 39–62.

Megarry, J. (2018). Under the watchful eyes of men: Theorising the implications of male surveillance practices for feminist activism on social media. *Feminist Media Studies*, *18*(6), 1070–1085.

Miller, K. C. (2023). Hostility toward the press: A synthesis of terms, research, and future directions in examining harassment of journalists. *Digital Journalism*, *11*(7), 1230–1249.

Motta Zanin, G., Gentile, E., Parisi, A., & Spasiano, D. (2020). A preliminary evaluation of the public risk perception related to the COVID-19 health emergency in Italy. *International Journal of Environmental Research and Public Health*, *17*(9), 3024.

Nakamura, L. (2015). Afterword blaming, shaming, and the feminization of social media. In *Feminist surveillance studies* (pp. 221–228). Duke University Press.

Narvaz, M., & Nardi, H. C. (2007). Problematizações feministas à obra de Michel Foucault. *Revista Subjetividades*, *7*(1), 45–70.

Nechushtai, E. (2023). Resisting the individualisation of risk: Strategies of engagement and caution in journalists' responses to online mobs in the United States and Germany. *Digital Journalism*, *11*(10), 1906–1923.

Noble, S. U. (2018). *Algorithms of oppression: How search engines reinforce racism*. New York University Press.

Perkowitz, S. (2021). The bias in the machine: Facial recognition technology and racial disparities. https://doi.org/10.21428/2c646de5.62272586

Posetti, J., Aboulez, N., Bontcheva, K., Harrison, J., & Waisbord, S. (2020). Online violence against women journalists. https://dspace.ceid.org.tr/xmlui/handle/1/1159

Rago, M. (2006). Foucault e as artes de viver do anarco-feminismo. In M. Rago & A. Veiga-Netp (Eds.), *Figuras de Foucault* (pp. 165–175). Autêntica.

Ramos, D. O. (2017). A influência do algoritmo. *Revista Communicare*, *17*, 70–85.

Rodriguez Garzon, S., & Deva, B. (2019). Sensafety: Crowdsourcing the urban sense of safety. *Advances in Cartography and GIScience of the ICA*, *2*, 1–8.

Savolainen, R. (2021). Assessing the credibility of COVID-19 vaccine mis/disinformation in online discussion. *Journal of Information Science*, *49*(4), 1096–1110.

Shock, N. W., Greulich, R. C., Andres, R., Arenberg, D., Costa, P. T., Lakatta, E. G., & Tobin, J. D. (1984). *Normal human aging: The Baltimore longitudinal study of aging*. US Government Printing Office.

Simões, R. B. D., Amaral, I., Santos, S., & Alcantara, J. (2022). Online violence against women: Reports from the COVID-19 pandemic experience. *Comunicação e Sociedade*, *42*, 179–203.

Slovic, P. (1993). Perceived risk, trust, and democracy. *Risk Analysis*, *13*(6), 675–682.

Souza, L. A. F. S. (2010). Disciplina, biopoder e governo: contribuições de Michel Foucault para uma analítica da modernidade. In L. A. F. de Souza, T. T. Sabatine & B. R. de Magalhães (Eds.), *Michel Foucault. Sexualidade, Corpo e Direito* (pp. 193–216). Cultura Acadêmica.

Stahel, L., & Schoen, C. (2020). Female journalists under attack? Explaining gender differences in reactions to audiences' attacks. *New Media & Society*, *22*(10), 1849–1867.

Terren, L., & Borge-Bravo, R. (2021). Echo chambers on social media: A systematic review of the literature. *Review of Communication Research*, *9*, 99–118.

UN Women. (2020). Online and ICT-facilitated violence against women and girls during COVID-19. https://www.unwomen.org/en/digital-library/publications/2020/04/brief-online-and-ict-facilitated-violence-against-women-and-girls-during-covid-19

van Dijck, J. (2014). Datafication, dataism and dataveillance: Big Data between scientific paradigm and ideology. *Surveillance and Society*, *12*(2), 197–208.

van Dijk, J. (2017). Confiamos nos dados? As implicações da datificação para o monitoramento social. *MATRIZes*, *11*(1), 39–59.

Velkova, J., & Kaun, A. (2021). Algorithmic resistance: Media practices and the politics of repair. *Information, Communication & Society*, *24*(4), 523–540.

White, K. (2002). *A sociology of health and illness*. Sage Publications.

Chapter 8

Doing Gender in WhatsApp Homosocial Groups

Cosimo Marco Scarcelli

University of Padova, Italy

Abstract

Digital media and mobile apps are constantly used concerning social interaction and maintaining social bonds. The most popular platform used for these practices is WhatsApp (Statista, 2022) a cross-platform instant messaging service for mobile devices. Like other instant messaging services, WhatsApp permits its users to create groups to have an interaction between (usually) a restricted number of people. This chapter will focus on young adults' everyday life and their mediated interactions using WhatsApp groups composed exclusively of people of the same gender. Considering these groups as communities of practices (Lave & Wenger, 1991) and gender as something that is doing with interaction (Butler, 2004; Connell, 2005; Mac an Ghaill, 1994), this chapter will concentrate on how young adults perform and (re)shape masculinities and femininities using mobile apps. Starting from the analysis of 46 online interviews with young adults living in Italy, this chapter will focus on homosocial practices in WhatsApp groups underling how gender identities are performed in these specific digital spaces, to what extent uses intertwine with WhatsApp's affordances and which kind of (the idea of) masculinities and femininities are reproduced by users practices. The interviews show how digital homosocial groups are usually carried out as a humourous act between friends, as a form of social consolidation, as an attempt to gain or maintain peer status or preserve hegemonic/dominant ideas of femininity or masculinity and as a safe space where performing what for some interviewees is the real essence of being men or women.

Keywords: Young people; homosociality; gender; masculinity; communities of practice

Introduction

Digital media and mobile apps are constantly used concerning social interaction and maintaining social bonds. The most popular platform used for these practices is WhatsApp (Statista, 2022) a cross-platform instant messaging service for mobile devices. Like other instant messaging services, WhatsApp permits its users to create groups to have an interaction between (usually) a restricted number of people.

The work focuses on homosocial practices among young adults (Flood, 2008) and their gender-making (Frosh et al., 2002; Mac an Ghaill, 1994) within private groups on WhatsApp consisting only of (heterosexual) men or women who know each other. In these spaces, as we shall see, boundaries are defined, particular discursive registers are used and specific content is shared. Practices that become part of the process of defining gender identity from the perspective that considers gender as performatively constructed (Butler, 2004) within social and relational dimensions (Connell, 2005; Kimmel, 2004).

The everyday lives of young men and women (West & Zimmerman, 1987, 2009) and their mediated interactions will be the privileged vantage point of this work, and the WhatsApp groups in question will be considered communities of practice (Lave & Wenger, 1991) where gender is learnt, modelled and performed.

The guiding theoretical beacon in the background is represented on the one hand by the sociological interpretation of youth cultures (Archer et al., 2007; Buckingham & Bragg, 2004; Nayak & Kehily, 2007; Ringrose, 2012; Willis, 1990) and on the other hand by the sociological approach to digital media (Couldry, 2012), which seeks to critically examine how gender-related social processes are enacted through digital media-related practices (Scarcelli, 2015a).

Digital Culture, Homosociality, Masculinity and Femininity

As danah boyd (2008, 2014) reminds us, digital media allow young people to redefine the boundaries constructed by adults by offering young people agency and spaces in which to construct and perform their identity (Hall et al., 1999) through bricolage practices (Willett, 2008), i.e. exploiting the potential of digital media and combining it with that of traditional media – or, in other words, media legacy. The spaces described allow young people to experiment with their selves also on the level of body, gender and sexuality (Buckingham, 2008; Metcalfe & Llewellyn, 2020; Scarcelli, 2015b; Tiidenberg & Gómez Cruz, 2015; Tiidenberg & van der Nagel, 2020). Experiments that can be linked to stereotypical – or hegemonic – ideas of masculinity and femininity (Connell, 2005; Connell & Messerschmidt, 2005), replicating them (Kapidzic & Herring, 2015; Metcalfe & Llewellyn, 2020; Ringrose, 2011), emphasising them (Döring et al., 2016) or subverting them (Cook & Hasmath, 2014).

WhatsApp enables one-to-one communication as well as the creation of groups to share messages, pictures and videos. Focusing on groups composed exclusively of members of the same gender it means to focus on homosocial interactions. Homosociality is the construction of – non-sexual – bonds between persons of the same sex (Lipman-Blumen, 1976; Sedgwick, 1985). According to

Odenbring and Johansson (2020), it is possible to distinguish analytically between horizontal and vertical homosociality (Hammarén & Johansson, 2014; Haywood et al., 2018). While the former refers to more inclusive forms of intimacy, with a consequent reconfiguration of hegemony and power relations, the latter is one through which bonds between people defend hierarchical relations and power structures, with a consequent strengthening of patriarchy and hegemonic masculinity.

A considerable body of literature has extensively explored the arrangement of men's relationships within homosocial contexts and the various tactics employed by men to perpetuate gender hierarchies and maintain male privileges. Scholars such as Bird (2018), Flood (2008) and Mac an Ghaill (1994) have contributed to this discourse.

Flood (2008) underscores the significant role of male–male relations in shaping the social and sexual interactions of young heterosexual men. He emphasises the policing of homosocial bonds against influences that might feminise or homosexualise, asserting that achieving sexual encounters with women becomes a means to status among men. Furthermore, sex with women serves as a direct medium for male bonding, with men narrating their sexual and gender experiences within storytelling cultures cultivated by homosociality (Flood, 2008).

The lack of intimacy in men's friendships, often associated with competition and exclusion, has been a prevalent topic in discussions on homosociality. Recent research, however, challenges this notion by presenting a more complex image of masculinity and friendship. For instance, studies on premarital rituals, such as the 'stag night', indicate changes in men's relationships (Hammarén & Johansson, 2014).

In contrast, there has been a noticeable gap in research exploring female friendships beyond desexualised relations. Sedgwick proposes an asymmetry between male and female homosociality, arguing that male bonding is primarily shaped by the exchange of women and the consolidation of men's societal power. However, Binhammer (2006) challenges this view, suggesting that women's relationships are not necessarily outside the dominant sexual economy but are integral to it, circulating within the same capitalist system as men. Consequently, relations between women are not by definition a challenge to Hegemonic masculinity.

To fruitfully interweave discourses on gender and homosociality with digital practices within WhatsApp chats, a final theoretical building block is represented by Paechter's (2003) suggestion to use the concept of communities of practice (Lave & Wenger, 1991; Wenger, 1998) as a tool to reflect on gendered performance and practices of doing gender. A process of social participation based, precisely, on practice and in which participation is understood as an inclusive process in which participants are active in the construction of identities concerning the community itself. To adopt this concept within a gender perspective is to argue that:

> ...the learning of what it means to be male or female within a social configuration results in shared practices in pursuit of the common goal of sustaining particular localised masculine and feminine identities. (71)

Looking at digital practices using the interpretative tools provided by Paechter's approach means analytically breaking down the barriers that groups such as WhatsApp's private ones can draw, technologically and symbolically, because of a gaze capable of reconnecting digital experiences with those outside the connected environments. A vision that is indispensable for relocating the tools of communication within everyday experience, which is inevitably intertwined with issues of gender and sexuality (De Ridder & Van Bauwel, 2015; Scarcelli, 2015a).

Methodology

The research underlying this chapter focuses on the management and testing of gender from the mediated spaces of everyday sociability. A qualitative approach was chosen to study the phenomenon and young adults' experiences from their points of view (Lobe et al., 2008) in order to illuminate the meaning they attribute to their practices.

In this case, such a perspective made it possible to explore in depth the experiences of adolescents and the complexity of meanings constructed in the intertwining of the gender identity dimension and that of the social web, as well as the universe of values, practices and cognitive dispositions of adolescents.

This work is part of a larger research project involving 46 young people aged between 20 and 24 years resident in Italy, selected through a theoretical sampling (Corbin & Strauss, 1990) that considered age and gender. The young people involved were recruited using the snowball technique. All the interviewees described themselves as cis-gender and heterosexual.

To gather empirical data, I chose to use the semi-structured interview technique. The choice stems from the very nature of the groups they wanted to study: private WhatsApp groups composed of only people who know each other. I am not, therefore, talking about particularly numerous groups or channels but about much more restricted realities made up of five to six people and difficult to observe except through the accounts of those who personally frequent them.

The interviews were conducted in the period between March and September 2021. Given the difficulty in being able to meet the interviewees in person due to the COVID-19 pandemic, online interviews in their synchronous variant (Janghorban et al., 2014) via Zoom.

The study was conducted following Silverman's (2013) ethical suggestions, namely: ensuring the voluntary participation of those involved, keeping the stories that emerged during the interview confidential, protecting the interviewees from harm and ensuring a climate of mutual trust between interviewer and interviewee.

The interviews – with an average duration of 60 minutes – were recorded and transcribed in full. They were subsequently analysed with the support of the ATLAS.ti software using thematic analysis as a specific narrative analysis model aimed at finding common themes between the interviewees and the reported experiences (Braun & Clarke, 2006; Riessman, 2002).

Female-Only and Male-Only Group Chats

Almost all of those who participated in the research stated that they were part of at least one WhatsApp group consisting exclusively of men or women. Before going into detail in the exposition of the research results, it is worth emphasising how the characteristics of WhatsApp groups become interesting to better understand the words of the respondents. This is especially so if we compare the peculiarities of the app in question with those of other platforms – such as Telegram (see, for example Semenzin & Bainotti, 2020).

In the first instance, the group has clear boundaries, all the members know each other and there are friendly ties between participants. In other words, we are not dealing with a group in which the public is unknown and this means that – as we will see shortly – on the one hand, there is a certain perceived limit within certain discourses in order not to incur symbolic sanctions from peers or other people.

Secondly, these groups have gatekeepers. WhatsApp only allows the administrator(s) to add new members. Many times, the interviewees, said that all group users are administrators, but let us not forget that we are still talking about rather small groups. Furthermore, the app warns when a new member is introduced into the chat or leaves it. This means that the group is closed and the perception that the young adults have is that this is a safe place in which to weave intra-gender bonds (Lyman, 1987). Of course, there is always the risk of someone sharing content with a third party, but this is an eventuality that the interviewees do not seem to consider fundamental.

Chatting 'as a Man' and 'as a Woman'

The interviews generally reveal a stereotypical utilisation of WhatsApp groups, and frequently, even within the accounts provided by the interviewees, there is a distinct differentiation between conversations 'among men' and conversations 'among women'.

The WhatsApp groups in question, then, turn into homosocial arenas in which the shared idea of femininity or masculinity dictates the posture and content within the group. This definition of gender boundaries becomes evident especially when the symbolic delimitations are, so to speak, threatened by the possibility of some men/women entering the group.

> [If a girl joined one of these groups] we would be less spontaneous I don't know how to tell you... yes even less crude (smiles), but it wouldn't be the same thing because some things then you can't send them because they are also specific things that also concern sex, things that also make you laugh anyway, we send them just for laughs but if there was a girl we wouldn't send them, it wouldn't be the same thing. (Carlo)

If a guy saw our chats, it would be a problem (smiles). I mean certain things I can only say to my female friends. (Paola)

The exclusively female/male WhatsApp groups function, in other words, as small communities of practice (Wenger, 1998) and as such have 'language, routines, sensibilities, artefacts, tools, stories, styles, etc.' (Wenger, 1998, p. 229). They represent a space that establishes a clear boundary between boys and girls that starts from an essential view of gender in which males and females are identified as separate by nature.

This type of discourse is also duplicated when discussing the substance of chats. For instance, I will provide an example focusing on humour, discourse about men and women and, lastly, the one related to support between friends.

Humour and Homosocial Complicity

According to the interviewees, WhatsApp groups are often used to convey funny content, both for women and men. Although they both use technically similar content (e.g. memes and links to Instagram or other internet pages), it seems that humour is declined differently among women and men.

When discussing about funny content, the women interviewed mostly referred to content concerning work or university, celebrities and domestic situations referring to the couples. Occasionally, a small number of participants brought up memes that joked about the dynamics between men and women, portraying males as awkward or subservient to their partners.

> They are silly memes, but they are funny... I don't know, for example the ones about exams we'll never pass. Or if something happens to someone famous that we maybe like... then we swap them. (Giulia)

> Every now and then, just for laughs, we send each other these memes about how males are..... I don't know, losing their temper immediately or doing things that make us angry. (Paola)

Conversely, when it comes to men, there is frequently a reference made to femininity and the dynamic within romantic relationships. References to women in this context are often related to sexuality. Memes connecting the menstrual cycle with aggressive behaviour or crude jokes about sexual activity were frequently used. Another recurring theme is the idea of the man losing power within a relationship and being reduced to simply obeying orders.

> Something that comes to mind is a recent humourous incident someone shared with me a few days ago, which left me in stitches. It involves a police officer, either a policewoman or a policeman in uniform, standing next to a car and stating, "It's 40 euros,"

indicating a fine, of course. The person inside the car responds with a humourous retort, saying, "OK, get in" [laughs].

Another instance involved sharing a meme with a friend who recently entered a relationship and became financially well-off. The meme featured a member of the British royal family and his wife gazing at him as if hypnotised, captioned with a witty remark like 'when he discovers you have no limit on your credit card'. (Ernesto)

Apart from what we talk about, in sharing funny content there seems to be a clear difference between women and men. For boys, humour continues to be an overtly expressed homosocial bonding element. For girls, hilarity seems to be an end in itself.

We share them for laughs. Then we move on to other talks. They are just moments…so…to laugh. Or to explain how we are, laughing… for example when we have exam anxiety. (Marta)

In the end, we are like that among friends. We're dicks. We always have a laugh. That's what you do with these groups more than anything else. You send these pictures, you laugh, you take the piss. You offend other people's mums (laughs). (Manolo)

As noted by Marta, for women, an emotional component is also integral. Consequently, the utilisation of humourous content serves as a means to convey and share emotions. Conversely, Manolo emphasises the gendered 'nature' inherent in the group's association with masculinity, where humour plays a central role in establishing and reinforcing homosocial bonds.

As other research has already shown (see, e.g. Ferrero Camoletto, 2013; Kehily & Nayak, 1997; Schnurr & Holmes, 2009), certain uses of language by men are capable of reproducing homosocial complicity (Flood, 2008). In particular, the use of humour is inextricably linked with the reproduction mechanisms of hegemonic masculinity (Ferrero Camoletto, 2013).

As we have seen, girls also use humour to make connections (Coates, 2007; Jenkins, 1985), but there is always a reference to emotional issues. Finally, it is interesting to note that men never talk about content on the male condition, except by referring to memes that speak about the men in the couple. Women, on the other hand, often mentioned other content capable of creating a more shared idea of femininity, namely that comes from creators (especially Instagram).

We also send each other links to stuff on instagram. Where we talk about women… but not just frivolous stuff. Also I don't know… the influencer talking about the fact that we women are on average paid less. Or stuff like that. Let's have a group, you know… solidarity among ourselves. (Camilla)

> Or even things for women let's say. Make-up, things for the body.
> to keep us beautiful or fit. (Silvia)

In this sense, we find, on the one hand, a series of contents with a more or less explicitly feminist subtext, on the other hand, videos or reels that refer to body care and thus bring back to a dimension of self-control of one's body.

Watching Boys, Watching Girls

In WhatsApp groups consisting only of men and women, one of the most frequently mentioned topics is the opposite sex. Girls said that boys were often talked about in their group, and boys said the same about girls.

> Well, it all comes down to girls. One way or another you end up talking about them. You know how boys are (laughs). (John)

> We talk about boys a lot too. In the sense of the ones we like or what they do, how they... behave. So we give each other advice. (Bianca)

The first difference between the two genders is that, whereas in groups of boys, references to other boys are rare, in groups of girls they often talk about other girls. In this case, the purpose is to gossip and often to judge the behaviour of other girls, when considered inappropriate or generally wrong.

> Well... then... I mean... let's talk about the other girls too. We gossip a bit... you know? We talk about what they did, who they went out with....... Sometimes we even criticise them. I'm a bit ashamed to say it, but sometimes we're a bit rude. But it's because we're among friends, so we're calmer. If someone dresses a bit badly, in short, it sometimes happens that we say to each other: 'Oh, did you see how Lucia was dressed today? (Bianca)

For men, as we will see later, the discourse on the feminine is not about advice or comparisons about differences, behaviour in general or anything else, but is mainly focused on women, with a meaning that is mostly related to desire and control.

In other words, alongside misogynistic jokes, we still often find rhetoric that describes women as sexual objects. Here, too, a distinction is made between a we (the group of men) and a they (the women), in which the group creates homosocial bonds at the (symbolic) expense of the woman in question.

In this case, different dynamics come into play. The first is the so-called digital girl-watching (Scarcelli, 2021): A photo – or video – of a girl is shared within the group, and comments ranging from sexual appreciation to slut-shaming follow. The comments may be accompanied by other photos of the same person, content that is easy to find in the profiles of unfortunate girls who, despite themselves, find themselves exposed to one of the characteristics of digital media, namely the presence of an invisible audience.

Thanks to the porosity that exists between one platform and another, narration and objectification are enriched by numerous visual elements, by practices that are not 'limited' to commenting aloud on a passing stranger – an act that is in any case a form of violence – but that create a kind of digital micro-dossier around the person observed at that moment. While Solove (2004) uses the term 'digital dossier' to refer to the possibility of large companies having access to our data, it is now possible for any user – on a smaller scale than the big players on the web (Amazon, Google, etc.) – to collect information and access other people's content by downloading various types of user-generated content – photos, videos, articles, etc. – and making them available to the public. Going back to what the boys told us in the interviews, this means being able to create real digital files containing mainly pictures of girls that you want to share in private chats and which could then be distributed elsewhere.

This could be pictures of girls known to at least one of the group members – the most common case in the interviews – and considered particularly attractive, or pictures of famous women, porn stars, models or strangers. In both cases, the comments are mainly, if not exclusively, directed at the woman's body and show us, as Ferrero Camoletto (2013) has already observed, how central it is for men to be able to demonstrate, in front of the rest of the group, their ability to control the girls' bodies and the gaze of the other men (Mac an Ghaill, 1994; Pascoe, 2007; Quinn, 2002).

As noted in a previous chapter, digital girl-watching takes place in three different ways. These modes, albeit with different meanings, also resonate within all-girl groups, as we shall see. First, there is slut-shaming, i.e. the often vulgar comments referring to the sexual activities or attitudes (often only presumed) of the person being talked about.

> Well... if I'm honest, we often slut-shame some of our colleagues. I don't mean all of them. The ones who are a bit more....... Flashy... a bit more... I don't know what word to use here... the ones who always dress a bit provocatively. Who act a bit provocative and post certain pictures a bit like that. So we exchange them and we say to each other... I'm a bit embarrassed in front of you... we say 'oh, did you see how slutty she is' or 'when she's in the office she doesn't look like that........ I'd like to have her like that on my desk tomorrow'. Or something like that. Come on, you understand. (Simone)

Even some of the girls in their groups repeat similar speeches. They reiterate that even among girls there is a certain control over the female body, which must not exceed certain (even if only supposed) limits. The punishment is to be labelled a bad girl.

> When we gossip, the names of a few colleagues who post these photos that are a bit... a bit hard, let's say. I mean, not porn, eh.

> But with a wink, with their bums in full view. And we laugh about it sometimes... other times we call them a bit excessive. What kind of idea do you want to give? Of course the idea you give is that you're a bit... slutty. (Gaia)

There is never any such talk when it comes to men.

A second type of digital girl-watching concerns the sharing of sexual models. In this case, we have a female counterpart that shows how within these groups even girls have to engage in behaviour that makes their heterosexuality explicit to other girls (Griffin, 2000).

The difference, however, lies in the nature of the talk. Although on both sides there are expressions of appreciation that are also related to sexual desire. In some all-male groups, these appreciations often lapse into rhetoric that continues to emphasise rape culture (Herman, 1989; Sills et al., 2016), objectifying the female body and apostrophising it with phrases that explicitly distance themselves from the idea of consensual intercourse. It works differently for women who make comments about men.

> When we were talking about this colleague, I remember sending each other the pictures she had on Instagram. One of my friends sent them and we immediately went to look at them on Instagram. She had her profile open so it was easy to see all the pictures and there were a lot of them where she was in a costume or something. And then this one was kind of showing off a little bit... So we made some jokes and I remember my friend, this guy's colleague, said 'tomorrow, as soon as she comes into the office, I'm going to put her up on the wall'. I was a bit surprised... I mean, it seemed like too much. But I didn't say anything. Obviously he just said that. (Federico)

> Well, one time a friend of mine went to a bar here in the city centre and saw this guy at the bar. Totally cool! So she immediately sent us the picture. And we commented on it. He was really cool, dark, tall, with green eyes. He looked like a model. So he sent it to us and said 'no girls, you have to come here'. (Carla)

A final mode is what we can call trophyisation. Again, there is a big difference between all-male and all-female groups. In general, when this type of practice is used in all-male groups, the person who shares the photo seeks the group's approval by showing the girl with whom he has had a sexual relationship or is dating, or by sharing intimate pictures sent by the girl.

> Once a friend of mine accidentally shared a video that someone had sent him. You couldn't see his face, eh... he removed it from the group soon after. But he wanted to be cool with us... so he wanted to show us this video of this girl he had met the night

> before and who was already sending him dirty videos (laughs). It wasn't a big deal... this one who was filming herself while pulling up her skirt in the bathroom... you could see a bit of her ass and a bit more. But you can imagine the comments afterwards. (Alberto)
>
> Look, it often happens that when one of us goes out with a really pretty girl, he sends us the photo to show off a bit. It doesn't always happen. So if you're lucky... because you need to be lucky... then you send everyone the profile picture of that girl. And usually we applaud in the group (laughs). (Michele)

These behaviours work for both men and women almost exclusively within homosocial groups. Outside these groups, sharing certain images is considered inappropriate or even wrong. This reinforces my view that these groups function as little islands where certain rules can be suspended because there is no fear of being sanctioned or of appearing deviant in the eyes of others, especially those of the opposite sex.

> Then we only do these things in this group, eh? If something comes out... I mean outside the group you lose the context and I think you risk being reported. In fact, from time to time I ask everyone to delete content. (Renato)
>
> If a friend of mine saw what we write to each other, he'd think we were crazy (laughs). Sometimes we look like little girls who are crazy about their idol and we're just talking about someone we met by accident. (Romina)

As already explained by Flood (2008) and taken up by Semenzin and Bainotti (2020), even in the case of WhatsApp groups, male connections feed the practices of violence, which in turn reinforce the bonds between men. A phenomenon, of objectification, which is certainly not new (Flood, 2008; Thompson & Wood, 2018), but which, intertwined with the affordances of the platform and the characteristics of digital media, finds new forms and forces (Renold et al., 2017; Ringrose & Harvey, 2015). Another example is that practices of objectification become ways in which hegemonic masculinity takes shape and is actualised (Rodriguez & Hernandez, 2018).

As can easily be observed, the practices we find in private WhatsApp chats where only men or women are present represent very specific performances towards other group members (Ferrero Camoletto & Bertone, 2017) and have as their background a certain kind of masculinity or femininity that is produced and reproduced through the display of (hetero)sexual desire (Pascoe, 2007). Women are often at the centre of these discourses, becoming objects of desire and control.

These practices of heterosexuality (Butler, 1990) show us some of how, even in digital platforms, masculinity and femininity are continually performed and claimed by respondents (Connell, 2005; West & Zimmerman, 1987). In other words, these groups become a means of highlighting and asserting one's gender identity in relation to a heteronormative view of desire within the peer group (Haywood et al., 2018; Kimmel, 2018).

WhatsApp Group as Support

A final aspect of relevance to gendering within female-only and male-only WhatsApp groups is the use of the platform to support other group members.

Here, too, the interviewees' accounts marked a clear dividing line between men's and women's use.

For men, these groups remain strongly associated with the performance of a certain type of masculinity, associated with joking and hegemonic masculine practices such as those we have described, in which the woman is mostly seen as a sexual object. The use of the group to share emotions or seek advice on affective issues is extremely rare (cf. Oransky & Marecek, 2009) and remains confined to one-to-one interactions in order to preserve a certain idea of masculinity that is still linked to a vision in which emotions are part of the feminine.

> This is not the place. If you need to talk about certain things, you do it with close friends, one or two at most. In these groups you end up badly if you open up. The teasing starts. Maybe not out of malice, but because they are groups made for something else. You don't expose yourself here. (Stefano)

> You're joking! No, no and then no! You don't talk about heart problems in a group or ask for advice. You talk to a friend. Then you laugh it all off. That's what certain relationships are based on. The other things you keep to yourself. (Mario)

In other words, it seems that homosociality in these groups cannot be transformed into bromance (Chen, 2012). Several interviewees stress that this is not the place for certain types of expressiveness. Women, on the other hand, often see the group as an emotional support.

> When my boyfriend broke up with me, this was the first place I wrote it down. I needed my friends, all of them! So I wrote there and they replied immediately. But it happens a lot, advice, not just where to buy something... but also how to behave. We help each other, we stay close. We also laugh. It's not a crying group (laughs) but it's not just a laughing group either. (Silvia)

The support the girls give each other is not limited to emotional support, but also becomes a mutual control of one's appearance or clothing. Something that is never mentioned by the male interviewees.

> We also help each other when we want to know how we look in an outfit... or when one of us is not really comfortable with her body and we send each other naked pictures of ourselves. But not for sexual purposes (laughs). To say, look how I look here, here I've put on weight. I have stretch marks. And we usually say to each other: 'But no love, you look beautiful'. Then you know that your friends are telling you that, but you still feel good. (Caterina)

Or, as Barbara says, it's a way of looking out for friends when they go out with someone they don't know. In this case, the affordances of the platform play a central role, as they allow you to share your location in real time so that others know where you are.

> Then I use this group a lot lately. I go out with a few guys and sometimes, I have to say, I'm afraid of meeting the wrong person, let's say. Someone who might want to hurt you. You know, on Tinder everyone is nice... well, not everyone (laughs). But how do you know it's not some crazy person who wants to kill you? So we always share the location in the group and give each other updates from time to time. It makes us feel safer. Then... if someone kills you, they still kill you. But it's still an extra feeling of security. (Barbara)

Conclusion

In the narratives with which the interviewees describe their presence and interactions within the WhatsApp groups, certain behaviours closely related to masculinity making were identified that we can intertwine with the characteristics of communities of practice described by Paechter (2003): the negotiation of meaning and the description of practice as a source of coherence in the community, a learning process, a boundary and the relationship between global and local.

In the private WhatsApp groups we observed through the interviewees' stories, there is indeed a constant production, reproduction and negotiation of what it means to be a man or to be a woman. As Paechter (2003) explains when discussing the negotiation of meaning, in order to be an effective member of the community – in this case the WhatsApp group – one has to share its fundamental meanings. The practices I have described are recognised by those who are part of the WhatsApp group and this happens through the mutual commitment of the members to a common project that results in a shared repertoire of performances. This creates consistency in what members can do or not do, what is important and what is not, what is worthy of attention and what is not, what is worth talking about and what is better not to say.

The practices of masculinity and femininity we have seen become part of a learning process in which there is continuous involvement in the development of the practice itself. We do not speak, therefore, of a passive process, but a dynamic one that is continually renegotiated by the members belonging to it. Languages, artefacts and values are shared and the boys often describe those places as safe from symbolic sanctions coming from others who, not understanding those expressions of identity, would deny them what they interpret as the true masculine essence.

Even more evident is another characteristic of communities of practice, as Paechter (2003) defines it, namely practice as boundary. Communities of practice cannot be understood independently of one another; by entering into the configuration of one of them, one also comes into contact with all the relations it forms with the rest of the social fabric.[1] Masculinity and femininity are defined, at least in part, in contrast to those outside the community of reference, in our case the WhatsApp group. The boundary between those inside and those outside a certain circle shows how situational gender differences are, something that can be emphasised at certain times – the male-only/the female-only chats – and ignored at others (Thorne, 1993).

Finally, the last aspect brings us towards the practice as the relationship between *global and local:* neither communities of practice nor the identities associated with them are formed in isolation. Masculinities and femininities, however local, do not form in a social and cultural vacuum; they are influenced by mass media, popular culture, normative backgrounds and all other forms of masculinities and femininities. Thus, although communities of practice are necessarily local, they incorporate within them practices that may be common to a much wider constellation such as the manosphere (Scarcelli, 2021).

References

Archer, L., Hollingworth, S., & Halsall, A. (2007). 'University is not for me – I'm a Nike person'. Urban working class young people's negotiations of 'style', identity and educational engagement. *Sociology, 41*(2), 219–237. https://doi.org/10.1177/0038038507074798

Binhammer, K. (2006). Female homosociality and the exchange of men: Mary Robinson's Walsingham. *Women's Studies, 35*(3), 221–240.

Bird, R. S. (2018). Welcome to the men's club: Homosociality and the maintenance of hegemonic masculinity. In E. W. Morris & F. Blume Oeur (Eds.), *Unmasking masculinities: Men and society* (pp. 14–23). SAGE.

boyd, d. (2008). Why youth (heart) social network sites: The role of networked publics in teenage social life. In D. Buckingham (Ed.), *Youth identity and digital media* (pp. 119–142). MIT Press.

boyd, d. (2014). *It's complicated: The social lives of networked teens.* Yale University Press.

Braun, V., & Clarke, V. (2006). Using thematic analysis in psychology. *Qualitative Research in Psychology, 3*(2), 77–101. https://doi.org/10.1191/1478088706qp063oa

---

[1] In this, Paechter's (2003) thought differs from Wenger's formulations, since for the English author the boundaries of masculinities – as well as those of femininities – are not formally fixed as Wenger (1998) describes.

Buckingham, D. (2008). Introducing identity. In D. Buckingham (Ed.), *Youth, identity, and digital media* (pp. 1–24). The MIT Press.
Buckingham, D., & Bragg, S. (2004). *Young people, sex and the media: The facts of life?* Palgrave Macmillan.
Butler, J. (1990). *Gender trouble: Feminism and the subversion of identity*. Routledge.
Butler, J. (2004). *Undoing gender*. Routledge.
Chen, E. J. (2012). Caught in a bad bromance. *Texas Journal of Women and the Law*, *21*(2), 241–266.
Coates, J. (2007). Talk in a play frame: More on laughter and intimacy. *Journal of Pragmatics*, *39*(1), 29–49.
Connell, R. W. (2005). *Masculinities*. University of California Press.
Connell, R. W., & Messerschmidt, J. W. (2005). Hegemonic masculinity rethinking the concept. *Gender & Society*, *19*(6), 829–859. https://doi.org/10.1177/0891243205278639
Cook, J., & Hasmath, R. (2014). The discursive construction and performance of gendered identity on social media. *Current Sociology*, *62*(7), 975–993. https://doi.org/10.1177/0011392114550008
Corbin, J. M., & Strauss, A. (1990). Grounded theory research: Procedures, canons, and evaluative criteria. *Qualitative Sociology*, *13*(1), 3–21. https://doi.org/10.1007/BF00988593
Couldry, N. (2012). *Media, society, world: Social theory and digital media practice*. Polity.
De Ridder, S., & Van Bauwel, S. (2015). Youth and intimate media cultures: Gender, sexuality, relationships, and desire as storytelling practices in social networking sites. *Communications*, *40*(3), 319–340. https://doi.org/10.1515/commun-2015-0012
Döring, N., Reif, A., & Poeschl, S. (2016). How gender-stereotypical are selfies? A content analysis and comparison with magazine advertisement. *Computers in Human Behavior*, *55*, 955–962.
Ferrero Camoletto, R. (2013). Laughing and talking about sex: A plural construction of heterosexual masculinities. *Health and Society*, *2004*(2), 59–76. https://doi.org/10.3280/SES2013-002004
Ferrero Camoletto, R., & Bertone, C. (2017). Between men. Investigating homosociality to navigate transformations of the masculine. *About Gender*, *6*(11), 45–73. https://doi.org/10.15167/2279-5057/AG2017.6.11.395
Flood, M. (2008). Men, sex, and homosociality. How bonds between men shape their sexual relations with women. *Men and Masculinities*, *10*(3), 339–359. https://doi.org/10.1177%2F1097184X06287761
Frosh, S., Phoenix, A., & Pattman, R. (2002). Young masculinities. Understanding boys. In *Contemporary society*. Palgrave.
Griffin, C. (2000). Absence that matter: Constructions of sexuality in studies of young women's friendship. *Feminism & Psychology*, *10*(2), 227–245. https://doi.org/10.1177/0959353500010002003
Hall, T., Coffey, A., & Williamson, H. (1999). Self, space and place: Youth identities and citizenship. *British Journal of Sociology of Education*, *20*, 501–513. https://doi.org/10.1080/01425699995236
Hammarén, N., & Johansson, T. (2014). Homosociality: In between power and intimacy. *Sage Open*, *4*(1), 1–11. https://doi.org/10.1177/2158244013518057

Haywood, C., Johansson, T., Hammarén, N., Herz, M., & Ottemo, A. (2018). *The conundrum of masculinity: Hegemony, homosociality, homophobia and heteronormativity*. Routledge.

Herman, D. (1989). The rape culture. In J. Freeman (Ed.), *Women a feminist perspective* (4th ed., pp. 20–44). Mountain View.

Janghorban, R., Roudsari, R. L., & Taghipour, A. (2014). Skype interviewing: The new generation of online synchronous interviewing in qualitative research. *International Journal of Qualitative Studies on Health and Well-Being*, 9(1), 1–2. https://doi.org/10.3402/qhw.v9.24152

Jenkins, M. (1985). What's so funny?: Joking among women. In S. Bremner, N. Caskey, & B. Moonwomon (Eds.), *Proceedings of the first Berkeley women and language conference* (pp. 135–151). Women and Language Group.

Kapidzic, S., & Herring, S. C. (2015). Race, gender, and self-presentation in teen profile photographs. *New Media & Society*, 17, 958–976. https://doi.org/10.1177/1461444813520301

Kehily, M. J., & Nayak, A. (1997). 'Lads and Laughter': Humour and the production of heterosexual hierarchies. *Gender and Education*, 9(1), 69–88. https://doi.org/10.1080/09540259721466

Kimmel, M. (2004). *The gendered society* (2nd ed.). Oxford University Press.

Kimmel, M. (2018). Hooking up: Sex in guyland. In E. W. Morris & F. Blume Oeur (Eds.), *Unmasking masculinities: Men and society* (pp. 261–271). Sage.

Lave, J., & Wenger, E. (1991). *Situated learning: Legitimate peripheral participation*. Cambridge University Press.

Lipman-Blumen, J. (1976). Toward a homosocial theory of sex roles. An explanation of the sex segregation of social institutions. *Signs: Journal of Women in Culture and Society*, 1(3), 15–31.

Lobe, B., Livingstone, S., Olafsson, K., & Simões, J. A. (Eds.). (2008). *Best practice research guide: How to research children and online technologies in comparative perspective*. EU Kids Online. http://eprints.lse.ac.uk/21658/

Lyman, P. (1987). The fraternal bond as a joking relationship. A case study of the role of sexist jokes in male group bonding. In M. Kimmel (Ed.), *Changing men. New directions in research in men and masculinity* (pp. 148–163). Sage.

Mac an Ghaill, M. (1994). *The making of men: Masculinities, sexualities and schooling*. Open University Press.

Metcalfe, S. N., & Llewellyn, A. (2020). "It's just the thing you do": Physical and digital fields, and the flow of capital for young people's gendered identity negotiation. *Journal of Adolescent Research*, 35(1), 84–110.

Nayak, D. A., & Kehily, D. M. J. (2007). *Gender, youth and culture*. Palgrave Macmillan.

Odenbring, Y., & Johansson, T. (2020). Just a joke? The thin line between teasing, harrassment and violence among teenege boys in lower secondary school. *The Journal of Men's Studies*, 1–17. https://doi.org/10.1177/1060826520934771

Oransky, M., & Marecek, J. (2009). "I'm not going to be a girl": Masculinity and emotions in boys' friendships and peer groups. *Journal of Adolescent Research*, 24(2), 218–241. https://doi.org/10.1177/0743558408329951

Paechter, C. (2003). Masculinities and femininities as communities of practice. *Women's Studies International Forum*, 26(1), 69–77. https://doi.org/10.1016/S0277-5395(02)00356-4

Pascoe, C. J. (2007). *Dude, you're a fag. Masculinity and sexuality in high school.* University of California Press.

Quinn, B. A. (2002). Sexual harassment and masculinity: The power and meaning of "girl watching". *Gender & Society, 16*(3), 386–402. https://doi.org/10.1177/0891243202016003007

Renold, E., Bragg, S., Jackson, C., & Ringrose, J. (2017). *How gender matters to children and young people living in England.* Cardiff University.

Riessman, C. (2002). Analysis of personal narratives. In J. F. Gubrium & J. A. Holstein (Eds.), *Handbook of interview research* (pp. 695–710). Sage.

Ringrose, J. (2011). Are you sexy, flirty or a slut? Exploring sexualization and how teen girls perform/negotiate digital sexual identity on social networking sites. In R. Gill & C. Schraff (Eds.), *New femininities: Postfeminism, neoliberalism and identity* (pp. 99–116). Palgrave.

Ringrose, J. (2012). *Post-feminist education? Girls and the sexual politics of schooling.* Routledge.

Ringrose, J., & Harvey, L. (2015). Boobs, back-off, six packs and bits: Mediated body parts, gendered reward, and sexual shame in teens' sexting images. *Continuum: Journal of Media & Cultural Studies, 29*(2), 205–217. https://doi.org/10.1080/10304312.2015.1022952

Rodriguez, N. S., & Hernandez, T. (2018). Dibs on that sexy piece of ass: Hegemonic masculinity on TFM girls Instagram account. *Social Media + Society, 4*(1), 1–12. https://doi.org/10.1177/2056305118760809

Scarcelli, C. M. (2015a). *Intimità digitali.* Franco Angeli.

Scarcelli, C. M. (2015b). "It's disgusting but…": Adolescent girls' relationship to internet pornography as gender performance. *Porn Studies, 2*(1–2), 237–249. https://doi.org/10.1080/23268743.2015.1051914

Scarcelli, C. M. (2021). Manosphere periferiche. Ragazzi, omosocialità e pratiche digitali. *AG About Gender – International Journal of Gender Studies, 10*(19), 1–34.

Schnurr, S., & Holmes, J. (2009). Using humor to do masculinity at work. In N. R. Norrik & D. Chiaro (Eds.), *Humor in interaction* (pp. 101–124). John Benjamins Publishing Company.

Sedgwick, E. K. (1985). *Between men: English literature and male homosocial desire.* Columbia University Press.

Semenzin, S., & Bainotti, L. (2020). The use of Telegram for non-consensual dissemination of intimate images: Gendered affordances and the construction of masculinities. *Social Media + Society, 6*(4). https://doi.org/10.1177/2056305120984453

Sills, S., Pickens, C., Beach, K., Jones, L., Calder-Dawe, O., Benton-Greig, P., & Gavey, N. (2016). Rape culture and social media: Young critics and a feminist counterpublic. *Feminist Media Studies, 16*(6), 935–951. https://doi.org/10.1080/14680777.2015.1137962

Silverman, D. (2013). *Doing qualitative research. A practical handbook.* Sage.

Solove, D. J. (2004). *The digital person: Technology and privacy in the information age* (Vol. 1). NYU Press.

Statista. (2022). WhatsApp – Statistics & facts. https://www.statista.com/topics/2018/whatsapp/. Accessed on April 14, 2022.

Thompson, C., & Wood, M. A. (2018). A media archaeology of the creepshot. *Feminist Media Studies*, *18*(4), 560–574. https://doi.org/10.1080/14680777.2018.1447429

Thorne, B. (1993). *Gender play. Girls and boys in school*. Rutgers University Press.

Tiidenberg, K., & Gómez Cruz, E. (2015). Selfies, images and the re-making of the body. *Body & Society*, *21*(4), 77–102. https://doi:10.1177/1357034X15592465

Tiidenberg, K., & van der Nagel, E. (2020). *Sex and social media*. Emerald Publishing Limited.

Wenger, E. (1998). Communities of practice: Learning as a social system. *Systems Thinker*, *9*(5). https://thesystemsthinker.com/communities-of-practice-learning-as-a-social-system/

West, C., & Zimmerman, D. H. (1987). Doing gender. *Gender & Society*, *1*(2), 125–151.

West, C., & Zimmerman, D. H. (2009). Accounting for doing gender. *Gender & Society*, *23*(1), 112–122. https://doi.org/10.1177/0891243208326529

Willett, R. (2008). *Consumer citizens online: Structure, agency, and gender in online participation*. MacArthur Foundation Digital Media and Learning Initiative.

Willis, P. (1990). *Common culture: Symbolic work at play in the everyday cultures of young*. Open University Press.

Chapter 9

Community Engagement With Health Messages on Reproductive Health in an Age of Misinformation and Political Polarisation: A Case Study of the US NGO Open Arms in Florida[1,2]

Carolina Matos

City University of London, UK

Abstract

How do young members of disadvantaged communities in countries like the United States, which has been affected by political polarisation and attacks from far-right populist politicians on women's rights, make sense of messages on reproductive health in the misinformation age? Following from the conclusion of a Global Challenges Research Fund (GCRF)-funded project which examined how 52 non-governmental organisations (NGOs) from across the world are making use of communications tools for advocacy on sexuality and reproductive health (SRHR), this study engaged with communities in Florida, US, in partnership with the NGO *Open Arms*, to assess how they consume media content on reproductive health, particularly on

---

[1] This research builds on a previous GCRF project, published as a manuscript by McGill Queen University Press (*Gender, Communications and Reproductive Health in International Development*, 2023).

[2] This chapter benefitted from the contribution of the research assistance of Songyi Liang, PhD student at the School of Communication, University of Miami, US, in the collection of data.

Young Adulthood Across Digital Platforms, 145–164
Copyright © 2025 Carolina Matos
Published under exclusive licence by Emerald Publishing Limited
doi:10.1108/978-1-83753-524-820241009

146   Carolina Matos

social media, within a context of proliferation of 'fake news'.[3,4] Applying a feminist methodological epistemology and a participatory approach which aims to 'empower' participants, two focus groups with males and females from diverse ethnicities, between 18 and 40 years of age, were conducted with *Open Arms* in July and August 2023. Findings revealed how groups are exposed to a lot of inaccurate news, misinformation and 'myths' around fertility treatments on the web, and how they feel there is a need for better scientific information on reproductive health in the media and on the internet, one which is also more 'entertaining' and which speaks directly to their experiences. This study concludes in favour of improving health literacy approaches as well as communications on reproduction health.

Keywords: Community engagement; NGOs; gender equality; social media; reproductive health; misinformation

Introduction

Gender politics and women's rights in the last decades have reached centre stage of the so-called sexual (and cultural) wars that have been fought in various countries throughout the world (Cornwall et al., 2008; Friedman, 2003; Matos, 2023), ranging from Eastern Europe to the United States. The last decades have seen substantial growth throughout much of the world, including in Europe, of 'populist' far-right political parties which have managed to intelligently navigate the anxieties and fears of large sectors of disenfranchised citizens, many dissatisfied with the limits of Western political democracy and its failure to deliver on promises of equality and social inclusion. They have managed to capitalise electorally on the climate of economic (and cultural) insecurity unleashed in the last decades particularly in the post-2008 and COVID-19 global recession and pandemic context, culminating in cultural backlashes against the advancements of the 'gender agenda' and other rights obtained during the decades of the 1980s and 1990s at the UN conferences, such as at the 1994 International Conference on Population and Development (ICPD) in Cairo and the 1995 Fourth World Conference on Women in Beijing (Cornwall et al., 2008; Correa et al., 1994; Friedman, 2003).

Politics around sexual and reproductive health and rights (SRHR) has thus started to take on centre stage in the political arena, entering even presidential campaigns throughout the world, even after 'populist' presidents like Trump in

---

[3]The GCRF has supported cutting-edge research which aims to address challenges faced by developing countries, such as the UN SDGs, with the aim of maximising impact to improve opportunities.

[4]This study draws from some of the data explored in the AEJMC paper 'Use of focus groups research on health communication messages on SRHR: experiences of "empowerment" from the global South in an age of misinformation on gender and minority rights' (August 2023).

the United States and Bolsonaro in Brazil left office in 2020 and 2022, respectively. Various ultra-conservative and religious groups have engaged in both online and offline protests against LGBTQ and minority rights, including targeting issues such as climate change, to the mandatory policies around COVID-19 vaccinations and women's reproduction. Feeling 'empowered' by (floating) voter support and resources, these groups often manipulate information in the mediated political and global public sphere, particularly on online platforms, inciting prejudice and stigmatisation around complex issues such as women's health, and which are still also subject to the impact of cultural, social or religious pressures. Thus information on reproductive health that circulates in the mediated public sphere is often ideologically manipulated, having an impact on women's rights to have access to accurate information that could assist them in making decisions and choices, thus feeding on to fears and cultural anxieties which can further lead to disengagement from the consumption of health communication messages as well as self-censorship practices.

Two focus groups with members of disadvantaged communities in the Miami-Dade country were thus conducted in July and August 2023 with the NGO *Open Arms*, a community centre in the Miami capital which provides various types of services. The sessions aimed to engage with younger segments of the population from diverse ethnicities and backgrounds, from students to the unemployed and particularly within the reproduction age, in order to better understand how they exercise their reproductive rights and how they consume communication messages at a time of growing polarisation around women's health rights. Social media networks and new technologies, such as *WhatsApp*, also are emerging as spaces for both obtaining accurate and scientific information about the topic as well as being sites where misinformation on SRHR circulates, seeking to create confusion and adding fuel to the polarised and ideological climate around reproductive health. Results showed also that there is some awareness on what constitutes 'true' or factual information from 'fake' stories and narratives, as well as an appetite for more accurate and 'attractive' information that can speak better to people's lived experiences.

A core question asked here was how does misinformation about women's rights affect people's perceptions, and how does this translate into impediments to the advancement of policies on reproductive health? The focus groups explored understandings around sexual and reproductive health and rights, and examined also the media consumption habits of the participants as well as their engagement with communications around SRHR matters. I argue here that not only communication messages on SRHR need to be improved, but also there is a need to improve discourses and rhetoric around reproductive health in the mediated public sphere so that people can exercise their rights more fully, something which is also dependent on better quality public information campaigns and NGO advocacy around the topic, but which also includes attention to investments in media and health literacy practices.

Before discussing the methodology and findings, the debate on how sexual and reproductive health and rights is articulated in the mediated public sphere is examined, including also the role of new technologies and social media in the advocacy on SRHR and the ways it can be used for social change.

The Debate on Sexual and Reproductive Health and Rights (SRHR) in the US and in the Floridian Context: An Assessment

The decision to overturn the *Roe v. Wade* legislation in June 2022 in the United States has since then had serious consequences on the lives of various groups of women in many different forms, affecting couples' decisions for choosing fertility treatments or not to problems created for women who want to terminate their pregnancies due to foetal abnormalities, among others. Although the measures have resulted in abortion bans in 13 US states, the tide has not favoured the electoral chances of the Republican party as perhaps previously anticipated, with the latter losing voters' support amidst a boost to the Democrat's chances of re-election in the 2024 presidential campaign.

The rise of 'populist' right-wing movements throughout the world has culminated in various push backs against the advancement of progressive policies on women's rights, with accusations made by conservative groups of the existence of a supposedly 'gender ideology' which has been 'imposed' by governments, the corporate world and progressives on the legislations of countries and their national policies throughout the world since the decades of the 1980s (Correa & Petchesky, 1994; Friedman, 2003; Harcourt, 2009). These attacks against reproductive health rights have been in the context of rising economic inequalities, giving rise to fear and anxieties against 'immigrants' and other minority groups, as well as resistance to advancements in the women's rights agenda.

In Florida, the governor Ron De Santis, a Republican frontrunner for the US presidency, has followed in Trump's footsteps and has made the 'cultural wars' the hallmark of his presidential bid. De Santis has been notorious for having attacked gender and LGBTQ rights, as well as race education and policy. In 2022 he signed a 15-week abortion ban passed by the Republican controlled legislature. He also passed the highly criticised 'Don't Say Gay' law, approving a ban on classroom instruction about sexual orientation and gender identity across all grade levels, including restricting gender-transition treatments for minors in clinics as well as introducing new guidelines on the teaching of Black history in Florida's state schools.

This highly politicised climate is thus also contributing to a growing distrust from communities of institutions, posing also a whole series of challenges on how people consume news and traditional media reporting on complex topics such as SRHR. The online sphere has thus emerged as both a space where there are more opportunities for access to specialised and trusted medical information on SRHR, either through specific websites or through information shared by NGOs working in the field, as well as being a site for the spread of polarised political information, misinformation and lies on SRHR. The choice of conducting fieldwork in Florida was thus due to some of these factors, and the fact that the state is, alongside others in the United States, such as Texas and North Carolina, a central place where political battles around 'sexual and cultural wars' are taking place among political groups, and who are also posing a threat to Western political liberalism and the institutions of democracy and governance.

Thus the Floridian NGO *Open Arms*, which took part in this research, is a community-based agency which provides services to the community of Miami-Dade County residents. It is involved in capacity building training as a means of diversifying funding and works with a series of partners, from the State of Florida Department of Children and Families to the City of Miami Beach. It aims to offer services to the community for them to be 'self-sufficient'. Among its core values, the organisation underlines that it is to improve the conditions of the social services for the economically disadvantaged people in the community'. It is to the feminist epistemological and theoretical concerns of this research, and to a brief examination of the literature on the forms of engagement with science and health messages, within the specific context of this research on SRHR advocacy communications, that I turn to next.

Feminist Epistemologies, Social Media Use and Engagement With Communication Messages on SRHR in an Age of 'Fake News'

The debate on SRHR in the mediated public sphere, both locally and globally, is still quite poor and subject to misinformation, stigma as well as ideological manipulation. This hinders the ability to provide in-depth, detailed and critical information on SRHR, permitting citizens to question messages, as well as making connections between reproductive health rights to issues of poverty, inequality and well-being. As it stands today debates on reproductive health, as well as on sexuality issues and bodily autonomy, are still largely restricted to public health professionals, NGO advocates and specialised feminist movements, mainly to those 'in the know', perpetuating 'echo chambers' and inequalities in knowledge and access to information and rights.

Compelled with media and health literacy problems that often members of disadvantaged communities can experience due to a lack of educational resources and access to health services, all of this can place an added risk on the capacity of community members to access quality information on reproductive health matters. This is due to them being exposed to misinformation and manipulation of messages in the mediated public sphere, particularly on online platforms. Many thus can have limited understanding of both their health and civic rights, often assuming from the information that circulates through the overall media that it is all about 'forcing abortion practices' by 'feminists that cultivate a culture of death'. There can thus be little understanding of how the acronym SRHR is an umbrella term that can encompass pregnancy issues, infertility treatments, comprehensive sexual education, maternal health and gender-based violence against sexual identities.

As Ratzan (2001) has argued, health is an essential component of global civil society. It is through the media and various communication channels that people have access to important information on health matters that affect their lives. Today many are getting information on reproductive health from a variety of media sources, from the private sphere of the family to educational professionals and the media, being thus highly susceptible to influence from media accounts or peer pressure. These findings share some similarities with others revealed in the literature on science communications (e.g. Scrimshaw, 2019, p. 265), which has shown how people process scientific facts through filters, including generational differences, culture, language, literacy and socio-economic status. Moreover, the reality is that people throughout the world, and particularly more in disadvantaged communities in developing countries, engage with media messages through a pattern that includes distrust of traditional institutions and a tendency to seek information for themselves on online networks, thus moving away from the mainstream media. There is a propensity to interpret facts differently, and to not necessarily act on information given. Information is thus processed amidst a series of personal and cultural values and beliefs, all of which are filtered through people's lived experiences (Scrimshaw, 2019).

The findings of the previous GCRF research revealed that there is still insufficient engagement with the affected communities and that there are problems with NGOs communicating on reproductive health. The conclusions of the project pointed to the need to assess the reasons for the current 'resistance' of the targeted groups, as well as the anxieties towards sexuality and reproduction issues due to cultural and social constraints, including political pressures and economic barriers. Some NGOs recognised that public health arguments, such as the mere adherence to advocating reproductive health based on 'facts', is not enough and is not 'winning hearts', at a particular time where emotions and cultural values around various political, cultural and social issues runs high amidst a context of increasing political polarisation and rise of opinionated commentary in the media and online sphere around a range of women's issues.

Many feminists have thus argued that the increased and active use of digital platforms for gender politics has influenced and shaped feminism in the 21st century by giving rise to different kinds of conversations and new configurations of activism. Despite assessments of the limitations of the internet in deepening democracy and combating structural inequalities, a key discussion has been the potential of the internet for citizenship, political mobilisation, debate in the global public sphere and the expansion of transnational feminist mobilisation and creative modes of protest. Digital platforms are seen as offering opportunities for the dissemination of feminist ideas, shaping discourses around gender and sexuality for instance, either through more conventional channels, such as through the advocacy practices of women's organisations and NGOs, or the activism of grassroots women's groups and of other individual bloggers, from politicians to social media influencers.

Feminist scholars in the last decades have examined the potential of new technologies for political mobilisation amidst the contradictions of these new technologies and how these can be seen as both 'empowering' and enabling as well as oppressive or 'precarious' for women (Fotopoulou, 2016; Mendes et al., 2019). Here the 'female body' emerges also as a site of *precariousness* within neoliberalism, with feminist politics being played out with all the contradictions of our current post-modern and capitalist age (Baer, 2016; Fotopoulou, 2016). In previous research, I (Matos, 2017), alongside other scholars (e.g. Harcourt, 2013; Khamis, 2015), examined the potential offered by new technologies, and particularly by social media platforms, to advocate for women in developing countries of the global South, particularly within the Latin American context. Similar to other authors (Fotopoulou, 2016; McPherson, 2015; Mendes et al., 2019; Michaeilidou, 2018; Wilkins, 2016), I conducted research on women's organisations to assess their advocacy communications efforts, and how they have sought to push for social change in the field of reproductive health (Matos, 2023).

Developing further from the results of the GCRF project, I have been concerned with also the *educational* potential of new technologies, and how these can provide more accurate and 'entertaining' information on SRHR that can be 'empowering' for women's communities and disadvantaged groups. Thus I am interested in assessing the potential of media, and of online communications in particular also, to strengthen health literacy skills, providing more avenues for marginalised communities to engage with health matters from a citizenship perspective so that these groups can exercise their rights. I argue here that this will thus better enable them to actively participate in the mediated public sphere of debate on SRHR, including in the *co-construction* of communication messages, content and campaigns on this.

Methodology

There has been a continuous rise of social and economic inequalities across much of the Western world in the last decades, with stagnation – and even reversal – of the conquests obtained in the area of women's rights and reproductive health, with the shift away from the 'population control' discourse to the *human rights* framework not having been fully realised 'on the ground' (Cornwall et al., 2008; Correa et al., 1994; Harcourt, 2009). Moreover, the persistence of structural social and gender inequalities also has not deemed the feminist political movement, as well as its critique of the dominance of empiricism in research (Harding, 1993; McHugh, 2020; Montell, 1999; Wilkinson, 1998), obsolete. The need to engage with marginalised communities *from their standpoint* (Harding, 1993) has remained more relevant than ever, particularly within a context where inequalities have not been fully tackled, with a lot of research coming from the Social Sciences still benefitting largely the upper strata of societies. Thus applying a *feminist epistemological standpoint* which argues in favour of 'situated knowledges' (Haraway, 1991) and the relevance of focus groups as an important method that 'empowers' less powerful participants (Harding, 1993; Montell, 1999; Wilkinson, 1998), I have sought to engage with women members of local communities, many who have been the prime targeted publics of health communication messages on SRHR in order to better understand how these groups interpret content.

Questions posed by feminists during the 1980s and 1990s also included the existence or not of a 'feminist method', as well as how research can be conducted more ethically, reducing biases and harm done to participants. Decades after the formulation of these critiques, these questions continue to be relevant for feminist researchers who are committed to conducting research that engages with real world problems, and which attempts to tackle gender inequalities globally. This research has previously done this. I have thus adopted here both a feminist methodological and theoretical epistemological perspective, as I believe that these intellectual concerns have not disappeared from the feminist debates within the Social Sciences, and perhaps are more relevant than ever in a context where neoliberalism has not fully delivered, becoming fragile to attacks from far-right groups.

This study conducted two focus groups with the local Miami NGO *Open Arms* during the months of July and August to examine how sectors of disadvantaged communities are making sense of health messages on SRHR within a highly politicised context, as examined previously. As active users of social media as a means of obtaining information on health-related issues, I was concerned with identifying patterns of engagement, talk and discourse online on media messages on reproductive health, particularly to try to understand how information is processed, how the participants understand these as well as how susceptible they are to manipulation. The NGO *Open Arms Community Centre* recruited the participants from the community programmes that they work with to be part of the focus groups sessions.[5]

Both focus groups were done online via Zoom. When it came to the power dynamics of both, the first group of the younger age range (18–24) saw a dominance of the two males in the conversation during the conduction of the focus groups in comparison to the other females. This was not the same with the older group (25–40), which consisted of all females and saw a more even discussion, although similar to the first, there were also some participants that had more knowledge and/or felt more comfortable to speak and to articulate their thoughts more than others. The consent from the participants was obtained orally before the session, guaranteeing them confidentiality and anonymity. Each participant received a small fee payment in the amount of 50 dollars as Amazon vouchers.

The focus groups were divided into two parts: the first part attempted to examine their knowledge on SRHR as well as to assess their forms of engagement with communications, particularly looking at the ways in which they sought out information on the web, and if they could tell if the information is accurate or not or if they were being subject to manipulation. The second part sought to evaluate their consumption patterns, particularly looking at the type of media they consume and the information that they find available on reproductive health. Questions included what vehicles they accessed, as well as how they sought out information on SRHR. Both groups were asked to image themselves as communication professionals, and how they would construct communication strategies and campaigns on reproductive health in accordance with their needs,

---

[5]See the full website of the organisation here: https://openarmscommunitycenter.org/

including being asked what they felt these communication messages lacked and how they would seek to improve them.

The PI and Co-PI conducted the sessions in a participatory and egalitarian manner. The first group had a total of eight participants who were predominantly Hispanic (only two were included as 'non-hispanic'), and half claimed to be 'white' and the other half 'Blacks'. The yearly income disclosed varied between 0 and 30,000 dollars, with the average income being 15,000. There were also two males in the first group, and all self-disclosed themselves as being 'students', with four also claiming to be 'employed'. None of them disclosed a disability or said they were unemployed. The second consisted of a total of six people between 25 and 40 years of age, and out of these, three claimed to be employed and the other three unemployed. All of them were of Hispanic ethnicity. There was one white participant, one American Indian and all the others were Black. The income disclosed ranged from 0 to 40,000 dollars annually, with most indicating an average income of 20,000.

The data collected from both focus groups was examined through thematic analysis. An Excel spreadsheet was created to include the categories, which consisted of a total of 10 phrases which aimed to capture the main themes explored in the sessions. These were: (1) *knowledge of SRHR*; (2) *women's problems and choice*; (3) *information/disinformation*; (4) *campaigns on SRHR*; (5) *media vehicles*; (6) *SRHR information on the internet*; (7) *talk on SRHR in the private sphere* (NGOs, doctors, schools, etc.); (8) *US and local media coverage*; (9) *personal narratives on SRHR;* and (10) *improvements in communications on SRHR*.

Findings and Discussion

The results of the focus groups showed some similarities with the sessions carried out in Brazil in July 2021, in partnership with the Brazilian NGO *Reprolatina* in Campinas São Paulo. Similarly to the sessions conducted in Florida, US, the all female groups in Campinas, from both age groups, managed also to make connections to the political climate of their countries (e.g. Bolsonaro in Brazil, De Santis in Florida within the legacy of Trumpian politics), and to the particularities of their local contexts, highlighting the impact of patriarchal thinking on knowledge and on assumptions on SRHR as well as overall attitudes on women's sexuality and reproductive health.

The groups in both local contexts underlined the need for more 'direct' communication campaigns that could speak directly to the everyday experiences of women. They also underlined the lack of circulation of information on the topic in the mediated public sphere. The results for both settings share similarities with the findings obtained from the GCRF project, which showed that many NGOs are seeking to combine 'hard facts', e.g. public health arguments, with 'emotions' and communication formats that make use of human interest stories to reach out to larger communities.

The presence of two males in the first group slightly skewed the tone of the conversations towards their perspectives over those of the female participants.

154 *Carolina Matos*

However, the PI and CO-PI worked to ensure everyone's inclusion. Many personal narratives and stories focused also on the proliferation of 'myths' and lies that circulated online. The participants also showed that they exercised critical thinking in relation to the messages that are available and that they consume, stating that the internet is their main source of information when it comes to SRHR matters, from conducting searches on websites, such as Google, to accessing specialised websites or engaging with influencers.

Both sessions started with a brief introduction of the research and what it was about, connecting to the previous results of the GCRF project. Participants had the opportunity to ask questions. Some also admitted to having prepared themselves, seeking information ahead of the focus groups. They thus revealed how they were eager to engage in 'safe spaces' where they could communicate their doubts and learn from others, while at the same time being asked to think critically about the role of media in reporting and communicating on SRHR. They revealed how they think reproductive health is not examined fully in public and private settings, either due to intergenerational differences, or also due to censorship practices exercised by public institutions, or due to a lack of in-depth coverage on the topic provided by the media.

Understandings Around SRHR and 'Women's Choice'

Regarding the first questions on how they understood SRHR, and if they could connect this to some problems faced by women, both groups showed themselves to have some knowledge, underlying issues of 'birth control' and 'to have sex to reproduce or not to reproduce'. The second group composed of women emphasised more 'women's rights', particularly the decisions that they take regarding their own bodies. In the focus group 2 however, participant 2 underlined that this referred to women's reproductive rights. Participant 3 underscored, however, the importance of power, and of women's rights to not only choose their pregnancy but also have rights to access healthcare and information:

> I think that sexual and reproductive rights are about the knowledge that women have about her own body, and her decision on her body and in her life, such as to live her sexual rights freely, and choose the partner and choose the precise time to get pregnant... (Participant 2)

> Well, I think rights is also about *power*, it is the way that women can have a say and be in control of her body. 'I am in control of what I want, what I need, and when I want to get married, with who I want to get married, when I want to have kids. How many kids do I want to have?....it's also about your right to a good health service....Do you need to have access to institutions of health where you can find whatever you need....., whatever you need is not only a doctor...... I'm talking about information. and

we need to have the right to information. I think that in these days, women have no right to information..... (Participant 3)

The issue of lack of knowledge on SRHR as well as poor information, in contrast to a more nuanced understanding of it, was explored by participants in both groups. A participant in group 2 mentioned the US overturning of the 1973 legislation *Roe v. Wade*, and the confusion it had caused. Other participants from the first focus group stated how issues on SRHR are explored more within the private sphere, but that this is often done under constraints. As participant 3 from the second focus group argued:

Is very well known that with the annulment of Roe versus Wade, women have been in a lot of trouble because they don't know how can they access......the institutions that they can have an abortion.....A lot of information.....a lot of wrong information. And we don't know where we can go if we want to have an abortion. And women are scared. Women are afraid of what can happen to them... (Participant 3)

The discussion of how the participants obtain information, both online and in the private sphere, is explored in the next section.

Information/Disinformation on SRHR in the Private Sphere and Online

The participants from both focus groups also tended to form a 'consensus' that there was poor information overall about the topic circulating in both the private and public spheres for different reasons, including a general sense of lack of in-depth coverage provided by the mainstream media, which often covered the topic in a political manner. Many mentioned that they actively seek information online, from doing Google searches to engaging with specialised groups on the topic. They claimed that this works as an antidote to a general lack of discussion in the private sphere, including among family members, as well as in educational settings. As Participant 2 from Group 2 mentioned, women do not have access to adequate quality information about SRHR either from local or national governments:

...there is misinformation, and lack of information, about precise topics such as sexual and productive health. Because women in various situations....don't know how to...and don't know where to go. Because they don't have the right information....I don't know the right way, but...women today don't have this information. (Participant 2)

Participant 2 from the second group talked more about the problems of lack of information on SRHR circulating in the family, and how more 'traditional' or elderly family members might inhibit talk. This was also agreed upon by Participant 4. She emphasised how women seek the internet to obtain more precise information, and to this extent, this can be 'empowering' for women, who can thus obtain knowledge that they can use to exercise their rights.

> ...most of...women....in rural places....don't have access to technology, to the Internet to find that information. In some situations all women have access...., but maybe they will need to Google it.... And maybe they can find the solution.....There are problems with location....we must have access to the Internet, but some don't have that way to solve their problems...... she will have to find some information from her family. But maybe not all families are the same. Maybe traditional families will not answer questions....in traditional families, the men are the head of the whole family, and they can decide what women can do... (Participant 4)

The focus groups were asked to explore more the communications that they receive, including public information campaigns, and to comment on the mainstream media's overall coverage.

Campaigns on SRHR and Media Coverage of Reproductive Health in the United States

The participants in both groups also struggled to remember any major public information campaign on SRHR, with some pointing to local campaigns on HIV/Aids as an example or also discussing the spread of various misconceptions about the topic instead in the online sphere, reinforcing the confusion and lack of information. Not anyone in the group could clearly remember any health communications campaign on women's reproductive rights. Both the United States and local Miami media coverage on the topic was deemed insufficient.

Participant 3 from focus group 1 talked about the topic being discussed in the mediated public sphere in a polarised manner, almost like a football match between opposing sides (e.g. the 'pro-choice' stance versus 'the pro-life' campaign). Participants revealed how it is hard to pinpoint a clear example of a successful information campaign. Participant 3 could not name the campaign that she was thinking about, which seemed to refer to the media coverage of pro and anti-abortion protests, and how people engaged with these. She was endorsed by the two male participants of the first group, who elaborated on some of the lies and myths that they had come across online:

> ...I feel it'd be like 'pro choice and against'.... But the whole campaign that happened ....I don't remember when it started...there was pro-choice and pro-life. That campaign is one example that....really stuck out like the past for like a while

now.......because I remember it through social media, mostly like everyone will post videos of them, protesting...there's people talking to the opposite team,...and then like their opinions and everything. So everyone will get that information from social media...., I remember seeing it...specifically on *TikTok*..... (Participant 3)

Participants 1 and 2 from the same group also stressed how a lot of information online is often unreliable. Many participants showed distrust of the information that they receive, including also a suspicion of institutions. The lack of more in-depth information provided by the media, and by public information campaigns, was reflected in the fact that participants struggled with particular health communication campaigns. It was also unclear if participant 2 was talking about a new type of contraceptive medicine. The participant underscored how they have mostly heard about campaigns on HIV, and not on reproductive health:

Yeah, I've seen that (campaign) as well....I'm sure it was backed....by the government health....But on *Instagram* there was this...so this like medical device to prevent pregnancy, and the women would like put it...I think you have....to inject it.......And then, like she puts it inside.... It was like being marketed pretty quickly, and on a lot of people who have been using it. It's like they were targeting.....Christians.... and it is more like natural birth control.....I don't get much info from like any kind of news......it's a bit like a friend...or people that I work with in film......But it's not anything about reproduction....the main focus that Florida has is the HIV free like Miami, HIV-free....A lot of billboards, and like local media, like on the bus....that's like the main focus.....not really anything on reproductive help, though I mean, yeah, just one part, like preventing.... (Participant 2)

The participants of the first focus groups also highlighted some of their experiences with false and misleading information online. Participant 3 for instance focused on reproductive narratives on the *TikTok* platform:

...mostly on *TikTok* is where you can see other women.....implementing other contraceptives....I remember seeing a girl talking about it, it was one that goes through her arm.....And then, like the pill and all the different ones which mainly targets women....like the feed that you're watching...the target is towards what you like and what your views are....You're going to see what you want and what your views are...... I would say for false information, it could be through social media. But I do believe it's also through shows, like TV shows....But if....someone with not that much information watches a

158   Carolina Matos

>show.....they're gonna try to copy. And they could do harm...more to themselves...like believing it. Anything you see like on social media, on shows....targeted towards women 'cause they carry the baby. They're the ones who have all the control.....Now you think there's more woman getting hurt by misinformation...yes. (Participant 3)

It is to the personal narratives told by the groups, as well as their suggestions for improvements in communication messaging, that I turn to next.

Personal Narratives, Storytelling and Improvements in Health Communication Messages

The second group also discussed the differences in the discussion of SRHR matters in the United States compared to Cuba, and the ways in which they seek to obtain accurate information on reproductive health online. Participants 1, 2 and 3 talked about their experiences engaging with some Cuban groups. Some noted how specialised websites can be a space for women to 'get together' in a kind of solidarity and 'sisterhood' fraternity, which is very much part of a 'feminist ideal', but which was not explicitly spelt out by the participants as such:

>...I have some kind of experience, but not in *WhatsApp* groups. Instead, in *Telegram*.... I have a Cuban family..., and classmates...that are in...some of these groups. There are specialists like psychologists, and they talk about interesting topics, about sexuality....some of the members are...friends, and they invite me. (Participant 2)

They also emphasised problems with debating SRHR matters, stressing the vacuum that exists between different generations. This leads to groups of women seeking to engage with others online whom they can connect with, and who can provide them with personal narratives and share their experiences. Participant 3 stated how the discussions among women on social media, including in *WhatsApp* groups, often feel like a 'fraternity':

>...I just recently came to the US. I lived in Cuba and in Cuba we have...groups of *WhatsApp* about women's....health. In that group we put our doubts...seeking the knowledge of other women.... But in those groups, there are no specialists.... It is the stories of other women. That's what I found the most interesting. Because in *Telegram,* I don't know why, it's more common to see people more prepared to share their knowledge. But in *WhatsApp* it is not the same, it's more like a fraternity....Sometimes that's good, because we can.....share our history....but it can go the other way....because there's a lot of

misinformation. Maybe we're trying to find the way to solve our problems......the person who tells what to does not have the right information....

Participant 3 further elaborated on the problems with the focus on personal stories, connecting these to the emphasis of opinions given by celebrities and social media influencers, indicating that this stress on individual accounts can cast aside 'scientific expertise', making room also for the proliferation of unsupported facts. There was also an emphasis on how the media do not provide proper context, including offering more solutions to women's SRHR problems:

> ...when Alex told us about this meeting, I went searching for information because I wanted to prepare myself...I was exploring the Internet, I found.....a lot of information not real, for example, many pages...with information that said that if women who need an abortion, they needed to go to an emergency room, they will be deported. And in the comments a lot of women said: "If I had to have an abortion in the U.S.A., I wouldn't go to a hospital or a health care institution, because I'm afraid that they would deport me... I...don't think that if anybody here needed an abortion they will be deported.....And on the other way you can have the right information from studies that have been undertaken by different universities..... you can find the right information....that will lead you to a good conclusion about what you're looking for....but the way that people consume....information has changed..., and you can see that in the way people believe more in *YouTubers* and influencers than a specialist...... People follow them more than the right information, the person who has the right information....the big media., the New York Times....none of that talk about what women can do.... no solutions...I think a lot of women go to big media looking for solutions....but they just put the problem. "Okay, this is what's going on right here. We are talking about this and Roe v. Wade, the importance of that".....So what can women do?...If they and talk about the problem, it is with a political agenda.... So there are no solutions....they're trying to lead us to think a way or another.... (Participant 3)

The participants in both groups also discussed where they access information on SRHR, with all of them emphasising social media, mentioning Google but also specialised websites. They also discussed 'the mainstream' media coverage, providing some suggestions on improvements in communication campaigns. A few newspapers were mentioned as vehicles for accessing information, such as the *New York Times*. The participants of the focus groups were also able to connect the difficulties of discussing SRHR in more depth with the national political climate. Participant 2 in focus group 1 underscored the polarised coverage provided by the media, with participant 3 adding that it does not help that the topic is not widely discussed in the private sphere due to 'self-censorship' practices:

> Well, the media definitely mentions (SRHR), like the current issues at hand and the ones that have the most conflict between.....the left and the right, so like birth control.....and how after like 9 weeks, there's no more abortion that a doctor can do. And there's like online stories about people who have had an abortion, and had to drive across 2 States and illegally do it..... But doctors are afraid to lose their licences... when I see the newspaper...I only see things that are happening with like the mayor's budget, and...But nothing on reproductive rights So I could tell you that for sure.....there is nothing on reproductive rights. From anything like the *New York Times* or the *Miami Times*..... (Participant 2)

> ...my teacher in my class, like in the school that I went to......She's not allowed to talk about it. It's why I want to mention now, because then we don't go in depth with information about...reproductive systems.... She did put out chapters.... But for her to talk about it, she said she didn't want to lose her licence......But now it's going to be more difficult for sexual reproductive systems. They're not going to be allowed to talk .... I do mean it's going to get worse.... (Participant 3)

The participants of group 2 also were very specific on the places where they do obtain information, with two participants (2 and 3) having engaged in a discussion over 'sexuality', e.g. if it is still seen as a taboo, and how this differs from the US context to countries like Mexico. Participant 2 talked about her work as an intern in a women's organisation while she was doing a masters in Mexico:

> ...we have one facility that is like a national facility of sexual education...... In this facility you can find all kinds of information about.....reproduction...I had the opportunity to take a master in Mexico.... I did an internship in a women's association...we talk about our experience....... I participated in like an internship with the team of the organisation to help women with knowledge about sexuality and reproduction...in drug situations.....I did research....in my masters about sexual and productive rights of the person of the same sex.....it was my research. And I have access to a lot of information, but not in social media, just in Google and websites.... (Participant 2)

> ...Is it a taboo?.....nowadays....it's not....Sexuality is...everywhere. So where is the taboo? People don't talk at home because they don't want to.....you go out and you see sex shops, and you see, magazines,

> social media has everything about sex. Why don't you talk? So there's no taboo.....They just don't talk because they don't want to.......They attire kids...in their own work, with their computer or their mobiles.....It's no taboo......But yes, in Mexico, it is. But here, no. It is in Cuba, of course.....maybe if I talk to my dad about sex he will slap me...in other cultures, you can see that's it's a toxic topic.....this is a big country, and there are a lot of types of families, and they keep their culture. So maybe it's hard to talk about sex..... (Participant 3)

Both groups were asked to imagine if they could participate in the co-construction of health messages and communication campaigns, and what they would seek to improve. All of them seemed to agree over the need to make information less political, more accurate and attractive. They suggested that celebrities and influencers should assist in advocating more on SRHR, indicating the need for science and health professionals to work more closely with communication teams to make their messages more meaningful, speaking directly to lived experiences. Participant 4 from group 2 stressed the importance of using various channels to communicate, such as radio, whereas participant 3 highlighted the need to use more relatable people to communicate in a way which resonated with audiences:

> ...The first thing is that the message, it's needs to look like the public.....what I am trying to say is that the main message of your campaign, It's gotta look like the people you're trying to reach....let's see, I'm a mother. I will say "I'm a young mother. I don't follow scientific information......maybe I will follow a lady who dresses like me......I would like to search for help in sexual health or reproductive health, and I will maybe follow her. I... will want to know what she's talking about......do you look at young people, and how they talk about their sexuality? They have cell phones....following a lot of people....They don't have the right information, but they follow them. And maybe you tell a teenager, "Hey, Why don't you look for these channels, they seem interesting? They talk about contraception methods and other information......" And they look and say, "that's boring. I don't like it", and they go to the other guy that doesn't know what he's talking about..... I think that it would be very good that the media....the scientific part of the issue looks for the influencers....to make...the content more attractive and...more fun. (Participant 3)

One participant in group 1 underlined how people should be more educated on this, and that some do not feel well equipped to talk precisely because of this, underscoring the importance of health literacy in people's capacity to debate. Similar to the previous group, when asked about how they would make communications better, they stated the need to make messages more 'attractive', including using new technological platforms such as *Apps* to provide more information as well as adopting more journalistic devices, such as *storytelling*:

...if somebody wants to speak out about it, they should be educated, and when people feel like they have a restraint on it, they don't. They know something about the topic....if like, I get taught a lesson, and then I have to teach it to somebody else. But I only get a portion of the lesson instead of the full whole.... (Participant 4)

I think there should be......a front runner or a model....somebody popular or famous, could help spread....unbiased information. And that could be something....trendy to do...Maybe they can just be supported or be sponsored by ....programs. So maybe it could be something....trendy....like a YouTube ad would help....and sometimes an ad that is like attractive and more informational could help......there's so many different media going on..... Maybe this could be like a middle ground then....People are quick to pick two sides on a political question....but maybe it should be more socially accepted to just look above both of them....because I know the Guardian is this newspaper, that online is unbiased. And that's like Apps as well....... that it's like you have to scroll a little bit longer to find their links or just go to their website first. So it's a lot more of a nice research that you have to be doing rather than just finding it. I guess then also to make it easier to access online. You have to kind of go out of your way to find unbiased information..... I think a lot of people....just go for the first media that they find and don't really delve into research and finding arguments against their own beliefs. Yeah, a lot of people don't really do that...what I would say is watch out where the misinformation is coming from, and the forms that they come in.....like the opinions they have on TikTok..... (Participant 2)

Conclusion

The results of this study have shown how members of disadvantaged communities in Miami, Florida (US) had some understanding of sexual and reproductive health matters. Participants from both focus groups were able to detect misinformation and inaccuracies in communications about the topic both offline and online, making connections between the poor debate around SRHR in the mediated (and global) public sphere with the local political polarisation and the difficulties of talk around issues of bodily autonomy and reproduction within the private sphere. Despite being inserted within a different local context, that of Miami Florida, the results had some similarities with the findings of the focus group study carried out in Campinas, São Paulo (Brazil), in partnership with the NGO *Reprolatina*, in July 2021, where participants also shared concerns of the negative impact of misinformation on SRHR matters on themselves, as well as on how this is contributing to hinder the advancement of women's rights.

Similar to the focus group sessions conducted in Brazil, participants from Miami also saw an impact of political populism on the conversations around SRHR in the mediated public sphere, including culminating in polarised media coverage and a proliferation of information/misinformation about the topic online. Thus due to the scarcity of reliable public information sources, individuals often seek emotional support and empathy through *personal* channels rather than relying on factual information to keep informed. However, in private communication settings, they also may come across misinformation, or experience the avoidance of certain topics by people due to various factors, from religious beliefs, and traditional norms, to intergenerational conflicts. This emphasises the importance of promoting public health campaigns.

The results from the focus groups carried out here thus showed that the participants consider it vital to: (1) improve the overall mainstream media coverage on the topic, to make it less polarised; (2) make better use of online networks and social media, with the scientific community, communication professionals and influencers joining more forces to produce information for the public interest that is free of vested interests, and which can be also more 'entertaining', thus speaking better to the lived experiences of women and also (3) women's groups and community members should be invited more to *co-participate* in the construction of health communication messages and campaigns so that they feel that they are having their voices heard and that their concerns are better taken into account by NGOs, public information campaigns and other governmental initiatives.

As I have argued here, feminist researchers have been enthusiastic about the potential offered by the internet for political mobilisation and advocacy around various issues. It is also vital to improve the health literacy skills of sectors of the communities, with NGOs working in the field conducting more workshops activities with the targeted groups to engage them more in the debate on SRHR matters, assessing also more closely the cultural, social and linguistic barriers that exist in an attempt to make them more *participatory* players in the co-construction of health messages on SRHR that can speak more to their lived experiences.

References

Baer, H. (2016). Redoing feminism: Digital activism, body politics and neoliberalism. *Feminist Media Studies*, 16(1).

Cornwall, A., Correa, S., & Jolly, S. (2008). *Development with a body: Sexuality, human rights and development*. Zed Books.

Correa, S., & Petchesky, R. (1994). Reproductive and sexual rights: A feminist perspective. In G. Sen, A. Germain, & C. C. Lincoln (Eds.), *Population policies reconsidered: Health, empowerment and rights*. Harvard University Press.

Fotopoulou, A. (2016). *Feminist activism and digital networks*. Palgrave Studies in Communication for Social Change.

Friedman, E. J. (2003). Gendering the agenda: The impact of transnational women's rights movement at the UN conferences of the 1990s. *Women's Studies International Forum*, 26(4), 313–331.

Haraway, D. (1991). Situated knowledges: The science question in feminism and the privilege of partial perspective. In *Simians, cyborgs and women: The reinvention of nature* (pp. 183–201). Free Association.

Harcourt, W. (2009). Reproductive bodies. In *Body politics in development: Critical alternatives in gender and development* (pp. 38–65). Bloomsbury Publishing.

Harcourt, W. (2013, May). Transnational feminist engagement with 2010 plus activisms. *Development and Change, 44*, 621–637.

Harding, S. (1993). Rethinking standpoint epistemology: What is 'strong objectivity'. In L. Alcoff & E. Potter (Eds.), *Feminist epistemologies* (pp. 49–81). Routledge.

Khamis, S. (2015). Gendering the Arab Spring – Arab women journalists/activists, cyber-feminism and the socio-political revolution. In C. Carter, L. Steiner, & L. McLaughlin (Eds.), *The Routledge companion to media and gender* (pp. 565–575). Routledge.

Matos, C. (2017). New Brazilian feminisms and online networks: Cyberfeminism, protest and the female 'Arab Spring'. *International Sociology, 32*(3).

Matos, C. (2023). *Gender, communications and reproductive health in international development*. McGill-Queen's University Press.

McHugh, M. C. (2020). Feminist qualitative research: Working toward transforming science and social justice. In P. Leavy (Ed.), *The Oxford handbook of qualitative research* (pp. 1–51). Oxford Handbooks.

McPherson, E. (2015). Advocacy organizations' evaluation of social media information for NGO journalism: The evidence and engagement models. *American Behavioral Scientist, 59*(1), 124–148.

Mendes, K., Ringrose, J., & Keller, J. (2019). *Digital feminist activism: Girls and women fight back against rape culture*. Oxford Studies in Digital Politics.

Michaeilidou, M. (2018). Feminist methodologies for the study of digital worlds. *International Journal of Media and Cultural Politics, 14*(1).

Montell, F. (1999, Spring). Focus groups interviews: A new feminist method. *NWSA Journal, 11*(1), 44–71.

Ratzan, S. C. (2001). Health literacy: Communication for the public good. *Health Promotion International, 16*(2).

Scrimshaw, S. (2019). Science, health and cultural literacy in a rapidly changing communications landscape. *Proceedings of the National Academy of Sciences, 116*(16), 7650–7655.

Wilkins, K. G. (2016). *Communicating gender and advocating accountability in global development* (pp. 85–123). Palgrave Macmillan.

Wilkinson, S. (1998). Focus groups in feminist research: Power, interaction and co-construction of meaning. *Women's Studies International Forum, 21*(1), 111–125.

Chapter 10

Views From Inside: Young Adults' Practices of Self-Governance on App-Based Platforms

Rita Basílio de Simões, Inês Amaral and Ana Marta M. Flores
University of Coimbra, Portugal

Abstract

This chapter focuses on the meanings that young adults ascribed to their practices on mobile app-based platforms, recurring to diary records. Combining their emic perspectives and etic knowledge, we sought to identify young adults' performances, emotions and beliefs to make sense of contemporary digital practices' social and cultural role. Research has shown that, along with ordering everyday experiences and providing convenience, ease and speed, digital technologies also establish asymmetrical relations between the different actors in the mediation process, with platform affordances enabling or constraining specific actions based on power relations. Adopting this critical standpoint, the conceptual frames they trigger, and the patterns of usages that young adult users regard as distinct and significant, we argue that normalising apps' daily practices should be seen as embedded in broader neoliberal governmentality.

Keywords: Mobile apps; everyday practices; diary methods; young adults; etic/emic; governmentality

Introduction

Smartphones have become ubiquitous companions in the hands of young adults, seamlessly woven into their daily lives. Mobile app-based platforms are no longer mere utilities; they serve as gateways to social connection, entertainment, education, finding romantic partners and financial management. This chapter, however, ventures away from the functionality mobile apps offer. It focuses on the more profound significance young adults ascribe to their bodily app usage, considering these technologies' crucial role in shaping social life. As digital practices continue to expand, it is also important to acknowledge their broader cultural relevance. Some research has been providing insights into mobile app usage across countries to understand demographic and geographic factors related to cultural values (Peltonen et al., 2018), while others have concentrated on local cultural mobile applications, shedding light on usability principles specific to cultural contexts (Antunes et al., 2023; Ariffin, 2017). Here, we focus on how mobile apps are incorporated into young adults' everyday usages, how they are domesticated to fit into routines and also how they constitute routines.

We combine an etic and emic perspective (Pike, 1990) to capture observable performances, emotions and beliefs from diary records and, simultaneously, to take the intentions behind users' activities and behaviours. The terms *emic* and *etic*, originally derived from the linguistic concepts of phonemics and phonetics, were introduced by linguist and anthropologist Kenneth L. Pike in 1954 to address incorporating non-verbal behaviour into linguistic descriptions. Phonemics pertains to the sound units that hold significance within a particular language, whereas phonetics encompasses the study of all discernible sounds across languages. The emic perspective focuses on the intrinsic explanations and meanings that participants ascribe to their own experiences. At the same time, the etic viewpoint encompasses descriptive data that can be objectively reported, even by observers with minimal understanding of the contextual nuances. In this research, the emic overlaps with the insider views of a group of middle-class, educated, cis-urban 16 young adults living in Portugal; the etic relates to how we, as researchers, look at how young adults incorporate mobile apps into their everyday lives as they are taken up and used as part of embodied practices.

Our etic perspective departs from critical inquiries into how digital technologies shape subjectivities, embodiments and practices. The commodification of personal data (van Dijck, 2013), the dialectical tensions between public and private (Seeliger, 2023) and the intensification of neoliberalism, or the emergence of 'technoliberalism' (Pfister & Yang, 2018), provide essential insights into how platform usages intersect with the broader structures of power in society. To better catch how the power dynamics are crossing the digital public sphere, we also proceed from Michel Foucault's (1991) concept of governmentality, which can be understood as both the (self-)governance of individuals and the multiple government rationalities that are engaged to govern the population. This means looking at practices of self-governance intertwined with practices of regulating others' behaviours.

The emic perspective comes from ethnographic data. We resorted to digital diary methods to capture the records of experiences, thoughts, feelings and behaviours of 16 young adults over 3 weeks. We seek to understand the meanings they construct around their digital practices and the extent to which these practices were shaped by corporate power and neoliberal discourses. Through its first-person accounts, we examine the discourses and emotional tapestry woven into their app usage and the beliefs that shape their online behaviour.

In what follows, we begin by situating the study within the theoretical underpinnings from which we depart, which relate to the framework of a broader project to which it belongs. The MyGender project investigates how young adults integrate mobile apps into their daily lives and how these apps influence their gender and sexual identities. Here, we interrogate how the apps they use are entrenched in the negotiation of their everyday lives and subjectivity.

Young Adults and App-Based Platforms Practices

Digital technologies have reshaped how individuals interact, communicate, work and engage with the world. Notably, mobile app-based platforms have transformed different dimensions of everyday practices (Berry, 2017). Their proliferation has blurred the boundaries between physical and digital realities, leading to the coalescence of online and offline experiences of heavy users, as is the case of young adults to whom much research focusing on the usages has turned (Abreu & Campos, 2022; Antunovic et al., 2018; Ash et al., 2020; Cooper, 2023; Khadir et al., 2021; Simões et al., 2023). Studies in these domains stress how mobile apps facilitate the organisation of daily activities, from scheduling appointments and managing tasks to accessing essential services and everyday routines, enhancing efficiency and integrating technology seamlessly into individuals' daily lives.

As platforms for self-expression and collective identity, mobile technologies are also deemed to influence young adults' communication patterns through heavy use of text messaging and social media (Cooper, 2023), sometimes with concerns (Khalaf et al., 2023; Samra et al., 2022). Simultaneously, mobile phones and platforms have become central to young adults' lives, serving as spaces for identity performances and expression, albeit with limitations imposed by platform functionalities (Alcaire, 2024; Antunes et al., 2023; Flores & Antunes, 2023). Social media apps, in particular, are seen as capable of shaping young adults' daily social activities in tandem with negotiating gender and sexual identities (Simões et al., 2023).

Another significant aspect of mobile technology is its capacity to order and structure everyday experiences in a continuum. Researchers have highlighted the importance of studying the transformation of everyday experiences to understand the implications of organisational work practices and structures (Yoo, 2010). The impact of digital technologies on individuals' experiences both inside and outside formal education settings, for instance, has been a subject of interest for educators seeking insights into students' technology experiences (Bennett & Maton, 2010). Still, there is much to explore regarding the broader sociocultural significance of young adults' daily management practices with app-based platforms.

Through algorithms, personalised recommendations and predictive analytics, apps tailor content and services to individual preferences, shaping users' interactions and, ultimately, their perceptions of the world. This means that, while generating convenience, integrating digital technologies into everyday activities creates a dependency on private corporations which own the platforms and may also exploit users' data for monetary gains.

In the face of users' data and generated content being commodified and app usage being transformed into a source of profit, individual actors and private corporations occupy different places in the chain of value, even though digital technologies' democratic value rests notably on the idea of universal access and horizontal communication relations. When users' data, content and usages are commodified and transformed into a profit source, we can see neoliberalism in Foucauldian terms (1991) as a productive power that shapes corporations and people's practices. In this context, the data plays a 'constitutive' role in governance (Foucault, 2008). That is, the data contributes to the social creation and shaping of both corporations and their clientele.

At the same time, since people's everyday routines are continuously coded and rendered manageable and manipulable (van Dijck, 2013), power differentials emerge in various forms, beginning with the disparities in control over data. Digital platforms' collection and utilisation of personal data not only creates asymmetrical power dynamics between users and technology companies, but the commodification of user data enables corporations to influence individuals' behaviours, preferences and decision-making processes, often without transparent consent or adequate safeguards for privacy.

Users are subjected to market rationality and may also be seen as economic actors who act and perceive themselves accordingly (Brown, 2006). Thus, they can be addressed as self-entrepreneurs self-governing their lives across platforms.

Self-Governance of Practices

Looking at digital technologies as connecting broader power relations to neoliberal forms of governmentality, as described by Foucault (1991), can help explain the evolving landscape of self-management in almost all aspects of everyday life through mobile apps. This includes social media profile-checking practices to gather or confirm information about people (Gangneux, 2019), but also all sorts of self-surveillance practices through apps designed to monitor sexual activity and performance (Simões & Amaral, 2022) or personal health (Hasan et al., 2022; Lupton, 2019). Neoliberalism, as a governing ideology, plays a pivotal role in shaping individual practices, which have increasingly become more personalised while being influenced by dominant behaviours and societal structures such as gender, class and race. For instance, the presentation of the self on social media platforms is shaped by socially sanctioned norms, despite the apparent autonomy in constructing and performing one's subjectivity (boyd, 2015).

Likewise, the phenomenon of self-branding accentuates individuals' entrepreneurial spirit and self-motivation while concealing the underlying mechanisms required to conform to hegemonic standards, encompassing self-discipline and regulation, which are also underpinned by corporate influence. These contemporary forms of self-governance should not be viewed as imposed but rather as ingrained and internalised behavioural patterns widely normalised in social practices. According to Foucault (2008), the existence of an individual is contingent upon discursive inscription in broader patterns, as discursive formations fabricate the subject they discuss. This process occurs through intricate power dynamics and the multitude of interpersonal connections that shape the upbringing of individuals across different life stages. So, the mechanisms of discursive control work to standardise populations through knowledge dissemination, surveillance, observation and experimentation, albeit by 'individualising' individuals within confined spaces like cells and classroom settings or social network profiles. Consequently, the internalised practices engender an 'individual' complicit in their own formation as a subject. In this context, narratives of neoliberal self-optimisation propel individuals to eagerly capture, monitor and track various performance and bodily metrics, all with market value, to enhance different facets of their psychological and physical well-being (Depper & Howe, 2016; Lupton, 2016; Sanders, 2016). Notably, this happens under the guise of free choice and a presumed willingness to act in accordance with their self-defined rules. Self-tracking thus serves as a tool of disciplinary power and biopower, normalising specific behaviours and constructing arbitrary interpretations of personal data while also intensifying self-surveillance (Lupton, 2014; Simões & Amaral, 2022).

Methodology

Articulating the above insights with the meanings that young adults ascribed to their practices on mobile app-based platforms, we sought to identify young adults' performances, emotions and beliefs to address how self-governance digital practices have become taken for granted. We specifically interrogate how young adults make sense of the role of app-based platforms in their everyday lives and, ultimately, how they shape contemporary subjectivity.

We employed qualitative methods to gain insights into young adults' discourses and practices through their own eyes. We used digital diary records chosen for their ability to capture immediate responses and minimise memory bias compared to interviews or focus groups. The participant group was comprised of 16 individuals between 19- and 30-years old living in Portugal (Table 10.1). The sample was predominantly educated, urban, cisgender and white, with some diversity in sexual orientation. We aimed to create user-friendly and comprehensive diaries to encourage participation and ensure rich data collection.

Digital platforms were chosen for their flexibility in response formats, allowing participants to express themselves through text, visuals or audio/video recordings. These platforms offered a potentially more private and comfortable space for self-expression than traditional interviews (Baker, 2023), with experiences recorded closer to real-time (Jarrahi et al., 2021). Through this methodology, we sought to collect qualitative data on participants' regular updates concerning their interactions with mobile apps, particularly regarding how those interactions impacted their subjectivity ties. Additionally, we aimed to understand their experiences with technology intrusion and its presence in daily life. Specifically,

Table 10.1. Summary of Participant Profiles.

Participant	Gender Identity	Age
D1	Female	21
D2	Female	22
D3	Female	22
D4	Female	30
D5	Female	26
D6	Female	25
D7	Male	29
D8	Male	26
D9	Male	26
D10	Female	21
D11	Female	19
D12	Male	23
D13	Male	19
D14	Male	27
D15	Female	19
D16	Female	27

Source: Authors.

we focused on identifying daily digital practices and casual occurrences associated with mobile app use among young adults in Portugal.

During the planning phase, we prioritised user-friendliness. Informal language was used to minimise the burden of participation and reduce the potential pressure associated with university involvement, as observed in Carter and Mankoff (2005). Offering diverse response formats was crucial for ensuring inclusive and varied expression. We aimed to empower young adults to be the authors of their narratives, encouraging honest and unconstrained diary entries.

We tested several digital platforms and opted for two familiar platforms: the latest versions of Google Docs and WhatsApp. Individual Google Doc files, accessible only to the participant and research team, allowed for text entries, various media formats and colour, fonts and layout customisation. Each document included general instructions and contact information for participants.

WhatsApp served as a parallel channel for collecting audio and video entries. We sent prompts encouraging reflection at minimal intrusive intervals, varying message times and frequency. The digital diaries were envisioned as a tool for participants to share details about their day or elaborate on prompts received via WhatsApp. The call for participants was disseminated through various channels, including MyGender's social media platforms, monthly newsletters and the host university's institutional channels.

We conducted individual online appointments to brief each volunteer on the project goals and responsibilities. Participants received an information document with instructions and contact details and the opportunity to ask questions about the process. Data collection spanned 3 weeks, from 13 March 2023 onwards focusing on everyday short-term reflections on the previous day. Regular prompts were sent via WhatsApp addressing daily experiences and interactions, perspectives on digital practices and actions, online presence management and opinions on potentially polarising figures in social activism. Data from the digital diaries was then systematically analysed through a thematic analysis (Braun & Clarke, 2006) using version 2020 of MaxQDA software.

Our approach aligns with established qualitative research practices to understand everyday experiences and thought processes within youth populations (Bennett et al., 2003). However, we further enrich our data by applying both etic and emic perspectives. So, to describe and explain how users make sense of their mobile app-based practices, our analytic departure was a theoretical background that frames the kinds of situations we observed and participant accounts of the situations in their own terms.

Findings and Discussion

Identifying recurring axes of themes in participants' performances and reflections using the principles of thematic analysis (Braun & Clarke, 2006) resulted in a matrix of themes. This chapter focuses on productivity, online identity and e-relationships.

The theme *of productivity* refers to young adults describing or reflecting on the value they place on their daily mediated activities. Recordings of feeling productive or achieving goals are included here. The theme *of online identity* relates to how young adults express and describe their online behaviour and the profiles they create on social media platforms. This includes discourses and practices of 'netiquette' and the use of 'real' or 'alter-ego' profiles. *E-relationships* likely refer to how young adults report on and manage various digitally mediated relationships. It comprises close friendships, acquaintances or even romantic relationships lived through online platforms. In what follows, we discuss these themes that emerged from our emic data and are embedded in broader neoliberal governmentalities.

Practices of Governing the Productive Self

The focus on *productivity* is a constant in the everyday records of our group of participants. Women and men depict and, sometimes, reflect on their mediatic activities, realising or mentioning the instrumental value of what they do daily and evaluating their lives according to the efficiency they achieve in accomplishing the number of tasks carried out in a given period:

> By the way, the week went well! I managed to do everything needed and the assessments were successful, in addition to managing my time and doing good work. The most important thing is to strive to learn and create even more! (young man, 19 years old)
>
> I had a very productive day! I was still able to work outside the house in the morning and, at the same time, catch a little sun. The afternoon was spent in meetings and the night working. (young woman, 22 years old)

These accounts, often pursued with a sense of entrepreneurship and autonomy, suggest that our participants experience pressure to live a perfectly productive life that can be presented through a curated online image of proficiency (Ehret et al., 2018). Ultimately, it also translates into unpaid labour and self-exploitation (Andrejevic, 2011; Hesmondhalgh, 2010). Young adults may face a growing disparity between narratives emphasising autonomy, creativity and self-fulfillment and the actual working conditions characterised by instability, long work hours, casualisation and precariousness (Gill & Pratt, 2008; Hesmondhalgh, 2010).

By enabling individuals to maintain flexibility, constant connectivity and the ability to work remotely, digital technologies have become aligned with the emerging paradigm of the flexible workforce (Gregg, 2011) and the discourse of its positive effect on self-management.

Framed by a neoliberal etic perspective, the productivity goal has many pitfalls. Young adults occupy a prominent position within the domain of precarious employment (Standing, 2011). Although precariousness is not unique to youth and isn't uniformly experienced by all individuals within this group, it has become increasingly prevalent among certain segments of middle-class youth. The widespread adoption of digital technologies has notably shaped experiences of precariousness, ushering in new modes of amateur and semi-professional production while championing the ideals of 'creativity'. Conversely, the diaries sometimes also reveal anxieties or frustrations associated with feeling unproductive due to comparisons with others' online portrayals.

Participants' records also give accounts of how *online identity* is understood, and, again, they express specific forms of neoliberal governmentality. In general, all show strategic crafts to present themselves in certain matters. While it is not surprising because one's reputation online may influence offline opportunities of courses of life, it is interesting to see how their engagement online results from a deliberate personal investment to manage their own symbolic value as subjects in the market labour. They carefully curate the content they publish instead of acting impulsively; they use pseudonyms and different online personas to properly fit the type of social network.

> I use another identity on several social networks because I don't want to adopt this part of me and leave my true identity more hidden. And I feel more free to say whatever I want and adopt

> another persona. (...) I plan a lot about what I'm going to post. It changes depending on my state of spirit/tastes/personal identity - I use my name or my nickname. The image is always different in all social networks. (young woman, 25 years old)

Participants seem to understand the self as entrepreneurial, active, decisive, independent and responsible (Kelly, 2013). Online identity is something that should be actively constructed and benefit from networking and self-promotion. Notably, while self-governance is normalised, the engagement with the platform's metrics also enables individuals to participate in the governance of others. Managing impressions, often trying to craft a 'professional self, is part of broader patterns of governmentality and has the platform' affordances as a powerful ally.

Managing e-Relationships

This picture can be applied to what happens in the field of mediated relationships. Generally, participants show that they maintain the same relationships online and offline. At the same time, they show they recognise how social network sites can become a breeding ground for new forms of social connection, potentially providing companionship and fostering a sense of belonging. So, the diary entries offer insights into the positive aspects of e-relationships, including the importance of building a strong professional network as a tool for getting relevant information for self-progress.

Practices of e-relationships are also understood as embedded in a context where boundaries between work and leisure have been blurred (Vaast & Káganer, 2013). Through their affordances, digital technologies change the frontiers between work and non-work time and space, reducing individual privacy. Participants usually normalise the overlapping of personal and professional lives, positioning it as an individual 'natural' and empowered choice, often overlooking the complex interweaving and balancing of work and life.

> While I'm at work, I talk to my girlfriend on WhatsApp, and when I'm not at work, I exchange memes with professional colleagues through various social networks (basically where the memes are). (young woman, 27 years old)

Certain records highlight the potential challenges and drawbacks associated with the erosion of privacy, particularly in light of the issues we have explored throughout the 3 weeks. While we aimed to gather accounts that reflect participants' perspectives (emic) to construct knowledge, we have also prompted participants to consider the implications of their routine interactions with app-based platforms by presenting them with issues framed from our standpoint (etic). At times, discussions on privacy revolved around concerns regarding risks posed by potential online harmful encounters and incivility (see Antoci et al., 2016) or the implications of disclosing personal information in the context of professional assessment. These risks merit careful consideration.

> There are certain social media networks that have certain specific uses and I want to protect my real identity and my privacy on my own initiative. In doing so, I opt for practices that I consider to be non-harmful, simply concealing some aspects that I consider unnecessary for the uses, such as knowing my original name or my location, mentioning them in private, which I want to and to whom I want to. (young male, 27 years old)

Adjusting privacy settings, using digital profiles judiciously, and creating alternative online personas are all seen as personal responsibilities, distinctly separate from the actions of large corporations that profit from shared data. Corporations act discreetly in the background, and their practices seem taken for granted.

Few participants acknowledge that corporations may compromise their privacy. Although privacy is always seen as an individual issue, some recognise the systematic collection of users' personal data and how corporations make life difficult for users when it comes to this matter. As one participant commented:

> It's important to emphasise that it's practically impossible for someone to read the terms assigned to us from the start and, obviously, violations of our privacy are easily perpetrated. Who hasn't bought a game and gone through the terms in a split second? Of course, it's easier to accept cookies than to go through a more time-consuming than go through a more time-consuming process to refuse them. By this, I mean that the inaccessibility to consult the practices carried out by applications and websites with regard to our data is unacceptable from an ethical point of view. (young male, 19 years old)

Conclusion

Drawing upon digital diary methods and relying both on outsiders' (etic) and insiders' (emic) descriptions and interpretations of daily mediated life, this chapter presents a picture of how app-based platforms are inscribed in young adults every day lives. We aimed to understand on a deeper level the underlying motivations and personal significance ascribed to these practices and what they say about subjectivity in contemporary society. Our findings show how digital life is self-regulated according to broader neoliberal forms of governmentally, where blurred boundaries between physical and digital, public and private, work and leisure are taken for granted, and users are constituted as active entrepreneurs responsible for managing their own (economic) value in society.

Examining young adults' practices on app-based platforms reveals a multifaceted landscape shaped by the interplay of digital technologies, neoliberal ideologies and individual agency. The pervasive integration of mobile apps into everyday life has transformed how individuals organise their daily activities and influenced their communication patterns and self-expression. Moreover, private corporations' commodification of user data has led to asymmetrical power dynamics, where individuals often unknowingly contribute to their own surveillance and exploitation in exchange for convenience and connectivity.

Drawing from Foucauldian perspectives on neoliberal governmentality, it becomes evident that the self-governance of practices extends beyond mere individual choices to encompass deeply ingrained behavioural patterns influenced by societal norms and corporate interests. The cultivation of online identities, the pursuit of productivity and the management of e-relationships are all manifestations of this neoliberal ethos, where individuals are encouraged to optimise themselves according to market-driven ideals of efficiency and self-promotion.

Furthermore, the findings from our qualitative research underscore the nuanced ways young adults navigate the digital landscape, balancing the benefits of connectivity with the risks of privacy infringement and data exploitation. Despite growing concerns about online privacy, there remains a prevailing sense of resignation and acceptance of corporate surveillance practices, reflecting a normalisation of data commodification in contemporary society.

Moving forward, it is imperative to critically examine the implications of app-based platforms on individuals' subjectivities and social interactions, particularly within neoliberal capitalism. By acknowledging the complex interplay between technology, ideology and individual agency, we can better understand the dynamics of power at play in the digital age and work towards fostering more ethical and equitable practices in the design and governance of digital technologies. Therefore, future research could delve into the long-term effects of app-based platforms on young adults' mental health and well-being, considering the constant negotiation between self-governance and external pressures within the neoliberal digital landscape. Additionally, exploring how marginalised groups navigate and resist dominant norms and power structures within app-based platforms could provide valuable insights into the potential for fostering more inclusive and socially just digital environments.

References

Abreu, J., & Campos, M. (2022). Exploring the impact of mobile apps on cultural practices: A qualitative study. *Journal of Cultural Studies*, *15*(2), 45–62.

Alcaire, R. (2024). Sexualidades, Identidades de Género e Interfaces. In I. Amaral, A. M. M. Flores, & E. Antunes (Eds.), *Apps e Jovens Adultos: Contributos para um Mapeamento de Práticas Mediadas* (pp. 41–55). UMinho Editora.

Andrejevic, M. (2011). Exploitation in the data mine. In C. Fuchs, K. Boersma, A. Albrechtslund, & M. Sandoval (Eds.), *Internet and surveillance: The challenges of web 2.0 and social media*. Routledge.

Antoci, A., Delfino, A., Paglieri, F., Panebianco, F., & Sabatini, F. (2016). Civility vs. incivility in online social interactions: An evolutionary approach. *PLoS One*, *11*(11), e0164286. https://doi.org/10.1371/journal.pone.0164286

Antunes, E., Amaral, I., Simões, R. B., & Flores, A. M. M. (2023). Who are the young adults in Portugal? Daily usage of social media and mobile phones, in a no-kids and no-independent housing context—Results from a representative online survey. *Youth*, *3*, 1101–1120.

Antunovic, D., Parsons, P., & Cooke, T. R. (2018). 'Checking' and googling: Stages of news consumption among young adults. *Journalism*, *19*(5), 632–648. https://doi.org/10.1177/1464884916663625

Ariffin, N. M. (2017). The impact of social media on youth: A case study of Malaysia. *International Journal of Humanities and Social Science*, *7*(1), 150–158.

Ash, G. I., Robledo, D. S., Ishii, M., Pittman, B., DeMartini, K. S., O'Malley, S. S., & Fucito, L. M. (2020). Using web-based social media to recruit heavy-drinking young adults for sleep intervention: Prospective observational study. *Journal of Medical Internet Research*, *22*(8), e17449. https://doi.org/10.2196/17449

Baker, Z. (2023). Young people engaging in event-based diaries: A reflection on the value of diary methods in higher education decision-making research. *Qualitative Research*, *23*, 686–705.

Bennett, A., Cieslik, M., & Miles, S. (Eds.). (2003). *Researching youth*. Palgrave Macmillan.

Bennett, S., & Maton, K. (2010). Beyond the 'digital natives' debate: Towards a more nuanced understanding of students' technology experiences. *Journal of Computer Assisted Learning*, *26*(5), 321–331. https://doi.org/10.1111/j.1365-2729.2010.00360.x

Berry, M. (2017). *Creating with mobile media*. Springer.

boyd, d. m. (2015). Social media: A phenomenon to be analyzed. *Social Media + Society*, *1*(1). https://doi.org/10.1177/2056305115580148

Braun, V., & Clarke, V. (2006). Using thematic analysis in psychology. *Qualitative Research in Psychology*, *3*(2), 77–101. https://doi.org/10.1191/1478088706qp063oa

Brown, J. (2006). The influence of market rationality on user behavior: A study of economic actors. *Journal of Consumer Psychology*, *16*(4), 321–335.

Carter, S., & Mankoff, J. (2005). When participants do the capturing: The role of media in diary studies. In *Proceedings of the CHI'05: SIGCHI Conference on Human Factors in Computing Systems*, Portland, OR, USA (pp. 899–908).

Cooper, C. (2023). The influence of the mobile phone on young adult communication. *Professional Communication and Translation Studies*, *10*, 12–20. https://doi.org/10.59168/htnk9894

Depper, A., & Howe, P. D. (2016). Are we fit yet? English adolescent girls' experiences of health and fitness apps. *Health Sociology Review*, *26*(1), 98–112. https://doi.org/10.1080/14461242.2016.1196599

Ehret, C., Boegel, J., & Manuel-Nekouei, R. (2018). The role of affect in adolescents' online literacies: Participatory pressures in BookTube culture. *Journal of Adolescent & Adult Literacy*, *62*(2), 151–161. https://doi.org/10.1002/jaal.881

Flores, A. M. M., & Antunes, E. (2023). Uses, perspectives and affordances in mobile apps: An exploratory study on gender identity for young adults in social media platforms in Portugal. *AG About Gender*, *12*, 35–63.

Foucault, M. (1991). Governmentality. In G. Burchell, C. Gordon, & P. Miller (Eds.), *The Foucault effect—Studies in governmentality* (pp. 87–114). Harvester Wheatsheaf.

Foucault, M. (2008). *The birth of biopolitics: Lectures at the Collège de France 1978–1979*. Palgrave Macmillan.

Gangneux, J. (2019). 'It is an attitude': The normalisation of social screening via profile checking on social media. *Information, Communication & Society*. https://doi.org/10.1080/1369118X.2019.1668460

Gill, R., & Pratt, A. (2008). In the social factory? Immaterial labour, precariousness and cultural work. *Theory, Culture & Society, 25*(7–8), 1–30.

Gregg, M. (2011). *Work's intimacy*. Polity Press.

Hasan, N., Bao, Y., & Chiong, R. (2022). A multi-method analytical approach to predicting young adults' intention to invest in mHealth during the COVID-19 pandemic. *Telematics and Informatics, 68*, 101765. https://doi.org/10.1016/j.tele.2021.101765

Hesmondhalgh, D. (2010). User-generated content, free labour and the cultural industries. *Ephemera: Theory and Politics in Organization, 10*(3/4), 267–284.

Jarrahi, M. H., Goray, C., Zirker, S., & Zhang, Y. (2021). Digital diaries as a research method for capturing practices in Situ. In G. Symon, K. Pritchard, & C. Hine (Eds.), *Research methods for digital work and organization: Investigating distributed, multi-modal, and mobile work* (pp. 107–129). Oxford Academy.

Kelly, P. (2013). *The self as enterprise: Foucault and the spirit of the 21st century capitalism*. Gower.

Khadir, F., Ravindranath, V., & Sen, R. (2021). Factors that influence users in selecting mobile apps – A study on Facebook and Facebook Lite. *Journal of Public Value and Administrative Insight, 4*(1), 24–36. https://doi.org/10.31580/jpvai.v4i1.1571

Khalaf, A. M., Alubied, A. A., Khalaf, A. M., & Rifaey, A. A. (2023). The impact of social media on the mental health of adolescents and young adults: A systematic review. *Cureus, 15*(8), e42990. https://doi.org/10.7759/cureus.42990

Lupton, D. (2016). Self-tracking, health and medicine. *Health Sociology Review, 26*(1), 1–5. https://doi.org/10.1080/14461242.2016.1228149

Lupton, D. (2014). Quantified sex: A critical analysis of sexual and reproductive self-tracking using apps. *Culture, Health & Sexuality, 17*(4), 440–453. https://doi.org/10.1080/13691058.2014.920528

Lupton, D. (2019). 'It's made me a lot more aware': A new materialist analysis of health self-tracking. *Media International Australia, 171*(1), 66–79. https://doi.org/10.1177/1329878X19844042

Peltonen, E., Lagerspetz, E., Hamberg, J., Mehrotra, A., Musolesi, M., Nurmi, P., & Tarkoma, S. (2018). The hidden image of mobile apps: Geographic, demographic, and cultural factors in mobile usage. In *MobileHCI '18: Proceedings of the 20th International Conference on Human-Computer Interaction with Mobile Devices and Services* (Article No. 10, pp. 1–12). https://doi.org/10.1145/3229434.3229474

Pfister, D. S., & Yang, M. (2018). Five theses on technoliberalism and the networked public sphere. *Communication and the Public, 3*(3), 247–262. https://doi.org/10.1177/2057047318794963

Pike, K. L. (1990). On the emics and etics of Pike and Harris. In T. Headland, K. L. Pike, & H. Marvin (Eds.), *Emics and etics: The insider/outsider debate* (pp. 28–47). Sage.

Samra, A., Warburton, W. A., & Collins, A. M. (2022). Social comparisons: A potential mechanism linking problematic social media use with depression. *Journal of Behavioral Addictions*, *11*(2), 607–614. https://doi.org/10.1556/2006.2022.00023

Sanders, R. (2016). Self-tracking in the digital era. *Body & Society*, *23*(1), 36–63. https://doi.org/10.1177/1357034x16660366

Seeliger, M. (2023). When Twitter blocked Trump: The paradox, ambivalence and dialectic of digitalized publics. *Philosophy & Social Criticism*, *50*(1), 239–254. https://doi.org/10.1177/01914537231203921

Simões, R. B., & Amaral, I. (2022). Sexuality and self-tracking apps: Reshaping gender relations and sexual reproductive practices. In E. Rees (Ed.), *The Routledge companion to gender, sexuality, and culture* (1st ed., pp. 413–423). Routledge. https://doi.org/10.4324/9780367822040-41

Simões, R. B., Amaral, I., Flores, A. M. M., & Antunes, E. (2023). Scripted gender practices: Young adults' social media app uses in Portugal. *Social Media + Society*, *9*(3). https://doi.org/10.1177/20563051231196561

Standing, G. (2011). *The precariat: The new dangerous class*. Bloomsbury Academic.

Vaast, E., & Káganer, E. (2013). Social media affordances and governance in the workplace: An examination of organizational policies. *Journal of Computer-Mediated Communication*, *19*(1), 78–101. https://doi.org/10.1111/jcc4.12032

van Dijck, J. (2013). *The culture of connectivity a critical history of social media*. Oxford University Press.

Yoo, Y. (2010). Computing in everyday life: A call for research on experiential computing. *MIS Quarterly*, *34*(2), 213. https://doi.org/10.2307/20721425

Index

Agreements, 48
Algorithmic bias, 66
Algorithmic governance, 113–114
Anti-vax theories, 115
Apple App Store, 96, 99, 101
Apps, 96, 161–162
    app-based platforms, 175
    development industry, 69
    ecosystems, 59, 64–65
    presentation, 101
    stores, 96
    usage, 7, 9–10
    young adults and app-based platforms practices, 167–168
ATLAS.ti software, 130
Authenticity, 86

Behavioural approach, 77–78
Biases in Portuguese Google Play Store, 61–69
Big Social Data, 29
Biopolitics, 120

Co-PI, 153
Colour, 62
Communication, 95
    mediator, 95–97
    strategies, 152–153
Communities of practice, 140
Community engagement with health messages
    campaigns on SRHR and media coverage of reproductive health in United States and Abroad, 156–158
    debate on SRHR in US and Floridian context, 148–149
    feminist epistemologies, social media use and engagement with communication messages, 149–151
    findings, 153–162
    information/disinformation on SRHR in private sphere and online, 155–156
    methodology, 151–153
    personal narratives, storytelling and improvements in health communication messages, 158–162
    SRHR and 'women's choice', 154–155
Constant connectivity, 83
Context collapse, 84
Convergence culture, 21
Corporate power, 166
Couple apps, 97, 105
    dating and mingle, 102
    discursive positioning of, 101–104
    fostering emotional and physical intimacy in pursuing healthy relationship, 102–103
    gendering couples, 104
    hearts and bodies in red spectrum, 101
    organising and keeping up with events and friends, 103–104
COVID-19 pandemic, 26, 80–81, 103, 115
Critical technology studies, 78
Critical thematic analysis, 81
Cultural norms, 64–65
Cultural significance, 167
Curation methods, 66

Data collection, 97
Data economy, 28
Data hoarding model, 29

Index

Dating
  apps, 84–85, 88
  and games, 67–69
Deep mediatisation, 10
Diary records, 9
Digital age, 27–28, 36
Digital citizenship, 24
Digital communication, 3–4
Digital cultures, 10–11, 23, 26, 59, 128, 130
Digital detox, 26–27
Digital diary methods, 166, 174
Digital disconnection, 26–27
Digital dossier, 135
Digital engagement, 29
Digital environment, 4, 58
Digital environments, 96, 113–114
  'couples' apps, 97
  date of release, categories and actor type, 97–99
  discursive positioning of couple apps, 101–104
  games, lifestyle, entertainment and more, 99–100
  method and data collection, 97
  from private sector, 100–101
  romantic couples and mobile apps, 95–97
Digital girl-watching, 134–136
Digital identity, 3–4
Digital inclusivity, 59
Digital interfaces, 76
Digital intimacy, 7–8, 52
Digital landscape, 28–29
Digital literacy, 22
Digital media, 2, 67, 76, 128
  technologies, 10–11, 20–21
Digital methods, 59
Digital natives, 20–22, 28–29
Digital platforms, 5, 36–37, 39, 169–170
Digital practices, 130
Digital profiles, 174
Digital sociability, 21–22
Digital socialisation, 20, 22–23
Digital spaces, 58, 83
Digital stores, 58–59

Digital surveillance technologies, 8
Digital technologies, 3–4, 7, 27–28, 38–39, 58, 68–69, 94–96, 167–168, 173
Digital tools, 59–61
Digitalisation, 25–26
Discursive strategy, 116
Disinformation on SRHR in private sphere and online, 155–156
Diversified strategies, 105
Docile body, 117
'Don't Say Gay' law, 148
DownThemAll, 59–61

E-relationships management, 171, 173–174
Email, 82
Emic perspective, 166
Emotional intimacy in pursuing healthy relationship, 102–103
Empirical data, 81
Etic perspective, 166
Everyday practices, 167

Facebook, 81–82, 88
Facebook Messenger, 82
Fake News, feminist epistemologies, social media use and engagement with communication messages on SRHR in age of, 149–151
Female body, 112
Female-only group chats, 131–139
Female/male WhatsApp groups function, 132
Femininity, 38, 89, 128, 130, 139–140
Feminists, 149–150
  framework, 112
  materialism, 6
  media studies, 7
  method, 151–152
  movements, 149
  scholars, 150–151
  thinking, 118–119
Floridian context, debate on SRHR in, 148–149

Focus group sessions, 152–153, 163
Fourth World Conference on Women in Beijing (1995), 146

Games, dating and, 67–69
GCRF project, 150–151
Gen Z, 25
Gender, 2–3, 37, 52–53, 58, 62, 78, 80
  advocacy, 150–151
  app icons, colour and gendered alignments, 61–64
  and biases in Portuguese Google Play Store, 61–69
  binary, 65–66
  chatting 'as a man' and 'as a woman, 131–132
  dating and games, 67–69
  digital culture, homosociality, masculinity and femininity, 128–130
  disparities, 4
  dynamics, 36
  equality, 146
  female-only and male-only group chats, 131–139
  gender binary, 65–66
  gender-based online harassment, 39
  gendered gaze, 64–65
  humour and homosocial complicity, 132–134
  ideology, 148
  across mediated mobile interfaces, 5–10
  methodology, 130
  norms, 3
  performance of identity, 67
  perspective, 146–147
  politics, 4, 146
  representation, 10
  roles, 2
  stereotypes, 62–64
  studies, 62
  watching boys, watching girls, 134–138
  WhatsApp Group as support, 138–139
Gender across digital platforms
  mean levels of agreement on content creation and sharing patterns, 44
  mean levels of agreement on intimate and sexual digital lives, 47
  mean levels of agreement on several burden experiences of hate, harassment and bullying, 42–43
  mean levels of agreement regarding digital interaction and socialisation experiences, 45–46
  methodology, 39–41
  results, 41–53
  sample distribution, 40
  state of art, 37–39
Gender identities
  challenging uses and gratifications, 76–80
  dating apps, 85–88
  identity management, 83–85
  methodology, 80–81
  technology as extension of daily lives, 81–83
Gendered critical overview of technology, 76–80
Gendered gaze, 64–65
Gendered practices, 13
Gendering couples, 104
Google, 153–154
Google App Store, 66
Google Play, 96
  ecosystem, 68–69
  Scraper, 59–61
  Store algorithm, 64
Governmentality, 166
Gratifications theory, 4
Grindr, 86–88
Gynaecological medicine, 120

Health, 149–150
  communication messages, personal narratives, storytelling and improvements in, 158–162
  risk perception, 115

Hegemonic processes, 25–26
Heterogeneity, 95
Heteronormativity, 2, 67–68, 101
Heteropatriarchal system, 79
Heterosexuality, 137–138
Heterosexuals, 48–49, 58
Homosocial complicity, 132–134
Homosociality, 128–130, 138
Humour and homosocial complicity, 132–134

Identity
  management, 83–85
  performance of, 67
ImageJ, 59–61
Inclusive process, 129
Informal language, 170
Information and communication technologies, 4
Information on SRHR in private sphere and online, 155–156
Instagram, 81–82, 88
Instant messaging, 82
International Conference on Population and Development (1994) (ICPD), 146
Internet, 4, 58
  internet-based technologies, 21–22
Intersectionality of identity markers, 39
Intimacy in digital environment, 36

Learning process, 139–140
Lesbian/gay respondents, 50–52
LGBTQ+ identities, 84–85
'Liminality' concept, 84

Magic bullet theory, 77
Male-only group chats, 131–139
Masculinity, 38, 89, 128, 130, 139–140
Media, 20–21
  consumption, 6
  convergence, 35–36
  literacy, 121

Menstrual tracking apps under Foucault's concepts
  algorithms and power dynamics, 112
  menstrual tracking app functions and strategies, 115–117
  self-care or self-control, 118–120
  subjectivities and surveillance, 117–118
Misinformation, 147, 149
  on SRHR, 147
Mixed-method approach, 8, 59
Mobile application platforms (m-apps), 2, 5–6, 36, 76, 81–82, 112, 128
  gender and sexuality across mediated mobile interfaces, 5–10
  mediated interfaces and extension of self, 3–5
  mobile app-based platforms, 165–167
  romantic couples and, 95–97
Mobile devices, 20
Mobile platforms, 114
Mobile technologies, 2–3, 112, 167
Mobile-based technologies, 2, 6
Mobile-centric technologies, 2
Montage method, 62
MyGender project, 8, 29, 80–81, 88, 167
MyGender research, 83

Neoliberal governmentality, 175
Neoliberalism, 168
New media ecosystem, 4–5
NGO advocacy, 147
Non-neutral technologies, 96
Normative femininity, 64
Normative masculinities, 66

Objectification, 137
Onde Tem Tiroteio (OTT), 114
Online communications, 151
Online communities, 10–11
Online identity, 171–173

Online interaction, 7
Online intimacy, 38–39
Online neighbourhood social networks (ONSNs), 22–23
Online platforms, 38
Online racial discrimination, 39
Online spaces, 39

Paechter's approach, 130
Panoptic metaphor, 119
Panopticon, 119
Parenthood status, 54
Participatory platforms, 21
Period tracking apps, 118
Persona curation, 14
Personal narratives, storytelling and improvements in health communication messages, 158–162
Personalised recommendations, 167
Phonemics, 166
Phonetics, 166
Physical intimacy in pursuing healthy relationship, 102–103
Political anatomy, 117
Political power of technology, 26–28
Populist right-wing movements, 148
Portuguese adults, 37
Portuguese Google Play Store, 69
  arena of gendered app cultures, 58–59
  gender and biases in, 61–69
  methods and data collection, 59–61
Post-subcultural context, 25–26
Power, 120
  dynamics, 114
  relations, 8, 37
Predictive analytics, 167
Privacy concerns, 49–50
Privacy issues, 113–114
Private sector, 100–101
Private WhatsApp groups, 139
Productivity, 171–172
Pseudonyms, 14
Punishment, 119

Qualitative data, 80–81
Qualitative methods, 14, 169
Quantitative methodological strategy, 39–40
Quantitative methodology, 39
Queer masculinities, 66
'Queer' identities, 64–65, 67–68
Queerness, 66
  invisibility of queerness in everyday life, 67–69

Rankflow, 59–61
RawGraphs, 59–61
(Re) negotiating gender, 3
Red spectrum, hearts and bodies in, 101
Relational dialectics theory, 95
Relationship satisfaction, 96–97
Relationship spectrum, 96–97
Reproductive health, 146–147
  campaigns on SRHR and media coverage of reproductive health in United States, 156–158
  rights, 149
Reproductive rights, 147, 160
Role-playing games, 67
Romantic couples, 95–97
Romantic relationships, 93–94

Self-care, 118–120
Self-control, 118–120
Self-governance of practices, 168–169
Self-presentation, 14
Self-representation concept, 83
Self–expression, 9, 11–12, 14
Sexual and reproductive health and rights (SRHR), 13, 146–147
  and 'women's choice', 154–155
  campaigns on SRHR and media coverage of reproductive health in United States and Abroad, 156–158
  debate on SRHR in US and Floridian context, 148–149

in private sphere and online, information/disinformation on, 155–156
social media use and engagement with communication messages on, 149–151
SRHR-related information, 13–14
Sexual diversity, 80
Sexual identities, 7
challenging uses and gratifications, 76–80
dating apps, 85–88
identity management, 83–85
methodology, 80–81
technology as extension of daily lives, 81–83
Sexual orientation, 7, 48–52, 54
Sexual wars, 146
Sexualisation, 52
Sexuality, 62
across mediated mobile interfaces, 5–10
Smartphones, 94, 165–166
Social interaction, 5
Social media, 84
networks, 147, 174
platforms, 10, 20–21, 24–25, 28–29, 82, 84, 88
use and engagement with communication messages on SRHR in age of 'Fake News', 149–151
Social networks, 4, 93–94
Social norms, 8, 20–21
Social participation, 129
Social relationships, 36
Socialisation process, 10–11, 20
Society, 10–11, 79
Sterilisation surgery, 116
Subculture, 25–26
Subordinated masculinities, 66

Technological system, 78
Technological uses, 3
Technology, 28, 76

as extension of daily lives, 81–83
Telegram, 131
TikTok, 157–158
Twitter, 84

UN conferences, 146
United States
and abroad, campaigns on SRHR and media coverage of reproductive health in, 156–158
debate on SRHR in, 148–149
Uses and gratification hypothesis (UeG hypothesis), 76–78, 80

Visual digital objects, 61–62
Visual studies, 62

Western cultures, 58
WhatsApp groups, 13, 82, 128–129, 131–132, 134, 137–139, 147, 158–159, 170
Women, 133–134, 138
reinforcing societal pressures on, 59
SRHR and women's choice, 154–155
Women's rights, 146

Young adulthood/adults, 5, 29
and app-based platforms practices, 167–168
digital cultures, 23–26
digital socialisation, 20–23
findings, 171–173
managing e-relationships, 173–174
methodology, 169–171
parenthood status, 53
political power of technology, 26–28
practices of governing productive self, 171–173
self-governance of practices, 168–169
Young people, 128, 130
YouTube, 86

Printed and bound by CPI Group (UK) Ltd, Croydon, CR0 4YY

21/11/2024

14596994-0001